MAIMONIDES

Torah and Philosophic Quest

EXPANDED EDITION

MAIMONIDES

Torah and Philosophic Quest

EXPANDED EDITION

David Hartman

Foreword by Shlomo Pines

2009 • 5769
The Jewish Publication Society
Philadelphia

JPS is a nonprofit educational association and the oldest and foremost publisher of Judaica in English in North America. The mission of JPS is to enhance Jewish culture by promoting the dissemination of religious and secular works, in the United States and abroad, to all individuals and institutions interested in past and contemporary Jewish life.

The Jewish Publication Society
2100 Arch Street, 2nd floor
Philadelphia, PA 19103
www.jewishpub.org

Cover Design by Claudia Cappelli

Manufactured in the United States of America

09 10 11 12   10 9 8 7 6 5 4 3 2 1

ISBN: 978-0-8276-0911-2

Library of Congress Control Number 76-6305

JPS books are available at discounts for bulk purchases for reading groups, special sales, and fundraising purchases. Custom editions, including personalized covers, can be created in larger quantities for special needs. For more information, please contact us at marketing@jewishpub.org or at this address: 2100 Arch Street, Philadelphia, PA 19103.

To Bobbie

*In deep appreciation to Elliot Yagod,
who is truly the co-author of this book.*

*Without his intellectual input,
the book would not have been written.*

ACKNOWLEDGMENTS

I am fortunate in having been born into a religious family whose roots within the Jewish tradition are deep. My father, of blessed memory, was a man who found profound satisfaction in his Judaism; his great legacy to his children was the joy of song. He was not religiously dogmatic, and he and my mother created a Jewish home which was experientially based yet intellectually free. I am grateful both to them and to my brothers and sisters for the intensely Jewish environment in which I spent the formative years of my life. These positive, emotional grounds provided a secure foundation in the Jewish tradition, yet left ample room for me to roam freely in the world of ideas.

The teacher who first introduced me, in depth, to the world of Jewish philosophic and halakhic thought was Rabbi Joseph B. Soloveitchik. He has been, for me, the paradigm of one who strives to integrate the rigorous discipline of halakhic thought with the study of philosophy. He taught me all that I know and love in Halakhah; above all, he showed me how halakhic man can be intellectually honest. He was never afraid to raise uncomfortable questions, and preferred to continue grappling with a difficult problem rather than seek an easy solution. He taught me how one can struggle religiously, yet remain strongly committed to a tradition. It was his example that sustained me throughout my years of encounter with philosophy. It was he who encouraged me to broaden my halakhic horizons by embracing the world of philosophy.

In my philosophic studies, I was favored in being exposed to great teachers. Indeed, the five years I spent at Fordham University were an intellectual feast. Professor Robert Pollock's experiential orientation to philosophic thought has remained a permanent feature of my thinking. At McGill University, where I earned my doctorate, I was fortunate to have studied with Professor Chaim Perelman whose penetrating approach to the philosophy of law and the logic of legal reasoning left a lasting impression upon me. He encouraged me to investigate the nature of halakhic reasoning, and his influence may be noted in Chapter Three of this work. I am also indebted to Alan Montefiore for his exacting approach to moral philosophy.

The friendship and concern of Professor Raymond Klibansky, under whose guidance this work was undertaken, were a source of strength to me, and the rigorous demands of his scholarship provided important directions in my research.

The intellectual companionship of my former colleagues in the Department of Philosophy at McGill University will always be appreciated. Harry Bracken was a firm supporter on many difficult occasions, and his suggestions have immeasurably improved the quality of this work. Throughout the long period in which I applied myself so intensely to the study of Maimonides, I was blessed with a great student, Elliot Yagod. Together, he and I studied all the material dealt with in this work; I have benefited greatly from his clarity of thought, his keen powers of analysis, his disdain for intellectual compromise. Without his continual help and reinforcement, this work would not have been completed. In a sense, this book is his as well as mine.

I also was fortunate to have had a congregation that was willing to study Maimonides with me during the many pleasant years I spent in Montreal as rabbi of Congregation Tifereth Beth David Jerusalem. The deep concern of many members of the congregation for my development, and their continued interest in my welfare will always be appreciated.

I gained enormously from discussions I enjoyed over the years with Professor Shlomo Pines of The Hebrew University in Jerusalem. He, too, encouraged me to roam freely in my thinking—but always insisted that I remain within the thought-patterns of Maimonides. The interest of this master scholar is of the greatest importance to me, for I know that no contemporary work on Maimonides can ignore the searching criticism which emerges from his boundless knowledge of that philosopher's reasoning.

This work was completed in Jerusalem, the city of Jewish spiritual aspirations. My coming on *aliyah* and being able to devote all of my time to study and writing was made practicable through the kindness and warm friendship of Sol Lederman. He believed that my place was in Israel; he knows that Jewish intellectual creativity must emerge organically from the soil of Jewish history. His graciousness made it possible for me and my family to come home; my gratitude for his devotion to Jewish scholarship and his faith in me is beyond words.

Since settling in Jerusalem, I have enjoyed and benefited greatly from the friendship of many colleagues at the Hebrew University. The talks with Professor Eliezer Schweid helped sharpen my focus on the spiritual implications of my approach to Maimonides. Professor Efraim

Urbach was always available for discussions on the rabbinic roots of Maimonidean thought. Professor Nathan Rotenstreich spent long hours with me in a detailed analysis of much of the philosophic implications of this work. Professor Abraham Halkin read my manuscript with care and was singularly helpful in the area of Judeo-Islamic thought. Dr. Chaim Soloveitchik provided incisive criticisms, stemming from his knowledge of Halakhah and Maimonides. His numerous helpful suggestions have been incorporated into this work.

I am indebted to my editor, Priscilla Fishman, for her meticulous and devoted concern, to Vivian Mamlich for her patient typing of the manuscript, and to Bernard Steinberg for his invaluable aid in the preparation of the Index.

I must mention my children, Devora, Tova, Daniel, Adina, and Ranan, who encouraged me to continue despite many difficulties. Their love and patience gave me much needed support.

I owe more than I can express to Bobbie, my beloved wife, whose honesty and love enabled me to aspire to give voice to intellectual and spiritual longings throughout the years of our marriage. It is to her that I dedicate this first fruit of our long search together for spiritual roots grounded in intellectual integrity.

We live in an age which, unfortunately, is dominated by religious existentialist thought. It is my hope that this work on Maimonides will encourage renewed discussion on the political implications of halakhic thought. The political renaissance of the Jewish people enjoins an intellectual understanding of the significance of Judaism—for the individual and, above all, for the community.

Jerusalem
Ḥanukkah 5735

FOREWORD
Shlomo Pines

A main theme of the present work is the relation between Maimonides' halakhic writings—which are concerned with both norms of conduct and norms of religious beliefs —and *The Guide of the Perplexed,* which, in a sense, is a philosophical work for it purports to expound or to hint at the physical and metaphysical verities in a way which reduces the danger of philosophical truth to religion. David Hartman takes issue with a closely knit thesis in which it is argued that the legal writings subserve an exclusively practical end and, accordingly, contain no indications of Maimonides' theoretical views which, to some extent, can be gathered—with great difficulty—from *The Guide of the Perplexed.* He also posits that for Maimonides intellectual perfection, the knowledge of theoretical truth, is the highest end of man.

The tendency of Hartman's investigations is to prove that the connection between the halakhic writings and *The Guide of the Perplexed* is much closer than is admitted. In this context some quotations and references may be relevant.

The first chapter of the first book of Aristotle's *Politics* describes man as having—contrary to the other animals—

perception of good and bad, of right and wrong, and of the other moral qualities. The fact that men have this characteristic in common accounts for the existence of households and of cities; it renders possible political and social life. However according to the tenth book of the *Nicomachean Ethics,* this life is not the highest end of the superior man nor is it directly conducive to it. "For it is the activity of [the theoretical intellect] that constitutes complete human happiness. . . . Nor ought we to obey these who enjoin that man should have human thoughts and a mortal the thoughts of mortality" (1177b). According to the implications of this passage, thoughts about practical (for instance, political) matters would undoubtedly fall under the inferior category of "human thoughts." Aristotle explicitly states (ibidem) that the activity of the politician (as that of the warrior) does not constitute happiness.

Maimonides seems to be in agreement with Aristotle. This view comes out clearly in his allegorical interpretation of the story of Adam's fall (*Guide of the Perplexed,* I, 2). According to him, before his transgression, Adam was engaged in theoretical thought (i.e., only concerned with truth and falsehood), which is the highest state of man. It was as a result of his sin and the desires engendered thereby that he acquired the knowledge of good and bad. It is, in Maimonides' view, an inferior kind of knowledge, and this is in accord with the Aristotelian tradition. In fact, reference to Aristotle's *De Anima* (433a 14) and to the "Commentary" of this work by the sixth-century Christian philosopher, John Philoponus, shows that concern with truth is a property of the theoretical intellect, while knowledge of good and bad characterizes the practical intellect. Thus, in the passage which is cited, Maimonides, like other Aristotelians, affirms the superiority of the theoretical intellect. Other passages in the *Guide* seem to prove even more explicitly the inferiority of halakhic, i.e., practical, thought and knowledge to theoretical, intellectual activity. In the elaborate parable of the palace (*Guide,* III, 51), the philosophers, i.e., men who know physics and metaphysics, and the prophets who, by definition, are also philosophers, enter the castle while the halakhists are looking vainly for a way in. There is no question that strong evidence legitimates the thesis that in Maimonides' opinion the philosopher or potential philosopher, the prophet, and perhaps the philosopher-statesman on the one hand, and the (non-philosophical) halakhic scholar on the other, belong to two essentially different categories. Unlike the men belonging to the first category, the members of the second have no cognition of the true end of man which is theoretical knowledge. This thesis seems to imply that in Maimonides' view there is an equally essential difference between halakhic and philosophical writings (in which, in this context, the *Guide* may be included).

As has been indicated, this is a coherent theory which is borne out by a considerable number of statements by Maimonides. There are, however, some reasons for questioning it. I shall refer to one only; in my opinion, it is the most fundamental of them. It is the limitation of human knowledge as set forth in the *Guide.* If Maimonides' statements on this subject are not intentionally misleading—and there is no prima facie evidence to show that they should be discounted on this score—he believed that man is incapable of having positive knowledge of God; nor has he—according to some assertions of Maimonides—such knowledge of incorporeal substances other than God. Man can, moreover, only indulge in conjecture in attempting to understand the heavenly phenomena and the nature of the heavenly bodies. His scientific certainties are confined to sublunar physics. Now intellectual perfection, said to be man's final end, according to the *Guide,* is acquired through knowledge of physics and metaphysics. In the light of what has been stated, this affirmation raises obvious difficulties: the science of physics is only partly accessible to man, and human limitations are even more evident in metaphysics (called in Arabic and in Hebrew "the divine science"). The particular subject of study of this science is God and the incorporeal substances of which, as we have seen, according to Maimonides, man has no positive knowledge. According to this concept, philosophy, i.e., physics and metaphysics, would consist, to a considerable extent, in the cognition and demarcation of the limits of human knowledge. In other words, it would be a critical philosophy.

At first, this interpretation does not seem to fit with the Maimonidean statement that intellectual perfection is the final end of man. For this reason one would be tempted to dismiss it summarily if some views of al-Farabi, of whom Maimonides thought highly (he preferred him to all other Arabic philosophers), could not be adduced in support of it and to give it some credibility. Al-Farabi, who was well-known for his self-contradictions (referred to by the Arabic philosopher Ibn Ṭufayl), at some point in his intellectual evolution, appears to have asserted—perhaps under the influence of the Aristotelian doctrine concerning the relation between the *phantasma* and intellection —that, because of the incapacity of the human intellect to cognize incorporeal essences, man's happiness was to be found only within the sphere of politics. Hence, at this stage (as in Aristotelian parlance), "happiness denotes final end," al-Farabi seems to have denied that intellectual perfection is man's final end. These views, though irreconcilable with many passages in various works of Al-Farabi, may accord with his insistence (which goes beyond that of Plato's teaching concerning the return to the cave) that there is an essential identity between the philosopher, the king, the legislator, and the religious leader *(imam)*. Al-Farabi's apparent denial of the existence of intellectual happiness and of its being man's final end is clearly in accord with the interpretation of Maimonides' thought suggested above.

Nevertheless—in spite of the intellectual respectability conferred upon it by al-Farabi's authority—this interpretation appears to be doubtful; it seems to engender more difficulties than it solves, and some of these may prove to be insurmountable. It does, however, disclose a structural weakness in the coherent explanation of Maimonides' system criticized by it. The fact that David Hartman's reflections may lead to such questioning of fundamentals is one of several reasons for considering his work important.

CONTENTS

MAIMONIDES: TORAH AND PHILOSOPHIC QUEST

MULTIPLE RESPONSES TO THE CONFLICT OF PHILOSOPHY AND HALAKHAH

Maimonides considered the revelation of the Torah at Sinai to be the central shaping event of Jewish experience. Any work dealing with his philosophy must present the general attitudes and values to which he, a traditional Jew, was exposed in consequence of this assumption.[1]

The Torah provided the Jewish community with a historical memory of a living God who selected them from among the nations to be His people, through whom He would be sanctified in history: "And I will be hallowed among the children of Israel" (Lev. 22:32). This historical memory of divine election shaped Jewish reality by providing a set of normative frameworks organizing every facet of daily living. The community's food, social relationships, family structures, and festivals were organized according to the shaping directives of the Torah and their expanded exposition in the Talmud. The obligations of the community were clearly indicated.

The essential question in Judaism was not the nature of the good, for "It has been told you, O man, what is good, and what the Lord does require of you" (Mic. 6:8). The major concern was not theoretical virtue, but the human capacity to embody the will of God in action: Can I allow my instincts or the social pressures of the environment to deter me from the promise my community made to God to serve Him in all ways? The cognitive process was applied to a search through the norms of the Bible for new insights and interpretations that could serve situations requiring novel forms of action. The focus was always upon action, not upon theoretical truth. Belief in God was inseparably linked with a mode of behavior because by accepting the yoke of the kingdom of Heaven one was led to accept the yoke of the divine command. To do the will of God with all one's heart and soul was considered the highest achievement of man.

The Torah provided a conceptual framework for the understanding of nature and history. In itself, nature was not an object of pure inquiry except as a revelation of God's omnipotence. Nature revealed the power of God in shaping man's destiny. One looked to nature to confirm God's power in history and to inspire observance of God's Torah.

The Torah also provided Jews with the main political categories for understanding their condition in history. Their history was not defined by empirical, secular, political realities but by God alone. When they became His people and committed themselves to Him, their history was thereafter determined exclusively by their obedience or disobedience to His will. "Because of our sins have we been exiled from our land" was one of the important catchwords for understanding this historical condition. Not the secular powers of history, but divine punishment caused their exile. No secular power had control over their destiny. They were God's people and God alone was responsible for their fate.

Their historical memory of the eternal validity of the covenant enabled Jews to live with hope and with the inner conviction that their exile was only temporary. Ultimately they would return to their homeland if God so willed. Messianism was not grounded in man's faith in his own ability to shape and build a historical reality free from war and violence, but in the expressed conviction of Jews that God had a stake in Israel's historical destiny. Jews knew with certainty that God was not impotent in history, that secular power could not frustrate God in His designs. Each day they recalled the exodus from Egypt which reinforced their memory of God's supremacy over the secular powers of history.

The only action necessary before their condition in history could be changed was *teshuvah*, the turning to God and Torah. The Torah was the key "to life and the good." Would the community choose life and the good, or death and evil? In Jewish experience redemption was a historical event that would show itself in the changed historical condition of the people. The quest was not for individual salvation but for salvation of the entire community. Since God spoke to a whole people at Sinai, redemption would manifest itself in the altered condition of the community.

God was revealed through the life-history of the community: "I the Lord am your God who brought you out of the land of Egypt" (Ex. 20:2). The individual within the Jewish community recognized the primary role of community in shaping his spiritual self-consciousness. To separate from the community was to cut oneself off from the God of history. The divine will, history, community, action were therefore dominant and interconnected organizing principles of the daily life.

This brief introduction to Jewish self-understanding gives a proper perspective for understanding Maimonides. Maimonides lived by the Torah, wrote major works on Torah, and throughout his life endeavored to elucidate the talmudic world view. He wrote legal responsa answering the daily questions of a community committed to the obedience of God's will as reflected in the Torah. He devoted the major part of his intellectual life to expanding and clarifying this normative process. He did not question the imperative quality of the law, and he did not lose his inner certainty that ultimately the community would be redeemed by the lord of history. Maimonides was an observant Jew who participated in the great yearning of his people for messianic redemption.

This is admitted by all who write on Maimonides, but it is not always recognized as a necessary basis for the correct approach to his philosophical works. What significance are we to give to this historical, spiritual self-understanding of the tradition, to Maimonides' total devotion to the Torah, and to his intellectual concern for the law? To what degree did the way Maimonides lived influence the way he thought?

Does the imperative quality of Jewish theology seeing God in terms of will, become totally altered when Maimonides enters into the Greek philosophic understanding of God mediated by Islamic philosophers? In accepting the Aristotelian conception of nature, does Maimonides abandon the prophetic concern for history? Does the nature of Athens eliminate the possibility of the Sinai of Jerusalem? Does the importance Maimonides assigns to the laws of nature cause him to take up spiritual residence in Athens? Does God's wisdom, as revealed in nature, negate the possibility of His will being manifested in history?

Does the emphasis upon justice and kindness, upon imitation of God in terms of moral action, radically shift as Maimonides embraces the contemplative, spiritual ideal of Aristotle? Does philosophy with its demand for contemplative excellence weaken the prophetic demand for moral excellence? Does immortality grounded in intellectual perfection, negate the primacy of the moral? Is the primacy of community lost by the emphasis upon individual self-sufficiency achieved through intellectual perfection? Does Maimonides' yearning for immortality cause him to abandon the significance of messianism? Which city does Maimonides inhabit—Athens or Jerusalem?

Perhaps he inhabits neither city—not if they are understood as two polarized frameworks of theoretical and practical virtue. A new, yet old, Jerusalem may emerge once Athens enters into history. The concept of nature and the contemplative ideal inspired by a God who is revealed through the ordered laws of nature may grow in Jerusalem without destroying the city's unique quality. Athens may provide a wider understanding of what the Sinai-moment implicitly demanded. Once the outgrowths of Athens have taken root in the soil of Jerusalem both cities may not need to remain opposing spiritual poles. A new, spiritual synthesis with different categories may emerge. Man may remain fully within the way of Jerusalem and yet deeply appreciate and appropriate the way of Athens.

To judge whether Maimonides developed such a synthesis, we must first examine the options available to anyone who exposes his particular way of life, or tradition-based knowledge, to a spiritual world view possessing different conceptions of truth. By examining the possible responses to such a crisis of value, we can better appreciate the task Maimonides set for himself. Unless we understand the value-transmutations that may occur in such a crisis, and unless we appreciate that a spiritual vision in its openness to the world may grow and expand, I believe we cannot grasp the spirit of Maimonides' philosophy.

What inspires Maimonides' philosophic writings is concern for maintaining and enriching a particular way of

life that became threatened by the Greek spiritual outlook. Maimonides' philosophic audience is always the
faithful Jew who is perplexed by the clash of philosophy
and tradition. If one demands of the philosopher that he
come to his quest for truth with no particular loyalties, that
he philosophize without being rooted in any particular
culture, that he address no particular audience, then one
cannot attribute any philosophical value to Maimonides'
work. Maimonides' philosophy is significant only if one
accepts the fact that philosophy can be practiced within a
tradition. By recognizing the legitimacy of philosophy
within tradition, we can then examine that options are
available to someone who, while living within that tradition, is exposed to different world views.

OPTION 1

The way of insulation

One can meet the new threat and challenge of alien truths
by refusing to take them seriously. This other life-style,
since it is different, is considered insignificant. An attempt
to explain and justify one's own values within the categories of another culture presupposes that the rational
framework of the other must be taken seriously by one
committed to intellectual honesty. However, if by definition that which is outside one's culture is considered to
have no legitimate claim, then the necessity for justification and explanation ceases: I meet the challenge by justi-
fying the right to ignore it. I feel no compulsion to justify
myself in a strange language. I need not explain my
spiritual world view within categories which are not born
of my tradition.

This method of exclusion insulates an entire body of
knowledge from all serious challenges. All problems are

answered by denying legitimacy to the questions. In order to make this move of cultural insulation, one has to claim that one's culture not only defines what a person should do but also what is to count as genuine knowledge—a logical move of one who maintains that his body of knowledge and his way of life are guaranteed authenticity by divine revelation. If God is on his side, then lending significance to alien human claims is the height of irrationality. How can the intelligence of puny man challenge the wisdom and way of God? By committing oneself to a mode of living dictated by God, one excludes any possible claims which human reason can make unaided by divine revelation. Prophets do not have to explain themselves to philosophers. Prophets do not have to give reasons for their claims. They need but announce, "Thus has God spoken." Since God's thoughts are not man's thoughts, no common language exists between the human and the divine. There are no common criteria which enable one to question or to require of God that He justify Himself before a human tribunal. Contemporary experience shows that this cultural insulation, this way of exclusion, need not be supported by a divine revelatory claim. There are secular cultures which claim similar insulations from attack and need for justification for their systems of knowledge and values. Reference to God in a religious world can justify insulation; in a secular world naked claims of absolute power and superior-race theories can serve the same end.

OPTION 2

The way of dualism

One's tradition can be preserved by remaining behaviorally loyal to its values while nonetheless accepting the conflicting truth-claims of another system. This bifurcation is possible if the active, willing nature of man's being is severed from its reflective, rational aspect: My knowledge does not get in the way of my practices. My wisdom never interferes with my will. The life of the mind is permanently shut off from the life of action.

This can be justified by a specific evaluation of the significance of moral action. Although morality is necessary for perfecting life in society, it is insufficient for perfecting the rational nature of man: The outer forms my actions take do not really matter so long as they are socially useful and provide the tradition with a proper way of establishing a well-ordered community. In my search for truth I do not look to the moral and ritual demands of tradition. On the contrary, even if my tradition justifies the authoritative bases for its norms and the significance of its rituals by adopting meaningless and false cognitive claims, I adopt its moral actions and rituals without being disturbed by its spurious knowledge. The truths of theoretical reason need not falsify the claims of practical reason. The theoretical is the ground for knowledge; the practical is the ground for orderly political society. The search for truth does not demand that I openly reject the false knowledge-claims that are part of the tradition. My pursuit of intellectual excellence will find its fulfillment in the lonely life of the mind, in the private aspect of my life. It is in the non-social and private moments of life that I will act out my true humanity which is theoretical perfection.

If I never allow the two to become confused, my actions within society need not be disturbed by my private life. The separation of the public from the private self follows from a denial of any cognitive significance to ethical action. Moral norms, having a social function divorced from the concern for truth, are not evaluated and judged by reason. The commitment to truth need not challenge a moral system whose aim is social and political. Truth leads to self-perfection; moral norms lead to communal well-being. The way of dualism places morality within a category of health whose questions are wholly pragmatic: Do these norms create a healthy body politic? Functional rationality must be separated from truth. The functional is measured by its usefulness whereas truth, possessing intrinsic significance, is desired regardless of its social value. Only through the pursuit of truth does man become essentially human. Moral systems merely provide the necessary political conditions to further the pursuit of individual excellence.

The way of dualism protects the tradition from counter truth-claims by preventing any possible interaction between thought and action, by severing any connection between individual and social perfection. The god of metaphysics and the god of history are never confused. Ethics, ritual, freedom, and a god of will are justified within political categories and must never be subject to the categories of truth. The individual gives society his body as long as he is allowed to keep his mind.

In order to secure the life of theoretical virtue, one has further to promise that the realm of truth will not disturb the well-being of the society. Philosophy, which creates a new orientation to the world, is able to claim a man rooted to a tradition by offering him an independent life of the mind which does not affect his position within a social reality. He gives lip service to the cognitive claims of his action system, even if it contradicts his personal truth-system. He feels justified in doing so because he recognizes that action does not define the essential perfection of man. Because the ultimate criterion in evaluating an action-system is only its functional value, the faulty theoretical ground of the tradition need not affect his loyalty to truth. Even if the God of his truth-system cannot act in history, cannot create a world, nor interfere in the historical process, this does not prevent him from committing himself to a way of life which presupposes a God who acts in history.

Man's assent to this system and its theological claims is justified by its functionalism rather than by its truth. Knowing that he must live in community, he justifies the knowledge-claims of the community within political categories. Revelation and reason can coexist if revelation is placed within the practical domain and reason within a framework of truth. Socrates was the fool who confused philosophy with ethics and politics. Plato was naive to think that the philosopher can eliminate the darkness of the cave by his vision. Philosophy, with its emphasis upon theoretical virtue, must give up its intention of constructing a world based upon a system of truth.[2]

This separation of the mind—theoretical virtue— from the body—political virtue—would be more readily accepted if political virtue made no truth-claims and, vice versa, if theoretical virtue did not demand a specific way of life. There would be a semblance of intellectual integrity if the two realms were neatly separated. But if a system of political virtue does make knowledge-claims, and if a theoretical system does demand a specific life of action, then such separation suggests dishonesty.

This dishonest separation may still be tolerated because of an awareness that submission to social and political virtue is the only way of living in a crude world of mass ignorance. One is then condemned to live in this social and political world as a philosophic Marrano. He acknowledges that society requires fictions—e.g., God is concerned with individuals and their actions—in order that it may order its life. The ground of norms for mass man must be sustained and propped up by myths—e.g., revelation of a divine law with its promises of reward and punishment —which, although untrue, are necessary and acceptable because of their motivational value. It would be catastrophic to demand that society order itself according to an ideal system of perfection which only a few can achieve.

This elitism is an expression of concern for and responsibility to community. The awareness of the differences in human potentialities promotes a life-style for the philosophic Marrano who does not feel that he is dishonest since the difference "between man and man is greater than the difference between man and animal." The way of dualism is the way of aristocracy, of a responsible elite which does not perpetuate myths for its own perfection but for society. The essential feature which defines the way of dualism for a man committed to a specific tradition is a combination of openness to truth—regardless of the source and the implications of that truth—and complete behavioral loyalty to the norms of his tradition.

OPTION 3

The way of rejection

The third option contains elements of the second, yet is significantly different. Unable to sever thought from practice, as the person utilizing the previous option of dualism is able to do, the individual refuses to sacrifice his body for his mind. He chooses to reject his own tradition completely, since he cannot separate the system of moral and religious rituals from theoretical claims.

Individuals using options two and three agree that the

truths of reason are in complete disharmony with the cognitive principles of the tradition. Neither of them allows tradition to define truth. Put in religious terms, they both agree that knowledge-claims cannot be justified by an exclusive appeal to revelation, but must be scrutinized to determine whether they are agreeable to human reason.

A mind that is loyal to the claims of reason may find the claims of revelation degrading and insulting. The claim that divine thoughts are not human thoughts becomes, for this individual, not a justification for submission to revelation but a reason for its rejection. He finds himself incapable of accepting a divine truth which is false by human standards. Appeal to authority does not convince a mind that views loyalty to tradition as an obstacle to the growth of understanding. The independent human mind then becomes the judge as to what is to count as truth.

The first option, the way of insulation, rejected knowledge which is unconfirmed by tradition. The second option rejected the truth-claims of tradition but accepted its practical demands. The third option rejects both the cognitive and the practical on the grounds that it is impossible to sever the private, theoretical self from the public, active self. A man choosing the third option cannot subscribe to a tradition—even though that tradition only affects actions—if in order to justify those actions, he must posit specific theological claims (e.g., a god of history, revelation) which he knows to be false.

However the unified and integrated person may not have to reject tradition. There can be another way to resolve the conflict of tradition and reason.

OPTION 4

The way of integration

The fourth option regarding this conflict is one in which the individual takes both knowledge-claims seriously: the religious as grounded in revelation and in traditional authority, and the human as grounded in reason. He does not assume an either/or posture. He refuses to believe that man must choose between God's mind and his own. "Your thoughts are not my thoughts" does not lead irrevocably to the complete severance of religious knowledge-claims and rational human-claims; it does not imply the impossibility of common areas of discourse.

Divine revelation need not be in discord with human understanding. In fact where they share a common domain, in principle, they are never in discord. Man's rationality participates in the divine system of knowledge. There are not two truths.

This participation does not mean that man can grasp all that the divine mind knows. But to say that man does not know all that God knows is not to say that the divine mind can know, as truth, that which the human mind knows to be false. The two minds do not contradict one another. To say that God's thoughts are not human thoughts is only to admit the limits of human understanding, and does not imply that the two contradict each other. The statement merely denies any claim of the human mind ultimately to judge what may count as true and as false. The human mind is not the sole source of knowledge. There are limits to human comprehension. Nevertheless, that which stretches beyond the limits of human understanding does not negate that which is within its limits. That which the human mind knows to be logically impossible from within its sphere of competence cannot be proven logically possible by the claim that the divine mind knows it to be true.

The human mind is prepared to admit limitations and yet claim absolute sovereignty within the legitimate scope of its understanding. This paradoxical gesture which admits both the absolute competence and limitations of human rationality is always operative within the fourth option—the way of integration—a gesture which may be called restrained self-confidence. Revelation, as mediated through the tradition, does not cause the individual to doubt that which can be known within the human sphere. He feels confident that he can maintain a posture of critical loyalty to the tradition because he knows that the tradition encourages and values the use of human reason. God does not play tricks nor does He deceive the human mind. God cannot square the circle. God cannot make possible that which is logically impossible. It is the human mind which defines the logically impossible that God's mind never violates. The same logical rules that apply to human understanding apply to the divine mind as well. The individual within this fourth, integrative, option applies the principle of limit, which is not a principle of negation, to the religious knowledge-claims of his tradition.

When the individual discovers apparent contradictions between the claims of revelation and the claims of reason, does he doubt his own system of reasoning or the claims of tradition? He knows that what he knows is true. He knows that his religious posture does not demand of him to doubt his own mind's rational credentials. If truth is not determined exclusively by tradition then he can demand that tradition make itself intelligible within the categories of the established truths of reason.

The fourth way makes possible an integration between the claims of tradition and the claims of reason by expanding the possible meanings of religious language to include symbolic meaning. A literal understanding of one's religious language limits the possibility of its being modified by new intellectual claims. The key epistemological criteria used to determine whether one is to read the language literally or symbolically are defined by the claims of reason. Rational demonstrative truth has the power to alter the literal meaning of religious language. However in order for a reevaluation of religious language to be in harmony with tradition, and in order that it not appear as a total distortion, one must demonstrate that tradition itself justifies the use of symbolic interpretation. Unless the tradition has within it the category of symbolic language and an awareness that religious language can be understood in multiple ways, the encounter between demonstrative truth and tradition forces a total abandonment of the latter. In order to feel that the reevaluation is itself a traditional mode of understanding, one must show that the tradition has built into it the awareness that its own language can be taken symbolically.

The way of integration cannot be used by individuals who choose the first two options because they separate the individual's trust of his own mind from his loyalty to community. In the first option, community defines the individual's life; in the second, the individual and community reflect incompatible life-styles. The emphasis upon individual self-realization demands the severance of social excellence from individual perfection.

The way of integration requires not only a cognitive reinterpretation of tradition, but a recognition that the community itself points to the goal of individual excellence, a recognition that the normative system of the community encourages individuals to move ahead according to their spiritual capacities. What is involved in the way of integration, therefore, is a total attempt to reconstruct the meaning of the normative system. If the normative system does not point to individual excellence, then the way of integration has failed. The individual will still be acting within communal rather than individual categories.

The way of integration rejects the first option not only for its insistence on tradition as the criterion of truth, but for its concomitant behavioral emphasis on submission to authority. For the first option to succeed, for one to believe that the tradition claims both the actions and thoughts of an individual, one's own understanding must not be allowed to question the criteria and content of tradition, as mediated through community. One must have an obedient nature to admit that authority defines truth. To encourage this total regard for authority, the tradition must develop the capacity for obedience through its norms. If, however, the individual is encouraged to think, and if the mind's discovery of demonstrative truths is considered sufficient reason for rethinking the tradition, then something is set in motion. This is the individual who does not look upon obedience as the highest virtue, but recognizes that to understand is greater than to obey. The trust in human reason creates a new relationship to God: love based upon understanding. The way of integration will not revel in norms that are not reasonable, nor consider the soul to be spiritually nurtured when it is obedient to that which it doesn't understand. On the contrary, actions which grow from understanding will be seen as the highest level of religious achievement.

A whole new way of life emerges when we maintain that community does not define the contents of truth. A whole new person emerges when one is encouraged to explore freely in the world of nature and to discover truths which are demonstrable to all men, and when traditional authority must justify itself to all rational creatures by rational method. Once tradition needs to justify itself in the court of universal reason, it can no longer demand obedience to itself as the highest virtue nor can it regard such obedience as the way to spiritual excellence. Obedience is the method which a community can use if it insists that it alone has the truth and does not have to justify or to explain itself in categories and to people outside the tradition. Arguments from authority presuppose acceptance of the authority which derives in turn from a loyalty to the community which legitimates that authority.

He who lives within the way of integration will attempt to discover methods of making his tradition intelligible within a universal framework of intelligibility. To the degree that one can render one's tradition comprehensible to all people, to that degree one can argue that the way of reason and the way of tradition are harmonious. Even those areas which manifest the particular life-style of the tradition will be interpreted within categories that are intelligible to all reasonable men. It is not enough that the knowledge-claims of tradition be in harmony with universal claims of knowledge; the way of integration strives to make the practice of tradition comprehensible and meaningful to all men.

One last feature of the way of integration must be emphasized. As mentioned, the way of integration strives to harmonize reason and tradition within a framework of mutual enrichment. The spiritual values that the tradition holds to be important become enhanced through the way of reason. Reason provides both a guide to knowledge-claims within the tradition and an opportunity for the individual to realize the goal which the tradition holds to be important. The growth of knowledge moves one to a deeper understanding of the tradition; the goals which are present within the way of reason take on new dimensions as a result of the tradition.

There are trends within modern approaches to Maimonides which suggest that his thought should be understood from the perspective of dualism. Isaac Husik and Leo Strauss divide the works of Maimonides into two distinct parts: the philosophical, exemplified by *The Guide of the Perplexed*, and the legal, *The Commentary to the Mishnah* and the *Mishneh Torah*.

According to Husik, Maimonides never intended to communicate philosophy to those who were engaged in the study of law. Students of the Talmud were never bothered with the implications of philosophic thought:

> Maimonides did not write his philosophy for the masses, nor did he compose his *Guide of the Perplexed* for the simple and the pious, though learned, students of the Talmud and the other rabbinic literature. They were satisfied with their simple faith, and Maimonides was not interested in disturbing it. For them he composed his *Yad ha-Hazakah*, the code of the rabbinic law.[3]

According to Husik, Maimonides wrote two major legal works, which occupied most of his lifetime, in order to teach people with simple faith how to conduct their lives. Their minds were too naive to be bothered by the speculative problems of philosophy; these are the concern of the student of the *Guide,* and are not to be discovered in Maimonides' legal writings. Husik believes, that in the *Guide,* Maimonides shows his true self, i.e., his Aristotelianism. The theoretical interests of Maimonides, however, run into conflict when he tries to apply Aristotelianism to specific Jewish concerns:

> As we approach those problems in which the human interest is very strong and particularly as we draw nearer to specifically

Jewish doctrines, we shall find that the measure of inconsistency increases, threatening to disrupt the entire system. The theoretical and practical parts of Maimonides' teachings do not hang together satisfactorily.[4]

Torah, with its concern for the way an individual acts before his God, cannot be integrated with a conception of the world that is concerned with the development of theoretical perfection. Husik marvels that Maimonides did not recognize the fundamental incompatibility between Aristotelianism and Torah:

Maimonides is an Aristotelian, and he endeavors to harmonize the intellectualism and theorism of the Stagirite with the diametrically opposed ethics and religion of the Hebrew Bible. And he is apparently unaware of the yawning gulf extending between them. The ethics of the Bible is nothing if not practical. No stress is laid upon knowledge and theoretical speculation as such. . . . That the pentateuchal law is solely concerned with practical conduct—religious, ceremonial, and moral—needs no saying. It is so absolutely clear and evident that one wonders how so clearsighted a thinker like Maimonides could have been misled by the authority of Aristotle and the intellectual atmosphere of the day to imagine otherwise.[5]

Husik does not question the Aristotelian models of theoretical and practical virtue from which he tries to understand Maimonides. What he does question is Maimonides' "naive" belief that Aristotelianism can live together with Torah. A further illustration of this approach can be found in an article by Harry Wolfson on Judah Halevi and Maimonides:

Maimonides was not a rabbi employing Greek logic and categories of thought in order to interpret Jewish religion; he was rather a true medieval Aristotelian using Jewish religion as an illustration of the Stagirite's metaphysical supremacy. Maimonides adheres staunchly to the Law, of course, but his adherence is not the logical consequence of his system. It has its basis in his heredity and practical interests; it is not the logical implication of his philosophy. Judaism designated the established social order of life, in which Maimonides lived and moved and had his being; and it was logically as remote from his intellectual interests as he was historically remote from Aristotle. That, naturally, he was unaware of the dualism must be clear. Indeed he thought he had made a synthesis and had given scientific demonstrations of poetic conceptions. Therein he was like the Italian priest and astronomer, Pietro Angelo Secchi, who, while performing his religious services, dropped Copernican astronomy, and while in the observatory, dropped his church doctrines. Maimonides really saw no incompatibility between his Judaism and his philosophy; he was a Jew in letter and a philosopher in spirit throughout his life.[6]

Leo Strauss follows the approach of bifurcating Maimonides' legal work from his philosophical work.[7] His effort at showing that the *Guide,* as opposed to the *Mishneh Torah,* reflects the true opinions of Maimonides is just a further elaboration, although a more sophisticated one, of the view that Maimonides separated theoretical from practical virtue. The relationship of Torah to philosophy must be understood, according to Strauss, in only one direction. Law aims at establishing the proper political order through which the philosopher is able to realize his individual quest for theoretical perfection. Just as a healthy body is a necessary condition for a healthy mind, so too is Torah a necessary condition for the establishment of a healthy political state. The creation of this healthy community is only a means to the further end of theoretical perfection.

The law of Sinai is a necessary station on the road leading to theoretical perfection. Once the individual enters into the domain of theoretical reason he never again reconsiders the meaning of his Torah observance. He goes through the required motions of political man: he obeys the law, but he knows that his true identity is defined by his quest for theoretical perfection.

According to Strauss, Maimonides' insistence that the law commands us to philosophize is only a clever political ruse used to safeguard the philosopher from persecution. In order for a Jew to philosophize he must first gain approval and legitimacy from a legal system which has no use for philosophy.[8] To obviate the danger to Maimonides the Philosopher, Maimonides the Judge must show that the Torah commands one to philosophize. The community, however, must not be allowed to know Maimonides the Philosopher, but only Maimonides the observant Judge, for if it discovers the true opinions of Maimonides the Philosopher, it will recognize the fraud that Maimonides the Judge has perpetrated upon it.[9]

This dichotomy in Maimonides (judge-philosopher) explains the esoteric and exoteric character of his writings:

Exoteric literature presupposes that there are basic truths which would not be pronounced in public by any decent man because they would do harm to many people who, having been hurt, would naturally be inclined to hurt in turn him who pronounces the unpleasant truths.[10]

According to Strauss, Maimonides writes in his legal work as a responsible judge for a community whose beliefs he rejects as a philosopher.[11] In describing Maimonides, one must always distinguish between these two roles. What Maimonides qua philosopher says he will never, qua judge, admit. The philosopher-king of Plato, as understood by al-Farabi, is the model from which Strauss studies Maimonides' understanding of the Torah.[12]

Maimonides' concern for Torah is to be understood within the model of political philosophy:

The exoteric teaching was needed for protecting philosophy. It was the armor in which philosophy had to appear. It was needed for political reasons. It was the form in which philosophy became visible to the political community.[13]

Both Plato and Maimonides aimed at establishing a society which would not persecute those who strove for theoretical perfection. The philosopher-king knows that in order to maintain the well-being of the political state, it may be necessary to perpetuate noble lies; similarly, Maimonides, the Platonist, perpetuates noble myths, such as messianism, God of history, and reward and punishment, in order to harness the society and to motivate the members within it to be obedient to the law.

The political aspect of the Torah will be supported by beliefs which are untrue but necessary for those individuals who are not capable of living the life of a philosopher. The philosopher-king never reveals to the masses what only the few can know. Maimonides' private speech to his single student in the *Guide* is never revealed to his public audience in the *Mishneh Torah*. He knows, however, that the public may read his *Guide* and discover the private thoughts of the king. Therefore he must write in such a way that only a few will be able to fully understand the *Guide*.[14] One gains the impression from reading Strauss that the importance and excitement of studying Maimonides lies not in what he writes, for there is nothing essentially new in his philosophy that one could not discover in al-Farabi or Aristotle, but in the brilliant way in which Maimonides hides his true thoughts from the Jewish community. The art of his writing reveals to Strauss the essential gap that has always existed between a philosopher who searches for truth, and a society concerned with law and history.[15]

Maimonides' thought is important if placed within the framework of a sociology of philosophy which does not see the thinker reflecting his community but, rather, focuses on the gap between the individual and the public man. From the writings of Husik and Strauss we do not gain any sense of the Jewish importance of Maimonides' works. As an Aristotelian, Maimonides contributes nothing to a deeper understanding of Judaism. Maimonides can only teach the believing Jew who has studied philosophy that his religious practices need not conflict with that study. He in no way shows how commitment to Torah can be deepened by philosophy. As long as the Jew needs to be a member of his society it is important for him to observe the law. His Torah observance continues as an appendage to his private Hellenistic spiritual development.

The approaches of Husik and Strauss to Maimonides reflect their understanding of the either/or decision that an individual must make regarding the conflict of reason and revelation. Either one chooses to be an Orthodox Jew who believes in revelation in a fundamentalist fashion, or one becomes an Aristotelian. Either one accepts the way of biblical man and learns to obey the will of God, or one follows the path of Greek philosophy and reflects on the wisdom of God.[16]

Athens, which is reason, and Jerusalem, which is revelation, are polarized by such thinkers and one is left with no alternative. As Strauss explicitly states:

> Jews of the philosophic competence of Halevi and Maimonides took it for granted that being a Jew and being a philosopher are mutually exclusive.[17]

If Maimonides accepted the virtue of critical rationality and individual excellence, and if he believed that the study of nature could provide one with knowledge of God independent of revelation, he could no longer return to the world view of Jerusalem.[18]

Strauss, unlike Husik, believes that Maimonides was

aware of the incompatibility between Jerusalem and Athens. Maimonides knew that he was a political-institutional Jew whose devotion to Torah was based upon practical, political interests which had no relationship to his personal, spiritual quest. Maimonides' awareness of the incompatibility of being a Jew and a philosopher is the factor responsible for his writing exoteric and esoteric books. Strauss denies any possible philosophical connection between Maimonides' legal and philosophical writings: These works are so bifurcated that any attempt at unity would be a violation of Maimonides' true Aristotelianism.[19]

The chapters that follow seek to prove that Maimonides chose the way of integration, and that his total philosophical endeavor was an attempt to show how the free search for truth, established through the study of logic, physics, and metaphysics, can live harmoniously with a way of life defined by the normative tradition of Judaism. The primacy of action is not weakened by the contemplative ideal; a deeper purpose for the normative structure is realized instead once the philosophic way is followed. The contemplative ideal is not insulated from Halakhah, but affects it in a new manner. Sinai is not a mere stage in man's spiritual development, but the ultimate place to which man constantly returns—even when he soars to the heights of metaphysical knowledge.

As noted, the concern for individual excellence is in direct opposition to a world view which emphasizes the ideal of a holy people. Therefore, the relationship of philosophy to Halakhah as it bears directly upon the question of the individual and community in Maimonidean thought must be considered. The claim that Maimonides attempted an integration of philosophy and the teachings of his tradition will rest upon an analysis of the manner in which he established a genuine harmony between commitment to community and intellectual love of God.

PHILOSOPHY IN MAIMONIDES' LEGAL WORKS

In his introduction to *The Guide of the Perplexed* Maimonides explicitly states that he wrote the work for individuals perplexed by the apparent conflict between talmudic Judaism and philosophic inquiry.[1] Elsewhere he states that his legal works were addressed to the general community of halakhic Jews.[2] Husik and Strauss claim that Maimonides protected his halakhic reader from the disturbing influences of philosophy.[3] But as we shall see, Maimonides did not totally insulate the audience of his legal works from the importance and significance of philosophy.[4] Although one recognizes that Maimonides' *Guide* and his legal works were addressed to different audiences, one may yet reject the approach which would understand these two audiences as reflecting two incompatible spiritual outlooks. Maimonides, who placed a high value on philosophy, did not restrict himself to communicating his philosophic understanding of Judaism to perplexed students alone, but also attempted to lead the traditional halakhic Jew toward a philosophic orientation to Jewish spirituality. An examination of Maimonides' treatment of philosophy in his legal works will enable us to judge whether he was aiming at a unification of philosophy and

Halakhah or whether, in the legal writings, he was articulating the views of a tradition which had no use for philosophy.

Maimonides' first major legal work was his *Commentary to the Mishnah*. Saul Lieberman and Joseph Kafih have shown that Maimonides did not cease reediting and correcting this work after its completion in 1168.[5] One cannot claim, therefore, that it represents an early phase in the development of Maimonides' thinking. Also, it must be clear that a medieval Jew's commentary on a rabbinic work represents his personal understanding of Judaism. Revelation as expressed in the Bible was not the only basis upon which the traditional Jew organized his spiritual life; he accepted the Bible as understood and developed by the talmudic tradition.

In the introduction to his *Commentary to the Mishnah* Maimonides divides the subject matter of the Talmud into four categories:

 a) explanation of the Mishnah;

 b) legal decisions in situations of conflict either in the Mishnah itself or in interpretations of the Mishnah;

 c) matters relating to new legislation which was introduced after the redaction of the Mishnah;

 d) *derashot*—non-legal writing (subsequently referred to as Aggadah).[6]

Although the greater part of the Talmud deals with legal issues, Maimonides is quick to warn his reader not to undervalue the last category, Aggadah:

One must not think that it is of slight importance, or that it is of little use since it serves a very great purpose in that it includes deep allusions and marvelous issues, for if one engages in a deep examination of those *derashot* he will gain from them understanding of the absolute good regarding which there is none greater and from which will be revealed Divine matters and true matters, all of which were concealed by men of science and with which philosophers consumed a whole lifetime.[7]

This statement clearly articulates an approach to the Talmud and thus to traditional Judaism which not only rejects the view that Judaism is exclusively a legal system concerned with normative behavior, but emphasizes the primacy of Aggadah.[8] To appreciate fully the implications of this position in terms of Maimonides' understanding of Judaism, we should clarify the epistemology involved. Although one's epistemology is not sufficient to explain a way of life, it is a key factor which makes certain options possible while it excludes others. This is especially true when the various world views involve such concepts as revelation and human reason.

The two modes of discourse, Halakhah and Aggadah, are not identical. The normative legal framework is an elaboration of the revelation of the law which is specific to the Jewish community. Other nations do not share in this legal system and are not bound to recognize its normative appeal. This particularity, however, does not obtain to the teaching of truths contained in Aggadah.

In *The Commentary to the Mishnah, Hagigah,* Maimonides identifies the esoteric teachings of Judaism, *Ma'aseh Bereshit* (the Account of Creation) and *Ma'aseh Merkavah* (the Account of the Chariot), with the universal cognitive disciplines of physics and metaphysics.[9] This identification denies any intrinsic mystery to the hidden teachings. In principle, these teachings are capable of being understood by all men of reason because, according to Maimonides, the criteria upon which they are based are universal criteria of knowledge. The caution with which such teachings were handled by the tradition was due not to the fact of their requiring initiation into some unique esoteric logic, but rather to an awareness of the difficult and extensive intellectual training in logic and mathematics which such disciplines demanded.[10]

The point of this discussion is Maimonides' assertion that the epistemology of Aggadah is not unique and exclusive to Jews. One may question this position by pointing out that Aggadah does not speak in the explicit style of philosophic treatises. One may also indicate that many aggadic statements appear to contradict the claims of reason. Maimonides must defend his position by explaining such counter-evidence. Also, Maimonides' epistemology upsets a prevalent approach to Judaism which insists on the unintelligibility of Aggadah to the non-Jew. Certain norms of the Halakhah which are laughed at by the nations of the world (e.g., the ritually forbidden linsey-woolsey, the red heifer, the scapegoat), have trained the Jew to carry the burden of isolation from the rest of the world.[11] Similarly, one may argue, the Jew must carry the burden of accepting aggadot which are laughed at by non-Jewish scholars. The spiritual and political isolation of the Jewish people can reinforce and support Jewish insulation, both with regard to the practice of Halakhah and the acceptance of Aggadah. Maimonides deals with these problems in his introduction to *The Commentary to the Mishnah* and in his commentary to *Ḥelek*.

In *Ḥelek*, Maimonides describes two approaches to Aggadah which cognitively isolate the Jewish community from the universal world of rational discourse:

The first class is, as far as I have seen, the largest in point of their numbers and of the numbers of their composition; and it is of them that I have heard most. The members of this class adopt the words of the Sages literally, and give no kind of interpretation whatsoever. With them all impossibilities are necessary occurrences. This is owing to their being ignorant of science and far away from knowledge. . . . They think that in all their emphatic and precise remarks the Sages only wished to convey the ideas which they themselves comprehend, and that they intended them to be taken in their literalness. And this, in spite of the fact that in their literal significance some of the words of the Sages would savor of absurdity. And so much so that were they manifested to the ordinary folk, leave alone the educated, in their literalness, they would reflect upon them in amazement and would exclaim: "How can there exist anyone who would seriously think in this way and regard such statements as the correct view of things much less approve of them?" This class of men are poor, and their folly deserves our pity.[12]

Maimonides does not question the pious motive inspiring this group's literal acceptance of Aggadah. He shares the absolute allegiance to rabbinic authority that this group proclaims:

Three classes are deniers of the Torah. He who says that the Torah is not of Divine origin—even if he says of one verse, or of a single word, that Moses said it, of himself—is a denier of the Torah; likewise, he who denies its interpretation, that is, the Oral Law, and repudiates its reporters, as Zadok and Boethius did; and he who says that the Creator changed one commandment or another, and that this Torah, although of Divine origin is now obsolete, as the Nazarenes and Moslems assert. Everyone belonging to any of these classes is a denier of the Torah.[13]

Yet while Maimonides would define this allegiance in terms of legal matters, this group expands the idea of rabbinic authority to include Aggadah as well.[14] Torah, as a unity of Halakhah and Aggadah, would argue against separating thought from action. Why discriminate between what the rabbis legislate in Halakhah and what they preach in Aggadah?

Against this approach Maimonides appeals to the Torah, arguing that the Torah itself indicates the existence and legitimacy of universal criteria of truth:

For this is your wisdom and your understanding in the sight of the nations which shall hear all these statutes and say, "Surely, that great nation is a wise and discerning people" (Deut. 4:6).

If there are specific Jewish criteria of truth, how could this promise be realized?[15] If what counts for truth in this community is to be based exclusively upon rabbinic authority, how can the Torah expect those who are not bound by that authority to marvel and appreciate the wisdom of the community? There must exist, then, independent criteria of truth which neither Jew nor non-Jew can ignore.

A careful reader of Maimonides' proof-text would immediately discover that the wisdom which the world appreciates includes the laws of Judaism:

See, I have imparted to you laws and rules, as the Lord my God has commanded me, for you to abide by in the land which you are about to invade and occupy. Observe them faithfully, for that will be proof of your wisdom and discernment to other peoples, who on hearing of all these laws will. say, "Surely that great nation is a wise and discerning people." For what great nation is there that has a god so close at hand as is the Lord our God whenever we call upon Him? Or what great nation has laws and as perfect as all this Teaching that I set before you this day? (Deut. 4:5–8).

The student must await *The Guide of the Perplexed* for a full explication of how Judaism as a whole—its Aggadah and Halakhah—can be seen as worthy and capable of universal appreciation.[16] In his commentary to *Ḥelek* Maimonides deals only with Aggadah. He informs his reader that the literalistic approach which leads to insulation "robs our religion of its beauties, darkens its brilliance and makes the Law of God convey meanings quite contrary to those it was intended to convey."[17]

A second group of readers accepts a literalistic reading of Aggadah which leads, however, not to submission, but to derision and rejection:

> The second class of reasoners is also numerous. They see and hear the words of the Sages and accept them in their literal significations, thinking that the Sages meant nothing but what the literal interpretation indicates. They consequently apply themselves to showing the weakness of the Rabbinical statements and their objectionable character, and to slandering that which is free from reproach. They make sport of the words of the Sages from time to time and imagine themselves more intellectually gifted and possessed of more penetrating minds, whereas they, peace to them, are deceived, shortsighted, ignorant of all existing things, and consequently unable to comprehend anything. . . . They are more stupid than the first class, of which we have spoken, and more steeped in folly! They are an accursed class, because they put themselves in opposition to men of great worth, whose learning is manifest to scholars. If only they trained themselves in knowledge so as to know how necessary it is to use the appropriate speech in theology, and in like subjects. . . .[18]

Since this group views the rabbis as fools and simpletons, one may infer rejection of rabbinic legislative authority as well.[19] Maimonides' statement that "they are an accursed class" seems to suggest this. The fundamentalist understanding of Aggadah by a person unable to disassociate his thinking from the way he acts results either in total obedience to tradition, the way of insulation of the first class, or in abandonment of the tradition, the way of rejection of the second class.

Maimonides offers a third approach:

> The third class of thinkers is, as God lives, so very small in numbers that one would only call it a class in the sense that the sun is termed a species although it is a single object. They are the men who accept as established facts the greatness of the Sages and the excellence of their thoughts, as found in the generality of their remarks, where each word points a very true theme. . . . The members of this class are convinced also of the impossibil-

ity of the impossible and the necessary existence of what must exist. For they know that they, peace to them, would not talk absurdities to one another. And they are convinced beyond doubt that their words have both an outer and an inner meaning, and that in all that they say of things impossible, their discourses were in the form of riddle and parable.[20]

Maimonides' reader is an observant Jew who fully accepts the Halakhah as a self-contained system with a specific logic of legal interpretation and development. Yet, Maimonides' point here is that this need not prevent one from recognizing that aggadic discourse can be understood in a manner different from the way in which one understands halakhic discourse. The halakhic Jew can approach the Aggadah with knowledge gained from sources independent of the tradition; when Aggadah violates reason's understanding of the necessary or the impossible, he recognizes that Aggadah must be understood symbolically.[21] The reader who is a member of this group (the reader whom Maimonides wants to cultivate) manifests his reverence for the tradition by his painstaking attempts to uncover hidden meanings in the Aggadah. By recognizing that one must discover the point of a statement before one can judge it to be true or false, one can combine a serious allegiance to the tradition with a commitment to universal criteria of knowledge. To reject a rabbinic or biblical statement whose literal reading contradicts accepted truths is to misunderstand the meaning of that which one purports to evaluate.

Maimonides supports his approach to Aggadah by showing that a symbolic understanding of Torah texts is a traditional mode of understanding:

And how can we disapprove of their literary productions being in the manner of proverb and simile of a lowly and popular kind, seeing that the wisest of men did the same "by holy inspiration" i.e., Solomon, in the books of Proverbs, Song of Songs, and parts of Ecclesiastes? How can we disapprove of the method of placing interpretations on the words of Sages, and drawing them out of their literalness to adjust them to reason and make them accord with truth and the books of Scripture, seeing that the Sages themselves place their interpretations on the words of the text and, by bringing them out of their literal meaning, present them as parable?[22]

One does not, therefore, distort the tradition when one applies an approach toward understanding Aggadah that differs from the method used to understand Halakhah.

The acceptance of the symbolic approach to aggadic language immediately raises a question: Why did the tradition choose to speak in parables when it could have been explicit and literal? Maimonides offers the following explanation in his introduction to the *Commentary to the Mishnah:*

And they did this to marvelous issues, i.e., wrote in parables whose literal meaning may be contrary to reason; first, to awaken the understanding of students, and also to blind the eyes of fools whose hearts will never be enlightened, and even if the truth were presented before them they would turn away from it according to the deficiency of their natures, as it is [written] said regarding those like them, "One does not reveal to them the secret" (T.B. Kedushin 71a), for their intellect is not perfect to the extent required to receive the truth as it is. . . . And, thus, it is improper for the man of knowledge [perfect man] to publicize what he knows of the secret teachings other than to one who is greater than he or like him. Because if he would present it before a fool, if [the latter] would not deprecate it to his face, surely the matter will not find favor in his eyes. Therefore, the wise man said: "Speak not in the ears of a fool; for he will despise the wisdom of thy words" (Prov. 23:9). And also, it is not correct to teach the public but by the way of riddle and parable in order to include women, young men, and children, so that when their intellects reach perfection they will know the meanings [matter] of those parables. To this issue Solomon alluded in his saying, "To understand a proverb, and a figure; the words of the wise, and their dark sayings" (Prov. 1:6), and because of this our Sages, peace to them, spoke about Divine matters in riddle form. Thus it is proper for a person who happens to come across one of their statements, which he thinks is opposed to reason, not to attribute the deficiency to those statements, but to attribute the deficiency to his own intellect. And when he sees one of their parables whose literal meaning is far from his understanding, it is proper for him to be much grieved that he did not understand the issue so that all true statements became extremely distant [to his understanding]. For the intellects of men are as different as differences of temperament, and as the temperament of one man is better and closer to the mean than the temperament of another man, so too will the intellect of one man be more perfect and complete than the intellect of another man. There is no doubt that the intellect of one who knows a sublime matter is not as the intellect of one who does not know that matter, for the one is like an intellect *in actu* and the other an intellect *in potentia*. Therefore, there are matters [issues] which to a specific person are perfectly clear and correct, while to another person they are in the domain of the impossible, according to the extent of their level of wisdom.[23]

The tradition spoke exactly and explicitly when it legislated norms.[24] However it spoke symbolically when it was guiding the individual toward higher spiritual achievements. The ambiguity and obscurity of the parables is a challenge to the wise and a veil to the unlearned. When the tradition elaborated norms for the community it addressed itself not to the elite few but to the total community. Moses as well as every other member of the community is expected to obey the same law.[25]

The democratization of the spiritual which is the hallmark of the Halakhah is not, however, the complete picture of Judaism. For those individuals capable of deeper spirituality it provides an Aggadah:

For these matters are not among those that can be taught, and are not interpreted in public, rather they [rabbis] allude to them in books by hidden allusions. And if God removes the screens from the heart of one who is pleasing before Him, after he has prepared himself through study, [such a person] will understand of them according to his intellect. . . . And when God reveals to such a man whatever He reveals, he should hide [such knowledge] as we said, and if he alludes to something [of them] behold [he should do so] only to one whose intellect is perfected and whose righteousness is known as we have explained and clarified in many stories of the Talmud.[26]

The tradition, in its desire not only to legislate for community but also to guide individuals, was concerned with not exposing the road of spiritual excellence to those unprepared to understand or to appreciate the sublime teachings of *Ma'aseh Bereshit* and *Ma'aseh Merkavah*. The symbolic language of Aggadah enables the individual to cultivate his individual capacity for excellence within a community defined by a comprehensive, all-inclusive law.

The emphasis upon individual excellence and the spiritual well-being of community are two characteristics of the supposedly incompatible world views of philosophy and Judaism. Maimonides resolves this apparent conflict between philosophy and Halakhah by showing that the Talmud, through Halakhah and Aggadah, embraced both the individual and community.

It is mistaken to impute to Maimonides the introduction of Hellenistic teachings into Judaism when he maintains that not all men can be placed at the same level of spiritual excellence. Any superficial reading of the Bible or the Talmud would show that not every member of the community was on the same level as the prophets or the talmudists. Husik is mistaken in his claim that the Bible is exclusively a guidebook for action.[27] We are not told in the Bible that the difference between prophet and community is based solely on degrees of practice. Maimonides did not invent the idea of the rarity of excellence. He only offered us a way of understanding it.

After explaining why aggadic language is symbolic, Maimonides proceeds, in his introduction, to show the reader how to interpret an aggadic statement which is opposed to reason. If his concern had been solely epistemological, i.e., to show that Aggadah does not violate the conclusions of science and metaphysics, he should have selected an aggadic statement which appears to contradict reason's understanding of nature and then proceeded to interpret and to reveal that statement's compatibility with reason. There are many bizarre factual claims in Aggadah which could serve this purpose. The Aggadah which he chose to explain, however, is a model from which to evaluate the supposed incompatibility of the spiritual outlooks of Athens and Jerusalem.[28] This Aggadah is neither a factual nor a metaphysical claim. It is, instead, a succinct statement of a world view which would destroy any attempts to construct a unity of philosophy and halakhic Judaism: "God only has in His world the four cubits of the Halakhah" (T.B. Berakhot 8a).

To what does Maimonides appeal to convince his reader that this statement must not be accepted at face value, but requires a symbolic interpretation in order to reveal its hidden meaning? In dealing with a statement which presents a world view, Maimonides is unable to declare the literal meaning as false through an appeal to factual affairs or to some violation of demonstrable principles. Instead, he counters the literal sense of this statement by appealing to human models present in the tradition which would invalidate the purported way of life suggested by this Aggadah.

If Halakhah is the only way to God, which is the obvious meaning of the aggadic statement, how can one explain the relationship of men to God prior to the giving of the law? Maimonides, in an incredulous manner, asks whether one can seriously entertain the possibility that in the time of Shem and Ever and those living prior to the existence of Halakhah no one was able to approach God.[29] The Torah does not begin with Sinai, but portrays men relating to God prior to the revelation of the law. Only by understanding a way to God, independent of the revelation of the Torah, can we make sense of these human models. Maimonides presents the method of the philosophers to elucidate the nature of this spiritual way.[30]

The philosophic method develops from a teleological understanding of the world of nature. After discovering that the final cause of sublunar beings is primarily related to the service of man, the philosopher proceeds to analyze the purpose of man. To discover the human end, one must first reveal the essence of man. From among all human activities, the philosopher isolates that activity which is unique to man. Having done this he can then understand how true humanity can be achieved. Since rational activity distinguishes man from all other animals, and since the discipline of metaphysics deals with the most sublime object of thought, the philosopher concludes that man's purpose can only be realized in reflection on God. Intellectual disciplines have significance because they lead a person from knowledge of nature to metaphysics and, ultimately, to knowledge of the most perfect Being—God. This final step consummates man's quest to realize his absolute purpose.

The search for this end entails a way of life as well as a development in theoretical knowledge. It is self-evident, to Maimonides, that one cannot live an animal existence of exaggerated gratification of the senses while seeking at the same time to perfect one's intellect. Philosophers know that knowledge of God requires that man achieve moral excellence. The ideal of reason—the single-minded pursuit of knowing God—gives rise to an ethic which attempts to limit one's involvement with bodily needs to the extent necessary for intellectual fulfillment.

At this point Maimonides could have legitimated the way of the philosophers in the eyes of his halakhic reader by inventing some claim which attributed the philosophers' understanding of man's purpose to the influence of the prophets.[31] The identification of Aggadah with philosophic teachings would have been acceptable to pious students of the Talmud if Maimonides had claimed that the philosophers were influenced by the prophets. Maimonides, however, makes a definite point of stating that

... this matter was not made known through the Prophets alone, but also the wise men of the ancient nations, even though they never saw the Prophets nor heard their words, already knew that man is not whole unless he includes [within himself] knowledge and practice.[32]

The way to God resulting from human reasoning does not require the authentication of the prophets. If philosophy alone can lead to a pursuit of God, why then is Torah needed?[33] This question is not raised, but we shall deal with the way Maimonides might address himself to such a problem. What is crucial at this point is that the halakhic reader gain an appreciation of the importance of philosophy not only as a cognitive discipline, but as an important road to God.

Before examining Maimonides' interpretation of the aggadic statement, "God only has in His world the four cubits of the Halakhah," let us evaluate what Maimonides has established so far. He has shown that philosophic knowledge enables one to discover criteria for interpreting both the form and content of Aggadah. Maimonides does not elaborate upon the methods and teachings of philosophy in his legal works. This training must be initiated by the student through independent study. The teachings of Aggadah, which aim at the development of the individual's spiritual capacities, cannot be taught in works which attempt to clarify and to codify the normative tradition of Judaism. What Maimonides does in his legal works is to goad his halakhic reader toward the path of Aggadah by revealing to the reader how deeply he, Maimonides, values aggadic knowledge.

Whenever the opportunity presents itself in his *Commentary to the Mishnah*, Maimonides stresses the importance of his aggadic explanations. One does not need the complicated exegesis of Strauss to determine Maimonides' view regarding the primacy of his aggadic explanations in comparison to his legal commentary:[34]

And also we shall discuss something of this matter in tractate Avot, and we shall show you some indication of the agreement of the teachings of the greatest philosophers with the teachings of the Rabbis in all matters. And it is not appropriate in this place to discuss this issue. Rather my way at all times [is that] in all places where there is an allusion to matters of belief, I explain something, for it is more worthy to me to explain one of the principles than anything else.[35]

Maimonides does not hide his supreme evaluation of Aggadah. His holding back of a full explication of Aggadah in his legal works is based upon his love for the community and his profound awareness that there are stages of intellectual and spiritual growth which the student must undergo by himself before fully comprehending the path of spiritual excellence. A responsible guide in Aggadah waits to hear from his student before he teaches.[36] The student's capacity and level of appropriation will determine what the teacher imparts.

Maimonides has a model for this approach in the talmudic tradition:

And the Sages, peace to them, would hide from each other secrets of Torah. They related that one of the Sages happened to meet with people who were learned in the Account of Creation [*Ma'aseh Bereshit*] whereas he knew the Account of the Chariot [*Ma'aseh Merkavah*]. He said to them, "Teach me the Account of Creation and I will teach you the Account of the Chariot." They complied with him. After they taught him the Account of Creation he refused to teach them the Account of the Chariot. And he did not do this, Heaven forbid, out of jealousy nor because he wished to be greater than they, for these qualities are disgraceful even for the lowliest of men and all the more so for great men. Rather, he did this because he saw himself worthy of learning what they had and he did not find them worthy of learning what he had.[37]

Maimonides' method in the introduction of *Commentary to the Mishnah* is to point to the unified way of Judaism and philosophy. In *The Commentary to the Mishnah* Maimonides states that such a unity exists, and he locates within the tradition those human models whose example provides a basis for integrating the claims of Athens and Jerusalem.

In his introduction, Maimonides' model of pre-Mosaic man and his analysis of the philosophers' way may not be sufficient evidence to convince a halakhic reader of the importance of philosophic knowledge for his relationship to God. Such a reader might acknowledge the necessity of theoretical knowledge of nature and metaphysics prior to the availability of Torah law. However, both Maimonides and his reader live after Sinai. Halakhic Jews claiming to possess a clear statement of God's will expressed in a comprehensive normative system, are not compelled to decipher the secrets of nature in order to know God. After all, is not Maimonides writing a commentary to the *Mishnah*—a legal text to which Jews can turn to discover the necessary elaboration and clarification of divine commandments? After Sinai, the primacy of practice cannot be overlooked by any religious Jewish writer who addresses a halakhic audience. His points of departure and return must be located within Halakhah. Consequently, for a traditional Jew to accept the importance of theoretical knowledge for his service to God, he must be convinced that it also affects practice.

Maimonides, aware of the problem, proceeded to offer evidence that would point to the primacy of Aggadah after Sinai. He turned to the talmudic tradition for human models which suggested different approaches to halakhic observance. If one could show that the Talmud was cognizant of varying levels of halakhic practice, proof then will be established for showing how knowledge of Aggadah is, in fact, responsible for the different levels of halakhic practice.

Maimonides presents three different models of action.[38] The first model, which the prophets and the philosophers reject, is the person who imagines he can separate the perfection of his intellect from the way he conducts his daily life. The hedonistic intellectual is valued neither by the prophets nor by the genuine philosophers.

The second model is the person who fears God, acts with moderation, and conditions himself to practice the moral virtues. His only limitation is that he is not learned. From the context of Maimonides' previous discussion, as well as from the explicit statement in his commentary to Avot, we must understand this lack of knowledge to refer to knowledge of the sciences of nature and of metaphysics.[39] Maimonides claims that this lack of theoretical knowledge affects the nature of practice:

And so if a man is God-fearing, abstemious, keeps afar from the pleasures other than for the maintenance of the body, behaves in all natural matters in the way of moderation, and possesses all the good virtues, but has no knowledge, he too lacks perfection, although he is more perfect than the first because these actions of his are not the result of true knowledge and understanding [of what is most fundamental]. And, therefore, the Sages said, "A rude man [*bur*] is not one that fears sin—nor is a man that knows not Torah [*am ha-arez*] a *ḥasid*" (T.B. Avot 2:6).

And he who says of an *am ha-arez* that he is a *ḥasid* is but denying the teachings of the Sages who have made it absolutely clear and he is denying also reason. And thus you will find the commandment everywhere in the Torah, "Study them," and afterward "to observe them." Learning precedes practice, for through learning one comes to practice and practice does not bring about learning, and this is what they said, peace to them, "that learning [*talmud*] brings about practice" (T.B. Kedushin 40b).[40]

Here, Maimonides does not simply identify the *am ha-arez* by his lack of theoretical virtue. Theoretical and practical virtues are not two distinct and independent properties. Maimonides claims that the imperfection in the practice of the *am ha-arez* can be explained by his lack of theoretical knowledge of God. Just as insufficient knowledge of one's legal tradition is detrimental to action, so too is one's ignorance of the philosophic disciplines which provide an understanding of God. Maimonides fortifies these claims by referring to the talmudic statement which places learning before practice. Although the surface meaning of the talmudic statement would suggest that the knowledge referred to is that touching directly on practice, i.e., the study of commandments, the deeper meaning of *talmud* includes both Halakhah and Aggadah.[41] Both the *am ha-arez* and the *ḥasid* agree that their tradition maintains the importance of knowledge for practice. They differ, however, in their understanding of which body of knowledge has this effect.

For now, it is sufficient to stress that by identifying the *ḥasid* of the Talmud with the halakhic Jew who knows philosophy, Maimonides indicated that he did not abandon the centrality of the normative tradition by insisting on the primacy of Aggadah.

It is not only with regard to the interaction of theoretical reflection and behavior that Maimonides seeks precedent models in the Talmud. He must also show how the ideal of individual excellence can emerge in a tradition that is heavily concerned with community. The Torah covenant was between a total community and its God.[42] The community—as a whole—was addressed by God and challenged to become a holy people. How, then, can one maintain that Judaism subscribes to a conception of excellence which depends on individual intellectual capacities? The ideal of intellectual perfection isolates singular, gifted individuals and would thus appear to be incompatible with a tradition in which community is central. The philosopher discovers God as an outgrowth of independent reasoning. The burden of a covenant-community is not part of his consciousness. How, then, can a Jew make sense of Maimonides' characterization of the *hasid?*

Maimonides does not raise the problem of individual excellence in this manner. Given the truth that God does not create anything in vain, and that the purpose of man is knowledge of God, Maimonides asks why it is that we find so few individuals capable of reaching this goal.[43] Although this question differs from the one we raise, the manner in which Maimonides deals with his problem will resolve our issue as well.

Maimonides shows that the talmudic tradition knew of the rarity of excellence and was led to evaluate the importance of community in terms of such rare individuals:

Ben Zoma once saw a crowd on one of the steps of the Temple Mount. He said, Blessed is He that discerneth secrets and blessed is He who has created all these to serve me (T.B. Berakhot 58a).

Maimonides understands this statement to refer to Ben Zoma's singular human perfection. Another statement from the tradition says:

> Hezekiah further stated in the name of Rabbi Jeremiah who said it in the name of Rabbi Simeon ben Yoḥai, I have seen the sons of heaven and they are but few. If there be a thousand, I and my son are among them; if a hundred, I and my son are among them; and if only two, they are I and my son (T.B. Sukkah 45b).

Although the rabbis did not explain the basis for their statement, Maimonides attributes this affirmation to their acceptance and understanding of nature. As men acquainted with natural science, they accepted the principle of necessity which the study of nature imposes upon man. Just as one does not ask why there are exactly "nine spheres and four elements," so too one does not ask why the rarity of human excellence is a fact of existence.[44] Just as teachers of Aggadah and philosophers agree as to the criteria of truth which emerge from the science of nature, so too do they share a common conception of the rarity of human excellence. Reason's understanding of nature provides epistemological criteria of truth as well as an approach to life entailing a specific ethos and conception of man.

Maimonides is now able to interpret the aggadic statement, "God only has in His world the four cubits of the Halakhah." The superficial meaning is that Judaism is exclusively concerned with the knowledge of law and that such knowledge is sufficient for man's perfection. This external meaning has value for those unable to travel the road of the *ḥasid*. It trains the people of the community to live by Halakhah. This interpretation, however, is incomplete. Halakhah, to the *ḥasid*, encompasses more than law. Halakhah, as practiced by the *ḥasid*, is what the rabbis meant when they said, "God only has in His world the four cubits of the Halakhah." To the Maimonidean *ḥasid* Judaism is not only compatible with philosophy but, in a more positive sense, demands that one have knowledge of philosophy.[45]

Examination of Maimonides' introduction to his *Commentary to the Mishnah* shows that his view regarding the centrality of philosophy for Halakhah was not hidden from the community. Indeed, throughout his entire works Maimonides attempted to create a bridge leading from the Halakhah of the *am ha-areẓ* to the Halakhah of the *ḥasid*. This perspective recognizes the continuity of *The Commentary to the Mishnah*, his earliest work, and his final work, *The Guide of the Perplexed*. If the student of the legal works follows Maimonides' suggestions of the ultimate value of aggadic knowledge, he will meet his teacher in the *Guide*, where the way of the *ḥasid* is explained.

Viewed from this perspective, it can be seen that Maimonides' legal works attempt to affect a change in the way the whole community understands the halakhic path to God. Although Maimonides was aware that only few would reach the full understanding of the Halakhah of the *ḥasid*, this did not prevent him from attempting to begin this process for the entire community. One can not deny that Maimonides' halakhic works, as distinct from the *Guide*, are addressed to the general community; but one can deny that Maimonides, in his legal works, is only "the mouthpiece of the tradition."[46]

Further refutation of the view which isolates Maimonides' legal works from his philosophic concerns are a series of features of the *Mishneh Torah*:[47]

a) Maimonides begins his *Mishneh Torah* with a treatment of various philosophical themes.[48] Is this not a strange way to begin a strictly legal codification? Does it not suggest that Halakhah demands more than the obedient readiness to follow norms?

b) The proof for the existence of God is based on the premise of the eternity of the world.[49] Is this not unsettling to the traditional Jew's understanding of creation?

c) The first commandment of the Decalogue which identifies God as the redeemer from Egypt, "I the Lord am your God who brought you out of the land of Egypt, the house of bondage," is interpreted by Maimonides as a commandment requiring of man that he gain knowledge of God as the necessary Being and source of existence.[50] The first *mitzvah* does not consist in believing in God's power to interfere in the historical process, but in gaining a knowledge of nature which can lead one to demonstrative knowledge of God. Were Maimonides simply reflecting the traditional beliefs of a community which relates to God exclusively through His power in history, he would not begin his codification of Jewish law with this approach to the first commandment of the Decalogue.[51]

d) Strauss emphasizes the decisive difference between Athens and Jerusalem in terms of the place man occupies in the hierarchy of Being:

The most striking characteristic of the biblical account of creation is its demoting or degrading of heaven and the heavenly lights. Sun, moon, and stars precede the living things because they are lifeless; they are not gods. What the heavenly lights lose, man gains; man is the peak of creation.[52]

Yet Maimonides, in his "Jerusalem" work, writes of the insignificance of man in comparison to the heavenly bodies:

When a man reflects on these things, studies all these created beings, from the angels and spheres down to human beings and so on, and realizes the Divine Wisdom manifested in them all, his love for God will increase, his soul will be filled with fear and trembling, as he becomes conscious of his own lowly condition, poverty, and insignificance, and compares himself with any of the great and holy bodies; still more when he compares himself with any one of the pure forms that are incorporeal and have never had associations with the corporeal substance. He will then realize that he is a vessel full of shame, dishonor, and reproach, empty and deficient.[53]

e) Maimonides identifies "the image of God" with the human faculty of reason:

The vital principle of all flesh is the form which God has given it. The superior intelligence in the human soul is the specific form of the mentally normal human being. To this form, the Torah refers in the text "I will make man in My image, after My likeness" (Gen. 1:26). This means that man should have a form that knows and apprehends idealistic beings that are devoid of matter, such as the angels which are forms without substance, so that [intellectually] man is like the angels.[54]

In *Hilkhot Yesodei ha-Torah* and in *Hilkhot Teshuvah* immortality of the soul is linked to the intellectual faculty of man.[55] This is not a conception of man which a tradition concerned exclusively with normative obedience would emphasize.

f) The description of love and fear of God in chapters two and four in *Hilkhot Yesodei ha-Torah* is not related to the study of the law.[56] The two ultimate categories of the tradition's understanding of the service of God are presented in a manner which any individual, Jew or non-Jew, can embrace. The God who inspires this love and fear has no specific connection with the community of Israel since the God described in these chapters is He whose wisdom is manifest in nature.

g) Maimonides identifies the most sublime teachings of Judaism, *Ma'aseh Bereshit* and *Ma'aseh Merkavah*, with physics and metaphysics. The elite of the tradition, those who enter *pardes,* occupy themselves with areas of knowledge not specific to Judaism. A book which is supposed to be "the mouthpiece of a traditional community" would never claim that "alien" knowledge is a condition for achieving the tradition's highest goal. A traditional book would not state that Rabbi Akiva's greatness lay in his capacity to master the disciplines of physics and metaphysics.[57] Nor would such a book dare to suggest that physics and metaphysics are more significant than knowledge of "the permitted and the forbidden":

The topics connected with these five precepts, treated in the above four chapters, are what our wise men call *pardes* [paradise], as in the passage, "Four went into *pardes*" (T.B. Ḥagigah 14). And although those four were great men of Israel and great Sages, they did not all possess the capacity to know and grasp these subjects clearly. Therefore, I say that it is not proper to dally in *pardes* till one has first filled oneself with bread and meat; by which I mean knowledge of what is permitted and what forbidden, and similar distinctions in other classes of precepts. Although these last subjects were called by the Sages "a small thing"—when they say, "A great thing, *Ma'aseh Merkavah*; a small thing, the discussions of Abaye and Rava"—still they should have the precedence.[58]

A writer who felt the danger of exposing his philosophic interest to the community would have to be a masochist to make such a statement. Although Maimonides does not explicate the teachings of *Ma'aseh Merkavah* and *Ma'aseh Bereshit* in the *Mishneh Torah* as he does in the *Guide*, one must appreciate his frankness in these statements. Whereas the Orthodox Jew might tolerate various philosophical exegeses of the Bible, he would nonetheless rage against the suggestion that the elite of his tradition—his prophets and cherished sages —consummated their love of God in "non-Jewish domains" of knowledge. The Orthodox Jew would reject the notion that philosophy is of greater significance than the study of Halakhah.[59]

h) The most powerful argument against the supposed split in Maimonides' thinking can be derived from the way he treats the Song of Songs. The Song of Songs is perceived by the traditional Jew as a parable of the passionate love affair between God and Israel.[60] To the devout Jew, the Song of Songs is what intimate letters are to the passionate lover. In the *Mishneh Torah* Maimonides interprets the parable in terms of the love gained from the knowledge of God through nature.[61]

As was noted, the god who is revealed in nature cannot be limited to a specific relationship with Israel. Thus to interpret a book—traditionally believed to express the intimate love affair of God and Israel—as a book about the love inspired by God in all beings capable of intellection is to negate the unique status of Israel in this love-relationship. Similarly, this interpretation unequivocally destroys a spiritual way of life in which God is exclusively a lawgiver.

Man's ultimate relationship to God cannot be the exclusive experience of any particular historical community. Physics and metaphysics are disciplines which are accessible to all rational men. Reason, the image of God in man, does not separate the Jew from the non-Jew. "Beloved is man who is created in the image of God" (Avot 3:14). By making the passion of the Song of Songs a function of these philosophic disciplines, Maimonides broke the exclusivity of the love-relationship of the Jew with God:

Not only the tribe of Levi, but every single individual from among the world's inhabitants whose spirit moved him and whose intelligence gave him the understanding to withdraw from the world in order to stand before God—to serve and minister to Him, to know God—and he walked upright in the manner in which God made him, shaking from his neck the yoke of the manifold contrivances which men seek—behold! this person has been totally consecrated and God will be his portion and inheritance forever and ever. God will acquire for him sufficient goods in this world just as he did for the Priests and Levites. Behold, David, may he rest in peace, says: "O Lord, the portion of my inheritance and of my cup, You maintain my lot" (Ps. 16:5).[62]

What the previous discussion shows is that Maimonides was not simply attempting to secure legitimacy for philosophy. Had this been his motive in the *Mishneh Torah* he would never have made explicit claims which would shock the most sensitive religious feelings of traditional talmudists. Maimonides could have then chosen the path of some of our contemporary Orthodox Jewish scientists who neatly separate the world of science from religion. No talmudist of that era would take issue with the view that Torah taught true science before Aristotle. After all in the Mishnah it is written: "Study it [Torah] again and again, for everything is contained in it" (T.B. Avot 5:22).

In fact, if protecting philosophers was Maimonides' aim, he could have achieved this with an acceptable argument that the study of the sciences enhances man's appreciation of the wonder and majesty of God. But this was not his purpose. He placed knowledge of *pardes* above knowledge of the law and made it a condition for joining the ranks of the sages and prophets. He deliberately restructured the private love story of God and Israel. Maimonides exposed his legal reader to an understanding of Halakhah which enabled the reader to recognize the importance of objective study of the sciences for his personal observance of the commandments.⁶³ To claim, as Strauss does, that Torah has significance for Maimonides solely in terms of political categories, as an instrument of social order, is to miss the point of Maimonides' constant stress upon the importance of Aggadah for Halakhah.⁶⁴

The difference between the approaches of Strauss and others who overlook Maimonides' integrated methods and the course taken here will come into sharper focus when specific problems in the *Guide* are analyzed later. But there is yet another instance in the *Mishneh Torah* in which Maimonides offers a rationale for the existence of Torah as an integrated system of norms and philosophy. If Torah is not to be simply a redundant way of formulation of philosophy, one must understand why Halakhah is a vital component in integration. To do this, Maimonides' presentation of the conditions which preceded the giving of the Torah must be examined. If pre-Mosaic man could have appropriated the philosophic way to love of God, what made it necessary to introduce a Torah into history?

Before enumerating the laws of idolatry in the *Mishneh Torah*, Maimonides begins with a prolegomenon dealing with the historical origins of idolatry.⁶⁵ In this introduction, three stages of biblical history are discussed: a) the origins of paganism, b) the revolt of Abraham against his pagan society, and c) the election of Moses and the giving of the Torah.

Maimonides describes three stages in history which he believes led to the abandonment of belief in God. The process began from a mistake in the form of worship.⁶⁶ At first men believed in one God who governed the world through intermediary forces. Given this cosmology, they reasoned that just as a king is honored when respect is shown to his ministers, so too would God be pleased if men paid homage to His ministers, the heavenly bodies. This mistaken form of worship of intermediaries grew out of an honest mistake which resulted from a cosmology that perceived God as affecting the world through His intermediaries.[67]

Maimonides does not explain why this form of worship is mistaken. What Maimonides does is to show the reader how mistaken forms of worship are compatible with a true belief in God and, therefore, why the change from pure monotheism to the beginnings of paganism is not a radical one. This is characteristic of Maimonides' theory of human development which is presented in his theory of history in the *Guide.*[68]

The second stage in the process of abandonment begins when "prophets" claim that the authority of God legitimatizes a pagan form of worship:

In course of time, there arose among men false prophets who asserted that God had commanded and expressly told them: "Worship that particular star, or worship all the stars. Offer up such and such sacrifices. Pour out such and such libations. Erect a temple. Make a figure, to which all the people—the women, children, and the rest of the folk shall bow down."[69]

Mistaken forms of worship, which initially resulted from human thought, are now claimed to represent the will of God. It is interesting that wise men who appeal to reason do not succeed in making intermediary-worship practice universal. In the stage of wise men, there were no images to worship—only temples devoted to the worship of the stars. The false prophets, however, introduced figures and images, and succeeded in bringing about the popular forms of idol-worship.

The final stage emerges only after a long period, when the masses of people come to know only the images and the wise men know only the spheres. What begins as a mistaken way of honoring God concludes with the complete absence of God from the minds of men.

Maimonides does not claim that such a process is necessary and can be predicted by an analysis of some metaphysical or natural concept. The stages of this process of alienation are not links in a logical chain, but descriptions of a human process, one which results from a tendency in man to treat means as ends in themselves.

Maimonides also noticed this process of alienation in man's economic behavior. In his introduction to *The Commentary to the Mishnah,* he marvels at the involvement of man in economic pursuits which appear to have no relationship to human needs. Although human survival may be the initial reason for an economic activity, the reason is often forgotten once such activities are in motion.[70] Thus, spheres, stars, figurines, and images become exclusive objects of worship in much the same way that economic pursuits, which may have little connection with one's survival, dominate one's whole life.

One who understands the tendency toward alienation in human behavior will be able to appreciate why, as a means of honoring God, the worship of intermediaries must be rejected.[71] It is quite understandable how Maimonides can claim the testimony of reason in rejecting the claims of false prophets who demand the worship of intermediaries:

And we should not worry about his claim to prophecy nor shall we ask from him a miracle. And even if he performed miracles the likes of which we have never even heard so as to verify his claim, behold this [person] is punished by strangulation and one should not pay heed to those miracles, for the reason for the existence of those miracles is what Scripture said, "For the Lord your God is testing you" . . . (Deut. 13:4). For the testimony of reason which denies his prophecy is stronger than the testimony of the eye which sees his miracles, for it has already been made clear to men of reason that it is not proper to honor nor to worship other than the One who caused all beings to exist and is unique in [His] ultimate perfection.[72]

The testimony of reason can refer both to one's ability to reject theological claims which contradict demonstrative truth, and to reasoned arguments which are grounded in examination of human behavior. This point is crucial in Maimonides' presentation of Abraham:

The world moved on in this fashion, till that Pillar of the World, the Patriarch Abraham, was born. After he was weaned, while still an infant, his mind began to reflect. By day and by night he was thinking and wondering: "How is it possible that this [celestial] sphere should continuously be guiding the world and have no one to guide it and cause it to turn round; for it cannot be that it turns round of itself." He had no teacher, no one to instruct him in aught. He was submerged, in Ur of the Chaldees, among silly idolaters. His father and mother and the entire population worshiped idols and he worshiped with them. But his mind was busily working and reflecting till he attained the way of truth, apprehended the correct line of thought and knew that there is One God, that He guides the celestial sphere and created everything, and that among all that exists, there is no god beside Him.[73]

Abraham, Maimonides' model of pre-Mosaic man, illustrates a relationship of man to God that is not grounded in Halakhah. Maimonides, who claimed that talmudic Aggadah reflects the philosophical tradition in Judaism, utilizes Aggadah for his understanding of Abraham.[74]

The Bible introduces Abraham at the age of seventy-five and is silent about his activities prior to his calling. Maimonides appeals to the aggadic picture of Abraham which fills the gaps. Maimonides accepts the view that Abraham discovered God when he was forty years old and not when he was three. Maimonides ascribes Abraham's discovery of God to Abraham's relentless attempts to understand the nature and origin of celestial movements.[75]

Abraham rejected the teachings of his father and his environment solely on the convictions which he gained through reason. He is able to stand alone against the ethos of his generation because of the certainty he possessed from discovering demonstrative truth:

> For when something has been demonstrated, the correctness of the matter is not increased and certainty regarding it is not strengthened by the consensus of all men of knowledge with regard to it. Nor could its correctness be diminished and certainty regarding it be weakened even if all the people on earth disagreed with it.[76]

Reason not only provides Abraham with demonstrative knowledge of God but is also the source of his attack on idol-worship. Maimonides does not quote a biblical text to indicate that Abraham's missionary activity is the result of a divine command; rather, Maimonides writes, "having attained this knowledge he began to refute the inhabitants of Ur of the Chaldees."[77] The midrashic picture of Abraham provides Maimonides with an archetype of how the tradition understood reason's way to God. By reflecting on nature one comes to realize that without recognizing God as the source of existence, the universe is unintelligible. Equally crucial is that aggadic man feels compelled to challenge an idolatrous world. Abraham recognized the factor of human alienation in transforming the idol- and star-worshiper into a pagan:

> He realized that the whole world was in error, and that what had occasioned their error was that they worshiped the stars and the images, so that the truth perished from their minds.[78]

Abraham's arguments against idol-worship are intelligible to those who are made to understand the process of alienation, i.e., that "the multitude grasp only the actions of worship, not their meanings or the true reality of the Being worshiped through them."[79]

Although intermediary worship, as distinct from belief in God's corporeality, is compatible with truth, it is not compatible with one's responsibility to safeguard belief in God within the broader community.[80] Abraham appeals to this sense of responsibility toward community in his confrontation with the wise men of his generation:

He broke the images and commenced to instruct the people that it was not right to serve anyone but the God of the Universe to whom alone it was proper to bow down, offer up sacrifices and make libations, *so that all human creatures might, in the future, know Him*; and that it was proper to destroy and shatter all the images, so that the people might not err like these who thought that there was no God but these images.[81]

Maimonides selects only one biblical text in his treatment of Abraham, "And invoked there the name of the Lord, the Everlasting God" (Gen. 21:33). This text shows how man is driven to act on God's behalf without having to appeal to God's legislative authority. This is the paradigm text of aggadic man. This way of reasoning, including a concern for both thought and action, is the basis for Maimonides' description of the community forged by the patriarchs as "a people that knew God." The community of the patriarchs, embodying the way of Abraham, is organized around the knowledge of God provided by reason. Maimonides knew of other views in the tradition which presented the patriarchs as observing the laws of the Torah.[82] The model of God as legislative authority, however, is completely absent from Maimonides' description of the patriarchs.[83] The patriarchs are, for Maimonides, models of the aggadic personality to which he refers in his halakhic works.

Given the emergence of the Abrahamic way to God, what factors could explain the appearance in history of Moses and the legislative model of God?

When the Israelites had stayed a long while in Egypt, they relapsed, learned the practices of their neighbors, and, like them, worshiped idols, with the exception of the tribe of Levi, which steadfastly kept the charge of the Patriarch. This tribe of Levi never practiced idolatry. The doctrine implanted by Abraham, would in a very short time, have been uprooted, and Jacob's descendants would have relapsed into the error and perversities universally prevalent. But because of God's love for us and because He kept the oath made to our ancestor Abraham, He appointed Moses to be our teacher and the teacher of all the Prophets, and charged him with his mission. After Moses had begun to exercise his Prophetic functions and Israel had been chosen by the Almighty as His heritage, he crowned them with precepts, and showed them the way to worship Him, and how to deal with idolatry and with those who go astray after it.[84]

Abraham's community, based exclusively on knowledge of God, could not sustain its belief in God within a broader society which was idolatrous and pagan. The experience of the Israelites in Egypt revealed the inadequacy of sustaining a community solely on the basis of knowledge. Maimonides points to an actual—but not a necessary—process in history which created the need for Torah. He specifically notes that the tribe of Levi was able to withstand the influences of their environment.[85] Singular individuals can remain steadfast in their loyalty to God through Aggadah. However the community which is composed of a variety of people—not all of whom are scholars —cannot sustain its allegiance to God if it is not supported by a total way of life. Abraham instituted worship of God based upon knowledge. Moses was compelled to promulgate laws whose actualization reinforces and sustains this belief: ". . . He crowned them with precepts and showed them the way to worship Him. . . ."

God appointed Moses the legislative teacher of Israel. The mode of discourse changes correspondingly. Where Abraham appeals to reason and offers convincing arguments, Moses appeals to divine authority and legislates a comprehensive way of life. Abraham rejects practices which can lead to the forgetting of God, Moses introduces practices which support and reinforce the belief in God.[86]

Our analysis of Maimonides' introduction to the laws of idolatry now puts us in a better position to understand both his model of pre-Mosaic man and how the way of Aggadah leads to the way of Halakhah. If we are correct in claiming that integration is the model according to which one should understand Maimonides, we should also discover an account of how Halakhah is enhanced by Aggadah.

After describing laws dealing with the prohibitions against divination, astrology, magic, and necromancy, Maimonides writes in the *Laws of Idolatry:*

These practices are all false and deceptive, and were means employed by the ancient idolaters to deceive the peoples of various countries and induce them to become their followers. It is not proper for Israelites who are highly intelligent to suffer themselves to be deluded by such inanities or imagine that there is anything in them, as it is said, "Lo, there is no augury in Jacob, no divining in Israel" (Num. 23:23); and further, "These nations that you are about to dispossess do indeed resort to soothsayers and augurs; to you, however, the Lord your God has not assigned the like" (Deut. 18:14). Whoever believes in these and similar things, and in his heart, holds them to be true and scientific and only forbidden by the Torah, is nothing but a fool, deficient in understanding, who belongs to the same class with women and children whose intellects are immature. Sensible people, however, who possess sound mental faculties, know by clear proofs that all these practices which the Torah prohibited have no scientific basis but are chimerical and inane; and that only those deficient in knowledge are attracted by these follies and, for their sake, leave the ways of truth. The Torah, therefore, in forbidding all these follies, exhorts us, "You must be whole-hearted with the Lord your God" (Deut. 18:13).[87]

In this short but powerful statement Maimonides presents two approaches to the observance of the law. The approach of those who are ignorant of science is to obey the law exclusively because of divine authority. This attitude is similar to that previously discussed—the approach of those who accept aggadic statements as true even though those statements conflict with what could be observed in nature: Obedience to authority enables one to live by a tradition which has no connection with the structure of nature. Maimonides rejects this approach to Halakhah for the same reason that he rejects a literalist approach to Aggadah. Commitment to Torah is wholehearted only if the individual understands the laws and teachings of the Torah from a rational perspective. Although the model of the legal authority of God is introduced by Moses, and the Jew is now called upon to obey God's commandments, one must not think that obedience unsupported by reason's understanding of nature is a new path to God.[88] Commandments and truth form a unity, if one understands that Moses consummates—without altering—the way of Abraham.

The unification of Aggadah and Halakhah by Maimonides is an attempt to protect the tradition from the risks involved in separating the one from the other. Aggadah divorced from Halakhah cannot sustain a community in history. Halakhah organizes the community and thus enables its members to withstand the influences of competing ways of life. The mind's understanding of God gains living expression in the norms which structure one's daily activities. Halakhah continuously sets God before the individual:

A person should pay heed to the precept of the mezuzah; for it is an obligation perpetually binding upon all. Whenever one enters or leaves a home with the mezuzah on the doorpost he will be confronted with the declaration of God's unity, blessed be His holy name; and will remember the love due to God, and will be aroused from his slumbers and his foolish absorption in temporal vanities. He will realize that nothing endures to all eternity save knowledge of the Ruler of the Universe. This thought will immediately restore him to his right senses and he will walk in the paths of righteousness. Our ancient teachers said: He who has phylacteries on his head and arm, fringes on his garment, and a mezuzah on his door may be presumed not to sin, for he has many monitors—angels that save him from sinning, as it is said (Ps. 34:8): "The angel of the Lord encamps round about them that fear Him, and delivers them."[89]

Halakhah provides concrete symbols which remind a person of his ultimate task: to know God. Halakhah prevents the individual from becoming totally absorbed in the demands of economic and political survival. It provides, within the everyday framework, a means by which to achieve spiritual transcendence beyond the dehumanizing effect of mundane routines.

However, the minute symbolic details of Halakhah present a risk as well. The risk of a religious, legal tradition is that man may focus on what one must or must not do, and forget or misunderstand for whom these actions are performed.[90] Maimonides cannot tolerate the possible separation of Halakhah from God; the law must express the relationship of a man with God. He cannot overlook the person who observes the law yet conceives of God in corporeal terms.[91] To Maimonides, to believe that God is corporeal is to believe in that which does not exist. Maimonides can accept imperfect motives in one's performance of commandments—but he will not tolerate belief in God's corporeality.[92] Such a belief makes the halakhic mode a monologue—not a dialogue.

The *Mishneh Torah* begins with four chapters dealing with norms which cannot be separated from the understanding of God as He is revealed in nature. The existence, unity, and non-corporeality of God are presented as the content of norms even though they are demonstrative truths. One is wholehearted in fulfilling these norms only when he understands, through his own intellect, that God exists—is one and is non-corporeal. By beginning the *Mishneh Torah* in this way the halakhic Jew is forced to perceive God's reality as extending beyond the structure of the law.

Halakhah is a means to serve God. Maimonides, who is so sensitive to the problem of alienation, as is revealed in his treatment of the origins of paganism, is equally aware of the possibilities of alienation within Halakhah itself. In his "Treatise on Resurrection," he explains why he dealt with matters of belief in his legal works.[93] He was aware that one could become enamored and totally preoccupied with details of Halakhah at the expense of knowledge of God. His concern with the fundamental principles of Judaism in his legal works, and his insistence upon a correct conception of God in the *Mishneh Torah*, are not the result of philosophical intellectualism.[94] They are based, rather, on a fear that a student of Halakhah can become an expert in legal matters and a pagan in matters of belief.[95] The aggadic themes briefly discussed in the legal works are addressed to legal students in the hope that their passion for law will lead to a passion for God.

Thus far, we have argued against the alleged schism between Maimonides' philosophic and halakhic writings. There still remains the explanation of how the studies of nature and metaphysics alter the practices of the halakhic Jew. The talmudic student of Maimonides will have followed his guidance well by studying both the written and oral law and then devoting most of his time to Talmud, a study which includes *pardes*, i.e., physics and metaphysics.[96]

Insofar as we are dealing with a spiritual outlook, we must expect that such cognitive development will alter one's perception of self, nature, history, and God. Philosophy, to Maimonides, not only points to the contemplative ideal, but also suggests a method of changing the religious attitudes and perspectives of a person. This leads directly to an exploration of the *ḥasid*.

HALAKHIC AND AGGADIC CATEGORIES AND THEIR RELATIONSHIP TO PHILOSOPHICAL SPIRITUALITY

Maimonides' treatment of philosophy in his legal works establishes that the rational approach to God can be understood within the categories of the legal and aggadic tradition of Judaism. Maimonides is not trying to show the Jewish universalist—embarrassed by Jewish particularity —that Judaism is compatible with the universal way of philosophy. Rather, he tries to show pious Jews how their commitment to Halakhah can be enriched by a philosophical understanding of God.[1] Maimonides leads the halakhic Jew toward a unification of the particularity of Torah and the universality of philosophy. This goal constitutes the core of his concern as a Jewish philosopher.[2]

Maimonides can be misunderstood in two ways. One may emphasize his concern and love for the Torah and minimize the importance he ascribes to the study of philosophy. Or one may emphasize his philosophic spiritual ideal and ignore his commitment to Halakhah as being essential for understanding his philosophic thought. In either case, one misses the important connection between his philosophic and legal thought.

The integration of philosophy and Judaism was made

possible by the talmudic tradition.[3] "Jerusalem" to Maimonides was not defined solely by the Bible but included the vast corpus of talmudic writings. To establish the incompatibility of Athens and Jerusalem exclusively on the basis of the Bible, would be to misconceive Maimonides' understanding of Jerusalem; Maimonides employs numerous aggadot to support his non-literal approach to religious language. To Maimonides, the midrashic treatment of Abraham serves as a model of the way to God, based on philosophic reflection.

In chapter one it was noted that Maimonides took the talmudic model of the *ḥasid* as a paradigm of one who achieves the unity of the contemplative ideal and of halakhic observance. Maimonides made this seemingly exaggerated claim on behalf of both tradition and human reason: Without the perfection of theoretical virtue, as understood by the philosophers, one could not become a *ḥasid*.[4] This conviction can be buttressed by proving that the theological model which emerges from reason's understanding of nature makes the halakhic observance of the *ḥasid* intelligible.

In demonstrating a relationship between a person's actions and his conception of God, one must not expect to discover the same rigorous connection which one finds in a deductive argument. Logical entailment is not the model with which to understand the relationship of thought to action.[5] It is sufficient to show how conceptions of God influence and give direction to one's life. "Influence" and "direction" are categories which make intelligible the life-patterns set into motion by one's theoretical beliefs. Theoretical frameworks make some life-patterns more appropriate than others for an individual; they do not necessarily make alternate life-patterns logically untenable.

A religious man's conception of God informs him of how to act in His presence. He seeks a community of existence with his God and thus proceeds to structure his actions in a way that makes this possible. Man's understanding of his relationship to God, therefore, has an emphatic influence on the way he acts.

What an individual anticipates as a result of his observance of the commandments indicates how he perceives his relationship to God. If the world of philosophy is to be compatible with Judaism then the expectations of the religious Jew must be in keeping with the theocentric universe of reason. The Mishnah in Sanhedrin states that "All Israel have a share in the world to come."[6] This expectation of the world to come (olam ha-ba) provides Maimonides with a foundation from which to analyze the varying eschatological expectations of Jewish traditionalists.

Maimonides begins his introduction to Ḥelek by describing what people expect from God as a result of their commitment to Torah:

One class of thinkers holds that the hoped for good will be the Garden of Eden, a place where people eat and drink without bodily toil or faintness. Houses of costly stones are there, couches of silk, and rivers flowing with wine and perfumed oils, and many other things of this kind. . . . This set of thinkers on this principle of faith bring their proofs from many statements of the Sages, peace to them, whose literal interpretation forsooth accords with their contention or with the greater part of it.

The second class of thinkers firmly believes and imagines that the hoped for good will be the days of the Messiah, may he soon appear! They think that when that time comes all men will be kings forever. Their bodily frames will be mighty. . . . They also bring proofs for their statements from many remarks of the Sages, and from Scriptural texts which in their outward interpretation agree with their claim, or a portion of it.

The third class is of the opinion that the desired good will consist in the resurrection of the dead. . . . These thinkers also point for proof to the remarks of the Sages, and to certain verses of the Bible, whose literal sense tallies with their view.

The fourth class is of the opinion that the good which we shall reap from obedience to the Law will consist in the repose of the body and the attainment in this world of all worldly wishes, as, for example, the fertility of lands, abundant wealth, abundance of children. . . . The holders of this view point for proof to all the texts of Scripture which speak of blessings and curses and other matters, and to the whole body of narratives existing in Holy Writ.

The fifth set of thinkers is the largest. Its members combine all the aforesaid opinions, and declare the objects hoped for are the coming of the Messiah, the resurrection of the dead, their entry into the Garden of Eden, their eating and drinking and living in health there as long as heaven and earth endure.[7]

How are we to understand these expectations? Are they the fantasies of deprived persons who spin dreams of glory, power, and endless material gratification to escape from the misery of the present? Is there any basis in Judaism for assuming that these expectations are based on reality?

Reality, as understood by the believing Jew, is not determined only by empirical conditions. The unseen power of divine governance enters into the domain of reality. The prophets taught the Jew to interpret his history in terms of his relationship to God. The Torah explicitly states that there is a direct relationship between man's material well-being and his strict observance of the commandments. Crops grow or fail as a result of man's response to God's will.[8] Jews fast and engage in deep introspection when faced with natural calamities.[9] When they are defeated by the Romans they examine their past halakhic observance to discover reasons for their political humiliation.[10] The religious Jew inhabits a world in which he was delivered from the oppressive might of Egypt even though he lacked a well-trained army and he survived in a desert for forty years. The conception of God and history which results from such literal reading of the biblical covenant and aggadic literature molded the historical self-understanding of the Jew and expressed itself in hopes and expectations which, to outsiders, appear as exaggerated fantasies.

What is common to all the views which Maimonides presents is their firm literal understanding of Torah and Aggadah. But this literalist viewpoint not only presented Maimonides with cognitive problems, but was as well responsible for a religious perspective of God as primarily the master of material benefits which He would bestow on man. The community's lack of concern for what Maimonides believed to be the true end of Judaism, *olam ha-ba*, was symptomatic of the quality of relationship which existed between many members of the halakhic community and God. Maimonides attempted to change the community's perception of its relationship to God by convincing his readers that exclusive concern with material expectations was not in keeping with the true telos of Jewish tradition.[11] In order to achieve his goal, Maimonides had to convince his readers that by viewing *olam ha-ba* as the ultimate goal of Judaism, one came to somewhat different perceptions of the meaning and the significance of religious observances.

Before presenting his interpretation of *olam ha-ba*, Maimonides, in what appears as a digression, presents an extended simile of the methods which a teacher uses to motivate his student. However protracted, this simile helps illuminate what Maimonides believes to be a correct understanding of Jewish spirituality:

Now, O reader, understand the following simile of mine and then you will make it your aim to grasp my meaning throughout.

Figure to yourself a child young in years brought to a teacher to be instructed by him in the Torah. This is the greatest good he can derive in respect of his attainment of perfection. But the child, on account of the fewness of his years and the weakness of his intellect, does not grasp the measure of that benefit, or the extent to which it leads him toward the attainment of [spiritual] perfection. The teacher, who is nearer to such perfection than the pupil, must therefore necessarily stimulate him to learning by means of things in which he delights by reason of his youth. Thus he says to him, "Read, and I shall give you nuts or figs, or a bit of sugar." The child yields to this. He learns diligently, not indeed for the sake of the knowledge itself, as he does not know the importance of it, but merely to obtain that particular dainty —the eating of that dainty being more relished by him than study, and regarded as an unquestionably greater boon. And consequently he considers learning as a labor and a weariness to which he gives himself up in order, by its means, to gain his desired object which consists of a nut or a piece of sugar.

When he grows older and his intelligence strengthens, he thinks lightly of the trifle in which he formerly found joy and begins to desire something new. He longs for this newly chosen object[ive] of his, and his teacher now says to him, "Read, and I shall buy you pretty shoes or a coat of this kind!" Accordingly he again exerts himself to learn, not for the sake of the knowledge, but to acquire that coat; for the garment ranks higher in his estimation than the learning and constitutes the final aim of his studies. When, however, he reaches a higher stage of mental development, this prize also ranks little with him, and he sets his heart upon something of greater moment. So that when his teacher bids him "learn this section, or that chapter, and I shall give you a dinar or two," he learns with zest in order to obtain that money which to him is of more value than the learning, seeing that it constitutes the final aim of his studies.

When, further, he reaches the age of greater discretion, this prize also loses its worth for him. He recognizes its paltry nature and sets his heart upon something more desirable. His teacher then says to him, "Learn, in order that you may become a Rabbi, or a Judge; the people will honor you and rise before you; they will be obedient to your authority, and your name will be great, both in life and after death, as in the case of so-and-so." The pupil throws himself into ardent study, striving all the time to reach this stage of eminence. His aim is that of obtaining the honor of men, their esteem and commendation. But all these methods are blameworthy.[12]

The obvious point, and one Maimonides appears to labor, is that people are generally motivated to study Torah by the expectations of extraneous benefits. Why pursue the point with so many examples of extraneous rewards?[13] Why discuss the motivating power of nuts and figs, of pretty shoes, of money, honor, power? Maimonides' elaborate discussion of different forms of gratification corresponding to different levels of appreciation stresses the persistent self-interested motivation of human behavior. What changes with time is not the quality of motivation, but only the different forms which self-interest takes. One does not easily overcome the egocentric responses of the child. If one can accept the necessity to appeal to extraneous rewards he will understand the importance that people ascribe to biblical and talmudic materialistic promises.

Maimonides' method of integrating appeals to self-interest and disinterested philosophic worship is to treat them as two stages in a continuum of human development. There are no indications in the Bible that the blessings and curses of the covenant are related to a specific stage of religious worship.[14] The Bible does not reveal the difference between the rather usual man whose psychological makeup requires motivational appeals to material self-interest and the more uncommon man who has another orientation to worship. Maimonides, however, turns to the talmudic tradition for an understanding of levels of worship.

The talmudic tradition is highly sensitive to the necessity to transcend self-interest for service to God:

The Sages warned us against this also, i.e., against a man making the attainment of some worldly object the end of his service to God, and his obedience to His precepts. And this is the meaning of the dictum of that distinguished and perfect man who understood the fundamental truth of things—Antigonus of Soko—"Be not like servants who minister to their master upon the condition of receiving a reward; but be like servants who minister to their master without the condition of receiving a reward." They really meant to tell us by this that a man should believe in truth for truth's sake. And this is the sense they wish to convey by their expression *oved me-ahavah*, "serving from motives of love," and by their comment on the phrase "that delight in His commandments." Rabbi Eliezer said "in His commandments," and *not* "in the reward for performance of His commandments." How strong a proof we have here of the truth of our argument, and how decisive! It is a clear confirmation of the text we have previously quoted. And we possess a stronger proof still in their remark in Sifre: "Per adventure thou mayest say, Verily I will learn the Torah in order that I may become rich or that I may be called Rabbi, or that I may receive a recompense in the future world. Therefore does Holy Writ say 'to love the Lord thy God.' Let everything that thou doest be done out of pure love for Him."[15]

Although the rabbis disparaged the motive of self-interest, they recognized how rare the individual is who appreciates norms because of their intrinsic worth:

But our Sages knew how difficult a thing this was and that not everyone could act up to it. They knew that even the man who reached it would not at once accord with it and think it a true article of faith. For man only does those actions which will either bring him advantage or ward off loss. All other actions he holds vain and worthless. Accordingly, how could it be said to one who is learned in the Law—"Do these things, but do them not out of fear of God's punishment, nor out of hope for His reward"? This would be exceedingly hard, because it is not everyone that comprehends truth, and becomes like Abraham our father.[16]

One should note the parallel between the rarity of one who observes the commandments for their own sake and the rarity of one who has achieved intellectual excellence.[17] Despite the rabbis' emphasis on worship which is not based on self-interest, they were fully aware and responsive to the needs of those unable to attain this level.

The talmudic tradition elaborated upon the developmental process underlying the progression from worship based on *yirah* (fear) and *shelo lishmah* (observing commandments or studying Torah not for their own sake) to *ahavah* (love) and *lishmah* (observing or studying Torah for its own sake). This gave Maimonides a structure with which to understand the relationship between individual and communal levels of worship.

The rabbis, though committed to the need to transcend lower forms of religious experience, were careful not to develop a system catering solely to the elite.[18] Antigonus was censored by the rabbis for revealing publicly what few individuals were capable of accepting. One must be circumspect when discussing the highest level of worship—love—with individuals who have not gone beyond that which is based on self-interest. The danger is not that the unique man recognizes as false that which the community accepts as true, but, rather, such a person is exposed to that which he cannot psychologically appropriate.[19]

Maimonides describes the reactions to Antigonus' statement in his commentary to Avot:

This Sage had two disciples, one named Zadok and the other named Boethius. When they heard him deliver the statement, they departed from him. The one said to his colleague, "Behold, the master expressly stated that man has neither reward nor punishment, and there is no expectation at all." [They said this] because they did not understand his intention. The one lent support to his colleague and they departed from the community and forsook the Torah.[20]

One who evaluates the benefits of religious life in terms of self-interest will wrongly interpret statements stressing a disinterested worship of God as covert attempts to deny that God responds to man's condition. "There is no hope!" is the response of a man in need when he is told to love God for His own sake. One who, for whatever reason, is tied exclusively to the pursuit of his physical needs, requires a god who relates directly to his condition of deprivation. The rabbis responded to this situation by legitimizing even those actions not based on pure motives:

A man should always occupy himself with Torah and good deeds, though it is not for their own sake, for out of [doing good] with an ulterior motive there comes [doing good] for its own sake (T.B. Pesaḥim 50b).

Purity of motive was not the only criterion used by talmudic tradition to evaluate the religious significance of human behavior. Maimonides recognized that the Talmud's acceptance of imperfectly motivated actions was rooted in the belief that concrete action could lead to inwardness. Actions may lead to purity of motive even when initiated by impure motives.

Besides this understanding of the psychological consequences of behavior, the rabbis were also motivated by their realistic understanding of communal needs. What is important in a social reality is how people act toward one another. One must appreciate that beneficial consequences can derive from imperfectly motivated actions. The man who gives charity while stipulating in his mind that he does so in order that he is rewarded and that his son recover from illness, is nevertheless declared a righteous man by the tradition.[21] This person may be a philistine from the perspective of his motive, but at least the poor receive help. Those in need cannot wait until the individual heals his egocentricity. If one takes into account the needs of the poor and the deprived, one will be prepared to motivate action with a theology which promises abundant material rewards in return for compliance with religious norms.[22]

One does not require the teachings of Plato or al-Farabi to recognize the problem involved in attempting to embrace both individual excellence and responsibility to the community.[23] The esoteric-exoteric distinction between theological models is not so much a function of truth as opposed to falsity, as it is a function of a perceptive understanding of levels of worship. The rabbis' concern for excellence, *ahavah* and *lishmah*, was not compromised by their establishing minimal conditions in which all could participate, *yirah* and *shelo lishmah*.

Philosophy, for Maimonides, serves as an instrument for raising the individual from worship at the level of *yirah* to the level of *ahavah*.[24] Theoretical knowledge of God enables the individual to move from an observance based on self-interest to a purer observance of commandments. Philosophy offers the individual a God who is sought because of His perfection, and not only because He responds to man's physical helplessness. That Maimonides thought philosophy had this effect is clear from the way he treats its importance in his legal works. One may disagree with Maimonides' psychology and his conviction of the psychological consequences of philosophic development, yet one cannot ignore what he believed to be the human consequences of thought. To allege that philosophy is of little importance to Maimonides' halakhic reader, as Husik does, is to miss Maimonides' understanding of the direct bearing of philosophy upon one's relationship to God and the commandments. Philosophy directs the halakhic Jew from a relationship to God based on reciprocity to a relationship based on pure love.

The structure of the argument in *Ḥelek* reveals this understanding of philosophy. Immediately following a discussion of fear and love of God, Maimonides interrupts himself to describe the three approaches to Aggadah already discussed in chapter one. He concludes his description with the following statement:

If, O reader, you belong to one of the first-named classes, do not pay any attention to any of my remarks on this subject, because not a word of it will suit you. On the contrary, it will harm you and you will dislike it. For how can food of lightweight and temperate character suit a person accustomed to partaking of bad and gross fare? It would really injure him, and he would loathe it. . . . If, however, you are of those who constitute the third class, and when you come across any of the Sages' remarks which reason rejects, you pause and learn that it is a dark saying and an allegory. And if you then pass the night wrapped up in thought and dwelling in anxious reflection over its interpretation, mentally striving to find the truth and the correct point of view, . . . you will then consider this discourse of mine, and it will profit you, if God wills it.[25]

Why does Maimonides believe that he who reads Aggadah literally will find nothing satisfactory in his treatment of *olam ha-ba*? One may say that since Maimonides will offer a symbolic interpretation of many aggadot dealing with the messianic age, such a person would be repulsed by a non-literal conception of messianism.[26] This plausible explanation does not go far enough. Before one can appropriate the true meaning of *olam ha-ba* and then an approach to Torah grounded in disinterested love, one must be committed to universal criteria of truth independent of traditional authority. One must first understand nature from the perspective of independent reason, in order then to understand and to appreciate Maimonides' presentation of the relationship between the biblical God of history and the God of being.

The relationship of man to God described in the Bible is reciprocal. The lord of history issues norms to man and promises—in return for man's obedience—to satisfy all man's material needs. In a time when God's response to man is neither apparent nor visible, the expectation of an immediate historical response from God is replaced by messianism.[27] Messianism and the doctrine of the resurrection of the dead essentially reflect the same model of man's relationship to God as that found in the Bible; both doctrines merely postpone the time when God will reward those who comply with His will.

The world of philosophy, however, presents a different perception of religious life, one revolving around a conception of a God who inspires man's love wholly on His perfection. The lover of God, in this context, transcends history and longs for an intellectual communion with God. From Maimonides' perspective, Athens and Jerusalem would be incompatible if the tradition presented only messianism as the telos of halakhic observance. The fact that one can find statements in the tradition which place *olam ha-ba* above messianism was yet further proof to Maimonides that the philosophic ideal of contemplative love had an integral place in his tradition.[28]

To Maimonides, the ideal of *olam ha-ba* reflects the telos of the religious life of a person who has transcended his immediate physical needs and instead delights in the pleasures which the intellect affords. Maimonides' description of *olam ha-ba* in his legal works would be both unintelligible and undesirable to anyone who did not appreciate contemplative joy and disinterested love:

"In the world to come there will be no eating and no drinking, no washing and no anointing and no marriage; but only the righteous sitting with crowns on their heads enjoying the splendor of the Shekhinah." By their remark, "their crowns on their heads," is meant the preservation of the soul in the intellectual sphere, and the merging of the two into one as has been described by the illustrious philosophers in ways whose exposition would take too long here. By their remark, "enjoying the splendor of the Shekhinah," is meant that those souls will reap bliss in what they comprehend of the Creator, just as the holy *hayyot* and the other ranks of angels enjoy felicity in what they understand of His existence. And so the felicity and the final goal consist in reaching to this exalted company and attaining to this high pitch. The continuation of the soul, as we have stated, is endless, like the continuation of the Creator, praised be He, who is the cause of its continuation in that it comprehends Him, as is explained in elementary philosophy. This is the great bliss with which no bliss is comparable and to which no pleasure can be likened.[29]

The eschatological dreams of a community reflect their notions of happiness. Such dreams reflect what they consider to be the essence of human joy. Biblical descriptions of man's longing for material benefits would appear unrelated to a conception of man whose focus is upon his intellectual faculties. The concept of *olam ha-ba*, the domain of pure spiritual joy, enables Maimonides to assert that the Jewish tradition believes, that in addition to the satisfaction of man's everyday material needs, there is another satisfaction in the human joy of intellectual understanding. To Maimonides, *olam ha-ba* embodies the expectations of the man whose conception of joy involves more than the pleasures of physical self-interest.

The role of philosophy in transforming the individual's worship of God from one based on self-interest to one of disinterested love is, in part, a function of its capacity to inculcate notions of joy which transcend the pleasures of the body. The activity of intellectual reasoning brings about a new man insofar as it alters man's conception of what constitutes joy and happiness:

For we live in a material world and the only pleasure we can comprehend must be material. But the delights of the spirit are everlasting and uninterrupted, and there is no resemblance in any possible way between spiritual and bodily enjoyments. We are not sanctioned either by the Torah or by the divine philosophers to assert that the angels, the stars, and the spheres enjoy no delights. In truth they have exceeding great delight in respect of what they comprehend of the Creator, glorified be He. This to them is an everlasting felicity without a break.

They have no bodily pleasures, neither do they comprehend them, because they have no senses like ours, enabling them to have our sense experiences. And likewise will it be with us too. When after death the worthy from among us will reach that exalted stage they will experience no bodily pleasures, neither will they have any wish for them, any more than would a king of sovereign power wish to divest himself of his imperial sway and return to his boyhood's games with a ball. At one time he would without doubt have set a higher worth upon a game with a ball than on kingly dominion, such being the case only when his years were few and he was totally ignorant of the real significance of either pursuit, just as we today rank the delights of the body above those of the soul.[30]

Man is a complex being: he has a body which hungers for gratification and an intellect which seeks its own form of joy. These two conceptions of joy generate the different expectations which men bring to their religious life. The example of the king in the above quotation confirms what we have stated previously: The movement from a conception of religious life focusing on God's promises of material well-being, to a religious orientation focusing on the joy of intellectual contemplation of God, is not the result of discovering that the former is based on false beliefs but rather reflects a further development in man. The king does not play with a ball because it is "false," but because it is inappropriate to his new station. Different models of God become more appropriate to a person's religious life, depending on his conception of happiness. The belief in divine reward and punishment, although accepted as true, may be surpassed as a motivating force in religious life by a person who is able to love God.

In an age when men believed God affected history, they sought God's favor in order to alleviate their condition of material deprivation. The fact that the Jewish community at the time of Maimonides was subject to exile and political humiliation did not diminish their hopes that eventually God would respond to their needs. Maimonides' rationalism expressed itself in his belief, that despite these historical conditions, he could nonetheless elevate members of the community from their preoccupation with expectations of material satisfaction to a longing for the spiritual joy of *olam ha-ba*. *Olam ha-ba* is a description not only of the future life of the disembodied intellect, but also of an individual's evaluation of the significance of his everyday religious behavior.

The longing for *olam ha-ba* takes hold of an individual once he has experienced, in some way, the attraction and beauty of a non-reciprocal relationship with God. One who has not observed the law from the motive of love cannot fully grasp the significance of *olam ha-ba*.[31] To desire God for His own sake, even temporarily, is a condition for understanding what Maimonides describes as the glorious joy awaiting an individual in the world to come. In traditional terms one may speak of *olam ha-ba* as a "reward." Yet, were one to peel away the external meaning of "reward," he would discover that the good which *olam ha-ba* promises becomes significant only to a person whose motivation for observing the Torah has transcended the categories of reward and punishment.[32]

In many instances it may be difficult to distinguish the Halakhah of the person who obeys the Torah out of *yirah* from the Halakhah of one who follows Torah out of love. The observance of both may appear similar, but two distinct orientations to God are expressed. To Maimonides, *yirah* and the exclusive yearning for messianism place the human relationship to God within the circumference of human needs.[33] *Ahavah* and the longing for *olam ha-ba*, however, shift the focus of man's relationship to God. Worship becomes an act of self-transcendence, wherein man is drawn to God because of His perfection and not because of human deprivation and human crises. In worship based upon love, man enters the theocentric framework of cosmic intelligences.[34] Man's "significant others" are no longer other historical men, but pure intelligences whose sole interest is to know and to love God. An exclusive focus on one's capacity to know and to love the most perfect Being can lead one to feel intellectually inadequate when comparing his own comprehension of and devotion to God with that of the pure intelligences.

If it is the theocentric cosmic reality which the religious man seeks to enter, how is he to interpret biblical concern with history and community? The individual who aspires toward this higher form of worship cannot but feel the emptiness of the biblical conception of God.

Maimonides deals with this dilemma by explaining that the biblical model of divine-human reciprocity assumes another meaning once it is integrated with the eschatological scheme emphasizing the primacy of *olam ha-ba*:[35]

As regards the promises and threats alluded to in the Torah, their interpretation is that which I shall now tell you. It says to you, "If you obey these precepts, I will help you to a further obedience of them and perfection in the performance of them. And I shall remove all hindrances from you." For it is impossible for man to do the service of God when sick or hungry or thirsty or in trouble, and this is why the Torah promises the removal of all these disabilities and gives man also the promise of health and quietude until such a time as he shall have attained perfection of knowledge and be worthy of the life of the world to come. The final aim of the Torah is not that the earth should be fertile, that people should live long, and that bodies should be healthy. It simply helps us to the performance of its precepts by holding out the promises of all these things.[36]

Biblical eschatology is collective. *Olam ha-ba* as presented in the Mishnah is also formulated in communal terms: "All Israel have a share in the world to come." To Maimonides, all of Israel could share in the perfection implicit in *olam ha-ba*, but only if historical conditions were such that men were not overly concerned and burdened with the basic problems of survival. An individual's spiritual potential cannot be properly evaluated when the individual lives in social and economic hardship. This historical realism explains, for Maimonides, the biblical concern with man's material condition. The biblical description of the God of history is therefore compatible with the theocentric world view of philosophic reason. The concern for messianism supports the ideal of intellectual love of God:

The Sages and Prophets did not long for the days of the Messiah that Israel might exercise dominion over the world, or rule over the heathens, or be exalted by the nations, or that it might eat and drink and rejoice. Their aspiration was that Israel be free to devote itself to the Law and its wisdom, with no one to oppress or disturb it, and thus be worthy of life in the world to come.

In that era there will be neither famine nor war, neither jealousy nor strife. Blessings will be abundant, comforts within the reach of all. The one preoccupation of the whole world will be to know the Lord. Hence Israelites will be very wise, they will know the things that are now concealed and will attain an understanding of their Creator to the utmost capacity of the human mind, as it is written: "For the earth shall be full of the knowledge of the Lord, as the waters cover the sea" (Is. 11:9).[37]

As stated in chapter one, the way of Sinai does not emerge in competition to the way of Abraham, but as a support for it. Without the structure of Sinai, the way of

Abraham could not be realized for the community. The Torah trains the community to withstand the seduction of pagan environments. The goal of Torah is not only the abolition of idolatry, but also the positive ideal of love of God.[38] Law alone cannot bring about this ideal when the pressures of physical survival make it nearly impossible for a person to discover the joy of loving God for His own sake. One must alter the physical conditions of human history before one can hope for the liberating influence of reason to have any effect on community.

The Bible reflects this realism in its account of the exodus from Egypt. The liberation from Egypt preceded the revelation at Sinai. God does not address and challenge the community to become a holy people until the chains of slavery are broken. One must first be concerned with the political and economic conditions of the oppressed before one can expose them to higher aspirations.

Although singular individuals can realize their capacities despite adverse social conditions, Judaism did not construct a conception of what is possible based on what the elite few can achieve. To Maimonides, Torah was given to Moses despite the fact that the tribe of Levi was able to withstand the influences of Egyptian paganism.[39] Similarly, the ideal of love of God and *olam ha-ba* are provided with the support of political and social conditions, i.e., messianism, which would make this ideal realizable for the community. Just as the "tribe of Levi" leaves Egypt with the entire community and stands before Mount Sinai, so too does it await the coming of the messianic age—as does all of Israel. All of Israel longs for messianism because all of Israel has a share in *olam ha-ba*.

Maimonides' allegiance to messianism reflects his refusal to restrict *olam ha-ba* to the elite.[40] His conception of philosophical excellence was not insulated from his commitment to Torah and to community. Nowhere in Maimonides do we find anything parallel to the problem faced by the philosopher in Plato's *Republic* who must decide whether to return to the cave of community.[41]

Although community was central to Maimonides' thinking this did not imply that either he or the teachers of the Talmud accepted that everyone can achieve the same level of spiritual excellence. There are levels of worship, just as there are levels of intellectuality. The unique individual does have a place within the Torah community since the understanding of man in the Talmud is not based only on what is possible for the community. The talmudic teachers did not evaluate the potential of a community by the standard of the elite few; nor did they ignore what such people could achieve when the talmudists established a way of life for community.[42]

This is why messianism plays such a crucial role in Maimonides' legal works, as distinct from *The Guide of the Perplexed*. The legal works are primarily addressed to those members of the community who are subject to the influences of material conditions of history. The *Guide*, however, is addressed to individuals capable of realizing the ideal of love of God despite the political conditions of their community. The *Guide* is an attempt to train the individual to achieve the essential telos of messianism, *olam ha-ba*, within a non-messianic world. As a unit, the *Guide* and the *Mishneh Torah* reflect how the pursuit of individual excellence was meant to be cultivated along with a deep commitment to community.[43]

We have shown how the talmudic models of love and fear and the eschatological categories of *olam ha-ba* and messianism were used by Maimonides. He developed an approach to Judaism capable of dynamically integrating two theological models which emerged from the study of nature and the study of Sinai. We are now prepared to examine how the halakhic observances of the *am ha-arez* and the *ḥasid* reflect these two models.

Chapter one established, that according to Maimonides, the Halakhah and Aggadah of the Talmud reflect the tradition's way of guiding the community and the individual toward God. One can claim, as Strauss does, that Halakhah, more than the Aggadah, reflects the true picture of the Jewish tradition.[44] In emphasizing the primacy of Aggadah, therefore, Maimonides does not reflect the spirit of the tradition. However, the Aggadah was not Maimonides' only basis for establishing the significance of philosophy for the tradition. There are differences between the community and the uncommon individual—both in their understanding of Aggadah and in their practice of Halakhah.

Of course, there are many subtle distinctions within the internal system of halakhic obligation, but we will simply attempt to illustrate here two conceptions of Halakhah which reflect the practices of community and of the singular individual.

The concept of halakhic obligation in the tradition has both a collective and a singular meaning. Halakhah is a system of laws prescribing actions which every member of the community must follow. The obligatory character of the system is based upon the acceptance by Jews of the legislative authority of God and of those human authorities who are recognized as His legitimate agents.[45] Obligations based on the legal authority of God do not exhaust the scope of the Halakhah. Besides the precise, detailed system of standards which obligates every individual in the community to specific actions, in Maimonides' *Hilkhot De'ot* there is another description of the essence of halakhic life:

A man should aim to maintain physical health and vigor, in order that his soul may be upright, in a condition to know God. For it is impossible for one to understand sciences and meditate upon them, when he is hungry or sick, or when any of his limbs is aching. And in cohabitation, one should set one's heart on having a son who may become a Sage and a great man in Israel. Whoever throughout his life follows this course will be continually serving God, even while engaged in business and even during cohabitation, because his purpose in all that he does will be to satisfy his needs, so as to have a sound body with which to serve God. Even when he sleeps and seeks repose, to calm his mind and rest his body, so as not to fall sick and be incapacitated from serving God, his sleep is service of the Almighty. In thise sense, our wise men charged us, "Let all thy deeds be for the sake of God" (Avot 2:17). And Solomon, in his wisdom, said, "In all your ways acknowledge Him, and He will direct your paths" (Prov. 3:6).[46]

This description of how the halakhic Jew relates all of his activities to God is not a description of action grounded in legislative authority. The statement "Let all thy deeds be for the sake of God" is not a formula yielding precise legal norms of behavior. Its comprehensiveness reflects the aspiration of one who desires to sanctify every aspect of human conduct. Halakhic norms stemming from legislation are related to specific actions and specific times. "In all your ways acknowledge Him" embodies the aspirations of approaching God in any and every aspect of a person's behavior. The statement "In all your ways acknowledge Him" reflects the aspiring movement from man to God, as opposed to the legislative movement from God to man. The attempt to endow all of human action with religious significance leads the individual to seek a perspective which would enable him to say "I have set the Lord before me continuously."

This single-minded pursuit indicates that specific legal commandments addressed to community do not fully describe the Halakhah. In enhancing sleep and physical exercise with religious significance, one is not merely following a stated commandment. The all-pervasive longing for God—not simply obeying specified norms embodying His will—is the source of this comprehensive understanding of Halakhah.[47]

In Maimonides' *Eight Chapters* these two approaches to Halakhah are evident. In the fourth chapter, Maimonides discusses how the specific details of Halakhah develop a proper psychic balance for different virtues. He concludes his evaluation of the details of halakhic life with the following statement:

> If a man will always carefully discriminate as regards his actions, directing them to the medium course, he will reach the highest degree of perfection possible to a human being, thereby approaching God, and sharing in His happiness. This is the most acceptable way of serving God which the Sages, too, had in mind when they wrote the words, "He who ordereth his course aright is worthy of seeing the salvation of God."[48]

After showing how the Halakhah, through its precepts, makes possible the realization of moderation, Maimonides, in the fifth chapter, discusses the single-minded quest for God. His evaluation of this approach is quite different from what he writes in chapter four:

> Know that to live according to this standard is to arrive at a very high degree of perfection which, in consequence of the difficulty of attainment, only a few, after long and continuous perseverance on the paths of virtue, have succeeded in reaching. If there be found a man who has accomplished this—that is one who exerts all the faculties of his soul, and directs them toward the sole ideal of comprehending God, using all his powers of mind and body, be they great or small, for the attainment of that which leads directly or indirectly to virtue—I would place him in a rank not lower than that of the Prophets. Such a man, before he does a single act or deed, considers and reflects whether or not it will bring him to that goal, and if it will, then, and then only, does he do it.[49]

There is a clear difference between Maimonides' evaluation of halakhic prescriptions which develop moderation and his evaluation of the approach of one who follows a single-minded quest for God. He does not conclude his discussion of halakhic prescripts by claiming that "to live according to this standard is to arrive at a high degree of perfection which, in consequence of the difficulty of attainment, only a few, after long and continuous perseverance on the paths of virtue, have succeeded in reaching." The perfection of which he wrote in chapter four can be realized by all of the community. Single-mindedness, however, reflects the approach to Halakhah of one who worships God not only in following defined commandments, but also in all activities he undertakes.[50]

Maimonides' distinction between the specific norms of Halakhah and the more comprehensive Halakhah of "In all your ways acknowledge Him" is similar to his distinction between messianism and *olam ha-ba*. The specific norms of Halakhah aim at establishing a community which lives in accordance with virtue. Yet there is a further task to be realized: the single-minded quest for knowledge of God. Just as messianism aims at making *olam ha-ba* possible for members of the community, so do halakhic prescriptions create the conditions necessary for realizing the goal that all of human life could reflect divine service.

Singular individuals understand that what God requires of man cannot be exhausted within a precise, delimited structure of norms. They are drawn to a God who inspires action not only on the basis of His authoritative will, but by His infinite perfection. They do not solely look to the practice of community to determine what is expected from them. Their personal quest for spiritual excellence is a source from which they derive guidance for their behavior:

His restraining agency lies in his very self, I mean in his human framework. When the latter becomes perfected it is exactly that which keeps him away from those things which perfection withholds from him and which are termed vices; and it is that which spurs him on to what will bring about perfection in him, i.e., virtue.[51]

The difference between the unique individual and his community is not only reflected in his ability to develop a comprehensive understanding of Halakhah. Even within the circumscribed world of halakhic norms, one can discern both communal and individual orientation. The two halakhic categories reflecting this are 1) *din*—law which defines the line of legal requirement, and 2) *lifnim mi-shurat ha-din*—law which is beyond the line of legal requirement.[52] The following examples from the *Mishneh Torah* indicate how the Halakhah distinguished between action obligatory for every member of the community (*din*) and action practiced by individuals who were not content simply to fulfill the requirements of the strict rules of law (*lifnim mi-shurat ha-din*):

If one finds a sack or a basket, the rule is as follows: If he is a scholar or a respected elder who is not accustomed to taking such things in his hand, he need not concern himself with them. He must, however, examine his own conscience. If he would have taken these things back for himself had they belonged to him, he must also return them when they belong to another. But if he would not have overlooked his dignity even had they belonged to him, he need not return them when they belong to another ... If one follows the good and upright path and does more than the strict letter of the law requires [*lifnim mi-shurat ha-din*], he will return lost property in all cases, even if it is not in keeping with his dignity.[53]

If the majority of the inhabitants are heathen, the rule is that if one finds lost property in a part of town which is chiefly frequented by Israelites, he must advertise it. But if he finds it in a public highway or a large square or in assembly halls or lecture halls frequented regularly by heathen or in any place frequented by the general public, whatever he finds belongs to him, even if an Israelite comes along and identifies it. For the owner will abandon hope of its recovery as soon as he loses the property, since he thinks that a heathen will find it. Yet even though it belongs to the finder, if he wishes to follow the good and the upright path and do more than the strict letter of the law requires [*lifnim mishurat ha-din*], he must return the lost property to an Israelite who identifies it.[54]

If, on the road, one encounters a person whose animal is crouching under the weight of its burden, he is enjoined to unload the burden from the animal whether the burden is suited to it or too heavy for it. This is a positive commandment, for Scripture says, "You must nevertheless raise it with him" (Ex. 23:5). If the passerby is a Priest and the animal is crouching in a cemetery, he may not defile himself on its account, just as he may not defile himself in order to return lost property to its owner. Similarly, if one is an elder unaccustomed to loading or unloading, he is exempt, seeing that the act is not in keeping with his dignity. The general rule is as follows: In every case where if the animal were his own he would load or unload it, he must load or unload another's. But if one is pious [a *ḥasid*] and does more than the letter of the law demands [*lifnim mi-shurat ha-din*], even if he is a prince of the highest rank, still if he sees another's animal crouching under its burden of straw or sticks or the like, he should help unload and reload.[55]

It is clear that the tradition distinguished between practice stemming from a uniform law obligatory for each member of the community, and practice expressing the spiritual capacities of certain individuals within the community.

From Maimonides' characterization, the *ḥasid* differs from the *am ha-areẓ* in his approach to action as well as in his understanding of God. The former, in his practice, always goes beyond the strict requirement of law. The *ḥasid* understands God not only on the basis of the authority of Torah, but also from his study of physics and meta-physics.[56] Since Maimonides claims that one cannot be a *ḥasid* without philosophical knowledge of God, one can infer that there is an important connection between always following the path of *lifnim mi-shurat ha-din* and theoretical knowledge of God. How then are we to understand the connection between the conceptions of God of the *ḥasid* and the *am ha-arez* and their respective approaches to Halakhah?

When Maimonides describes how an individual Jew should treat a non-Jewish servant he writes:

It is permitted to work a heathen slave with rigor. Though such is the rule, it is the quality of piety and the way of wisdom that a man be merciful and pursue justice and not make his yoke heavy upon the slave or distress him, but give him to eat and drink of all foods and drinks. The Sages of old were wont to let the slave partake of every dish that they themselves ate of and to give the meal of the cattle and of the slaves precedence over their own. Is it not said: ". . . as the eyes of servants to the hand of their master, as the eyes of a maiden to the hand of her mistress" (Ps. 123:2)? Thus also the master should not disgrace them by hand or by word, because Scriptural law has delivered them only to slavery and not to disgrace. Nor should he heap upon the slave oral abuse and anger, but should rather speak to him softly and listen to his claims. So it is also explained in the good paths of Job, in which he prided himself: "If I did despise the cause of my manservant, or of my maidservant, when they contended with me . . . Did not He that made me in . . . the womb make him? And did not One fashion us in the womb" (Job 31:13, 15)?

Cruelty and effrontery are not frequent except with heathen who worship idols. The children of our father Abraham, however, i.e., the Israelites, upon whom the Holy One, blessed be He, bestowed the favor of the Law and laid upon them statutes and judgments, are merciful people who have mercy upon all. Thus also it is declared by the attributes of the Holy One, blessed be He, which we are enjoined to imitate: "And His tender mercies are over all His works" (Ps. 145:9). Furthermore, whoever has compassion will receive compassion, as it is said: "And [He will]

show you compassion; and in His compassion increase you"
(Deut. 13:18).[57]

In Maimonides' description of the law of the heathen
slave, there is a marked difference between action based
on the legislative authority of God (*din*), and action stemming from the imitation of the God of creation.[58] If an
individual were to conduct himself on the basis of the
strict requirements of the law, he would only refrain from
treating the Hebrew slave harshly. The ethical responsibility toward the non-Jewish slave results from understanding how God is related to all of creation. The legal category
of *din* channels one's perception of God within the particular juridical relationship of God to Israel. The boundaries
of one's obligations are circumscribed by God's legal revelation to the community of Israel. When the boundaries of
man's perception of God are expanded, he discovers that
the very existence of all men reflects an ethical attribute
of God. The boundaries of his ethical obligations, therefore, also change; he then finds himself unable to restrict
his ethical responsibilities only to individuals who participate in the juridical relationship with God.

The shift in man's understanding of God which we
have discussed in connection with the law of the non-
Hebrew slave should serve as an explanatory model for the
lifnim mi-shurat ha-din practice of the *ḥasid*. Knowledge
of God as the Creator of all life affects halakhic practice
both in terms of the scope of obligation (*lifnim mi-shurat
ha-din*) and the motives for observance of the commandments (*ahavah*).

He who lacks this knowledge of God is motivated to
fulfill the commandments on the basis of the expectation
of rewards and to follow only the strict requirements of
din.

The halakhic category of *din* can be understood as reflecting the behavior of one who cannot transcend the motivating principle of self-interest (*yirah*). Reciprocal responsibility defines the boundaries of one's understanding of obligation. Within this structure, the individual understands the meaning of responsibility to God and to other human beings to the extent that he can be shown that his own welfare is enhanced by such behavior. The *am ha-arez* knows that by conforming to the *din*, he is entitled to claim similar behavior from others. The *am ha-arez*, both in his theology and his halakhic practice, reflects the principle of reciprocity. Disinterested morality and disinterested love of God are beyond his comprehension. His God and his fellowmen must be bound to reciprocate to him for, otherwise, he cannot comprehend why he should be obligated to fulfill the law.

The halakhic category of *lifnim mi-shurat ha-din* reflects the behavior of one who has transcended the motivating principles of self-interest and legal obligations based upon reciprocity. Philosophical knowledge of God can—in a number of ways—help one to transcend the principle of reciprocity, which is an important feature of *din*. By transforming the individual into a person whose highest joy consists in knowing God—and not in material self-interest—the ground for requiring reciprocity as a ground for motivation becomes meaningless. The entire world view of the theocentric world of philosophic reason draws the individual to serve God not only because of His juridical authority, but also because of His perfection.

An understanding of the God of being would reveal that the principle of *hesed* ("overflow") is the organizing principle of reality. The entire chain of being, beginning with God and descending to lesser beings, is founded on the notion of overflow. This image—overflow—captures the idea of action yielding benefits to others, not on the basis of legal claims or reciprocal actions, but as a result of the benefits which spill over due to an excess of perfection. Maimonides, in the *Guide*, writes:

> We have already explained in the commentary on Avot that the meaning of *ḥesed* is excess in whatever manner excess is practiced. In most cases, however, it is applied to excess in beneficence. Now it is known that beneficence includes two notions, one of them consisting in the exercise of beneficence toward one who has no right at all to claim this from you, and the other consisting in the exercise of beneficence toward one who deserves it, but in a greater measure than he deserves it. In most cases the prophetic books use the word *ḥesed* in the sense of practicing beneficence toward one who has no right at all to claim this from you. Therefore every benefit that comes from Him, may He be exalted, is called *ḥesed*. Thus it says: "I will make mention of the lovingkindnesses [*ḥasdei*] of the Lord." Hence this reality as a whole—I mean that He, may He be exalted, has brought it into being—is *ḥesed*. Thus it says: "The world is built up in lovingkindness [*ḥesed*]"; the meaning of which is "The building up of the world is lovingkindness." And He, may He be exalted, says in an enumeration of His attributes: And abundant in lovingkindness.[59]

In the *Guide* Maimonides adopts the principle of overflow as the most adequate model for understanding God's relationship to nature.[60] The *ḥasid's* understanding of nature—as reflecting God's *ḥesed*—directs him to bestow benefits on others who have no legal claim on him.

Observing the commandments for their own sake and acting for the benefit of those from whom one does not expect a similar response derives from a commitment to the law influenced by the *ḥasid's* understanding of God's revelation in nature. One who acts beyond the strict line of the law cannot know if others will act in the same manner toward him. The *ḥasid* has no way of knowing whether others will treat his lost property with the same degree of concern as he treats theirs. Only law within the rubric of *din* can give this security, since all norms constituted by *din* are capable of being enforced by the courts.[61] The *ḥasid* is not bothered by a lack of certainty because his actions toward others spring from his commitment to imitate the God of *ḥesed*.

Maimonides' characterization of how a *ḥasid* responds to the way others treat him, is also the paradigm of a person who has completely transcended the idea of reciprocity. To Maimonides, *lifnim mi-shurat ha-din* is not only a description of types of legal behavior, but is also used to describe the nature of one's moral disposition and character structure.[62] The *ḥasid's* self-understanding is based on his philosophic knowledge of God. The way others within the community respond to him, therefore, is not as crucial for his self-respect as is his growth of knowledge and his ability to enter into the theocentric world of reason. Since he does not define himself in the manner by which others respond to him, his self-respect does not suffer when others treat him with disdain. Maimonides, in Avot, presents a graphic picture of the extent to which an individual can sustain his dignity irrespective of the behavior of others toward him:

I have seen in a certain book from among the books on ethics where it was asked of one of the esteemed saintly men—it was said to him, "Of all your days, in which day did you most rejoice?" He said; "On the day that I was traveling on a ship, and my place was in the lowliest of the places on the ship, [that is] among the bundles of clothes. On the ship were merchants and wealthy men. I was lying in my place and one of the men on the ship arose to urinate. I was insignificant and contemptible in his sight because in his sight I was very low, until he uncovered his nakedness and urinated on me. I was astonished at the firmness of the disposition of brazenness in his soul. As the Lord lives, my soul was not pained at his deed at all, nor was my power [to react in anger] aroused within me. Instead, I rejoiced greatly when I attained the limit where the contempt of that deficient man did not pain me and that my soul was not stirred up toward him." There is no doubt that this is the ultimate of humbleness of spirit —in order that one may remove from pride.[63]

The *hasid* has no need to seek revenge or to retaliate, for his dignity does not have its source in the response of others: "The practice of the righteous is to suffer contumely and not inflict it; to hear themselves reproached, not retort; to be impelled in what they do by love, and to rejoice in suffering."[64] He is beyond community in the sense that he is unaffected by the fears and threats which accompany the ordinary man's feelings of self-worth.

The law entitles a sage to safeguard his honor:

To safeguard his honor, the *hakham* may himself excommunicate a boor who treated him disrespectfully. For this, neither witnesses nor previous warning are necessary. The ban is not removed until the offender has appeased the *hakham*.[65]

Maimonides, however, qualifies this legal right when he writes:

Although a *hakham* has the right to pronounce the ban to safeguard his honor, it is not creditable for a scholar to accustom himself to this procedure. He should rather close his ears to the remarks of the illiterate and take no notice of them, as Solomon in his wisdom, said, "Also pay no heed to all the words that are spoken." Such too was the way of the ancient saints. They heard themselves reviled and made no reply. Yet more, they forgave the reviler and pardoned him. Great sages, glorying in their commendable practices, said that they never, for the sake of personal honor, imposed on anyone the lighter or severer ban. This is the way of scholars, which it is right to follow.[66]

The excessive humility of the *hasid* has its source not in self-debasement and weakness, but in the dignity and strength derived from one's knowledge of God. Moses, to Maimonides, is the model of one who achieved both the highest degree of philosophic knowledge and the highest degree of humility.[67] The *ḥasid's* method of response to others and to the law represents the development of a renewed man who has liberated himself from the tyranny of self-interest. He who has never left the orbit of community has no dignity or identity independent of the modes of response of others to him. The eyes of the *am ha-areẓ* are always focused on that which is external to him in order for him to know who he is and how he ought to act. Only from God's promises of reward and punishment is he able to discern the difference between right and wrong. He feels obligated to perform norms to the degree that he can observe that all members of the society are required equally to obey the same norms. He symbolizes political man who has not yet discovered the meaning of action based on individual excellence.

Maimonides was able, therefore, to find traditional support for a philosophical understanding of God both in the Aggadah of Talmud and in the behavior of the *ḥasid*. Maimonides recognized, that for a religious Jew, changing patterns of action must result from changes in his understanding of God. The conception of God as legislator is not adequate by itself to explain the *ḥasid's* approach to Halakhah. The unification of the legislative model of Sinai with the model of God as the creator and the sustainer of life explains, for Maimonides, the movement from an approach to Halakhah by one who follows the strict requirements of the law to an approach to Halakhah by one who goes beyond the strict rule of law.

From our analyses of the talmudic categories of love and fear, and of the halakhic categories of *din* and *lifnim mi-shurat ha-din*, we have shown that Maimonides believed that the talmudic tradition was fully aware of the differences between the capacities of the community and of the unique individual.[68] The distinction made in the Talmud between messianism and *olam ha-ba* enabled Maimonides to maintain that Jewish spirituality was not indifferent to the non-historical quest for God. The distinction between love and fear enabled him to recognize that the tradition did not address itself to one audience. Spiritual ideals in the tradition were understood in a way that would enable Judaism to contain and to give support to different people with different spiritual capacities. There were those who were encouraged by the sages to perform commandments even if their motivation for action was based upon self-interest. Serving God from fear, and not from pure motives, was but the first rung in the ladder of spiritual growth.

The Talmud reflects the educational methods of teachers who are able to adjust their teachings to the differing levels of their students. The talmudic rabbis did not sacrifice either the limited or the superior student in their program for religious development. The rabbis managed to keep them together in the community. They did not claim that the minimum was the maximum, nor did they seek to focus exclusively on the unusual capacities of intellectually gifted individuals at the expense of the large, more limited, sectors of the community.

The educational approach expressed in the Talmud is not found in the writings of the biblical prophets.[69] Prophets proclaim and thunder the word of God regardless of their audience. The rabbis, on the other hand, do not feel compelled to speak—whether or not their words will be understood.[70] They are patient and tolerant of the limited capacities of the community. Their task is to educate a community, not simply to set down noble ideals to which the community ought to aspire. They understand their task as implementers of the spiritual ideals of the prophets within the daily life of the community. As patient educators, they establish and develop a realistic way by which a community can relate to God. In their teachings, they do not mirror the uncompromising movement from God to man as does the discourse of the prophets. Rather they recognize the quite slow, painstaking efforts of humans who aspire to reach out toward God.[71] They reflect how difficult a task it is to build a spiritual community in accordance with the specifications of the divine architect.

The talmudic teachers, as distinct from the prophets, show us the importance of compromises and stages of development in man's religious growth.[72] The notion of obligation that emerges from the model of legislative authority reflects only the beginning of the Jew's approach to Halakhah. The *ḥasid's* approach to Halakhah is what the tradition hopes the community itself will ultimately realize. The rabbis were willing, therefore, to utilize multiple theological models in order to inspire observance of the Halakhah.[73]

Maimonides understood Jerusalem from the perspective of the Talmud. He knew that in appropriating philosophy he was expressing a definite spirit within the tradition and was not simply grafting on to it alien Greek tendencies. A suffering community waits for God's response in history. Maimonides, therefore, ends the *Mishneh Torah,* which is addressed to community, with the theme of messianism. However Maimonides knew that the Talmud, even under conditions of exile, described the halakhic approach of the *ḥasid.* He believed, therefore, that one can achieve disinterested love of God even under non-messianic conditions of history. Economic and political conditions of community do not necessarily define the spiritual capacities of individuals. Maimonides writes *The Guide of the Perplexed* for those who, in a non-messianic world, can approach Halakhah with the perspective of the *ḥasid*.[74]

———···⟨∞⟩···———

REASON AND TRADITIONAL AUTHORITY WITHIN HALAKHAH AND PHILOSOPHY

The previous chapters attempt to show, in opposition to Husik's approach, how Maimonides exposed the reader of his legal works to philosophy. He is not articulating a tradition which has no use for philosophy, but instead is portraying a halakhic way to God which must be united with philosophy.

There is yet another aspect of his works which supports this idea. A proper understanding of Maimonides' attitude toward authority is crucial for substantiating this orientation to his philosophy. A religious tradition which insists on uncritical subservience to its norms of behavior and beliefs tends to generate a specific human type which, in many ways, is incompatible with an intellectual love of God. Obedience to authority is not the basis for love—especially the love awakened by the perfection of the Beloved.

The individual guided by reason would find himself isolated within the community which demanded an uncritical acceptance of its beliefs. If such a person is to remain rooted in the community, it is crucial that the communal forms of spirituality, i.e., Halakhah, do not exclusively stress an obedience-orientation running counter to the independent spirit cultivated by reason. Political considerations may keep such an individual within the framework of community. Yet if the claim is made that such an individual can remain within his community for reasons which are essentially related to his personal spiritual outlook, we must show how the way of reason can flourish within halakhic Judaism.[1] The individual within Halakhah must have room to cultivate his independent reason; he cannot be asked to submit uncritically to the claims of authority.[2]

To fulfill a norm or to assent to a statement solely on the basis of authority is to cultivate a relationship nurtured by obedience. Imperatives can obligate an individual either on the basis of their content or on the authority of their author. Similarly, an individual can assent to statements of belief either because the statements appeal to rational criteria or because the individual possesses an unconditional regard for the authority-figure. In the latter case, one need not examine the content of belief before assenting. All that is necessary is to establish that the statement emanates from an accepted authority; the examination of what is said, for the most part, is irrelevant. Critical reasoning and evaluation, in fact, are dangerous and undesirable; they may introduce doubt and wavering when what is sought is unconditional compliance with authority.

We realize that this either/or dichotomy tends to oversimplify a problem that is more subtle than it is clearcut. Authority can take place within a context of shared values. It is these common values which both confer legitimacy on the person claiming authority and limit the scope of what he can do or say. As Peter Winch points out, the Pope, although often seen as an absolute authority—infallible in his decisions—could hardly maintain the allegiance of his church were he to claim that God does not exist or that cohabitation outside of marriage is a divine command.[3]

Despite this fact (which should caution one from emphasizing exclusively the notion of uncritical obedience in relationships based upon authority), one can still distinguish between the type of person developed by authoritarian systems and the type developed by systems whose appeal is to reason.[4] The former system is most compatible with the obedient personality, whereas the latter encourages the development of an independent person whose commitment is nurtured primarily by his own understanding. A relationship which allows for rational examination encourages an individual to appreciate the wisdom of the author of the norms and beliefs. When God's activities and dictates can be independently evaluated so that His wisdom becomes manifest to man, the groundwork is set for a relationship which is not based exclusively on obedience.

The Halakhah is a system of norms tracing its ultimate authoritative appeal to God;[5] the revelation at Sinai is the ground of the normative structure of halakhic legislation. Specific laws dictate the behavior of Jews in virtually all aspects of their lives. It is reasonable to expect, that since Halakhah is based on unconditional acceptance of divine authority, it would develop the obedient personality whose primary concern is to fulfill the laws of his tradition.[6] Yet, according to Maimonides, the telos of Halakhah is to create ideal conditions for the realization of intellectual love of God. Maimonides must therefore develop an approach to halakhic authority which will make it compatible with a spiritual life dedicated to philosophic knowledge of God. He must show that obedience to authority is not the sole virtue of Halakhah. If Halakhah encourages the development of a critical mind capable of independent reflection and evaluation, it cannot be exclusively characterized by appeals to authority which demand unconditional obedience.

Our analysis of the Maimonidean theory of halakhic authority will focus on how he restricted the use of appeals to authority within the Halakhah, and revealed instead areas of halakhic law which were independent of those appeals. Further analysis of Maimonides' epistemology in the *Guide* will also reveal that he sought to teach his reader to differentiate between norms and beliefs which must be accepted on the basis of the authority of tradition and those which appeal to reasoning, whether through demonstrative inference or through legal argumentation.[7] In doing so he showed that there are common principles operating within Halakhah and Aggadah which determine the legitimate scope of authority. His understanding of the relationship between authority and reason provides a frame within which the halakhic Jew can legitimately engage in those philosophic disciplines which nurture love for God.

Maimonides' treatment of authority, in his introduction to *The Commentary to the Mishnah*, begins with a discussion of the scope of prophetic authority. The prophet characteristically calls upon the authority of God to justify his claims. The limits of prophetic authority established within Judaism must be clarified if reason is to possess any legitimacy within the religious life of the tradition.[8]

Maimonides states that the prophet has full authority to decide political questions involving war and peace, economic policy and, if he deems it necessary, to temporarily suspend the laws of the Torah.[9] However, no prophet can suspend—even temporarily—the prohibitions against idolatry.[10] Regarding a "prophet" commanding participation in idolatrous worship, Maimonides writes:

. . . for the testimony of reason which denies his prophecy is stronger than the testimony of the eye which sees his miracles, for it has already been made clear to men of reason that it is not proper to honor nor to worship other than the One who caused all beings to exist and is unique in [His] ultimate perfection.[11]

Prophetic authority cannot demand obedience to that which is contrary to the testimony of reason.[12] Such demands would immediately prove the prophet to be false, regardless of miracles which might confirm his authority. Miracles do not convince rational men of the validity of such claims.

To Maimonides, such miracles are tests God sets before men. The tests may well be whether authority can be revered without such reverence leading to unconditional and indiscriminate submission, i.e., whether the Jew will abandon the testimony of reason when confronted with the claims of miracle workers. True loyalty to God is manifest by one who trusts his reason and refuses to follow authority indiscriminately.

A second limitation on prophetic authority prevents the prophet from permanently abrogating any part of Mosaic law. Maimonides appeals to the authority of Moses and Torah to explain the limitations set on the prophet's right to abrogate matters of Halakhah. He does not use the phrase "the testimony of reason" here as he does with regard to idolatry.[13] Rather he appeals to the testimony of the community of Israel who participated with Moses in the theophany at Sinai.[14] This event implanted a permanent conviction by which the community could withstand the seductions of miracle-working prophets who claim to supersede and negate the law of Sinai.[15] In the *Guide* Maimonides speaks of this conviction as the "certainty of sight."[16] The entire community "saw" God addressing Moses. Their participation in this revelation led them to accept Mosaic legislative authority, not on the basis of miracles, but on the firmer basis of their direct participation in God's revelation to Moses. The commitment to the Torah of Moses, which resulted from the "certainty of sight," imposes limits upon the authoritative pronouncements of post-Mosaic prophets.

In the *Mishneh Torah* Maimonides supports this limitation on prophetic authority by an analysis of the legal status of the prophet. He bases his position on the fact that miracles are not conclusive evidence of one's being a prophet:[17]

Hence one may conclude with regard to every Prophet after Moses, that we do not believe in such a Prophet because of the signs he shows, as much as to say that only if he shows a sign, we shall pay heed to him in all that he says, but we believe in him because of the charge laid down by Moses in the Torah that if the Prophet gives a sign "you shall listen to him"; just as the Lawgiver directed that a cause is to be decided on the evidence of two witnesses even if we have no certainty as to whether they are testifying to the truth or to a falsehood. Similarly, it is our duty to listen to the Prophet though we do not know if the sign he shows is genuine or has been performed with the aid of sorcery and by secret arts.[18]

Just as one accepts the evidence of two witnesses in a court, even though such witnesses may in fact be lying, so too does the law demand that one accept a person as a prophet on the basis of miracles. Although one is never absolutely certain whether witnesses are telling the truth, a judge is required to accept their testimony because this is the accepted legal procedure. Similarly the community must listen to a prophet even though there are rational grounds for suspecting miracles to be the works of clever sleight of hand.

Consequently a prophet cannot abrogate the laws of

the Torah, since it is the authority of this legal system that makes miracles acceptable evidence for assuming the role of prophet.[19] Whereas such prophets require the legal validation of the Torah, Moses' authority has been established not by the rules of a legal system but by the participation of the community in the theophany at Sinai. This experience yields an absolute certainty in Mosaic authority and must not be questioned by a prophet lest the grounds for his authority be undermined.

What is important, for our purposes, is that the prophet's authority takes place within a context limiting that which he can legitimately demand. A further restriction on prophetic authority emerges with the relationship of prophecy and the elaboration of Halakhah:

And know, that prophecy is not effective in the study and interpretation of the Torah and the inferring of laws by the thirteen hermeneutic principles; rather what Joshua and Pinḥas do in matters of study and argument is [the same as] what Ravina and Rav Ashi do.[20]

The appeal to prophetic authority in the elaboration and clarification of the laws of Torah is inadmissible despite the fact that the prophet, in calling upon revelation to decide an argument, is attempting to interpret the system, not to abrogate it nor to question Mosaic authority.[21] In matters of legal argumentation and decision-making, the prophet is like any man who uses arguments to defend his position.

One of Maimonides' reasons for excluding prophecy from halakhic argumentation involves a theory of halakhic reasoning which cannot permit the intrusion of appeals to prophetic authority:

And so, if a Prophet claims that God told him that the judgment [*pesak*] in any given commandment is such and that the argument of so-and-so is correct, behold that Prophet is killed; for he is a false prophet as we have explained, for there is no revelation of Torah after the first messenger [Moses] and there is no addition and no diminution, "It is not in the heavens" (Deut. 30:12). And God did not assign us to Prophets but he assigned us to wise men, masters of argument. He did not say, "And you shall appear before the Prophet"; rather He said, "And [you shall] appear before the levitical priests, or the magistrate . . ." (Deut. 17:9). And the Sages have dealt at great length with this issue and it is correct.[22]

Besides appealing to the paradigm-text which excludes legislative prophecy after Moses, "It is not in heaven," Maimonides presents what he believes to be the implication of the text, "And you shall appear before the levitical priests or the magistrate. . . ." The addition of this text, and the obvious distinction between "prophet" and "priests or magistrate" (masters of Halakhah), defines a fundamental difference between appeals to the authority of prophecy and to halakhic argumentation. The disparate logics of these two modes of discourse are, we believe, the basis of this Maimonidean concept. Maimonides is claiming that prophecy is excluded from halakhic procedures of argument and decision-making due to the epistemological status of halakhic reasoning. To substantiate and clarify this interpretation, we shall examine how Maimonides uses the text-category, "And [you shall] appear before the levitical priests, or the magistrate . . . ," in another section of his introduction.

Maimonides distinguishes between laws that stem directly from Sinai and laws that result from the application of halakhic rules of reasoning.[23] The former is subdivided into a) laws that, although known independently of biblical interpretation, can be supported in some way by exegesis or hermeneutic reasoning *(perush mekubal mi-Moshe)*, and b) laws which cannot be supported by either of these *(halakhah le-Moshe mi-Sinai)*. The common characteristic of these two types of laws is that they appeal to the authority of God and thus, with regard to them, no disagreement is possible. Any law which appears to have come from Sinai is accepted as normative; one must only prove that the chain of transmission was never broken and that the transmitters were trustworthy.[24] The presence of disagreement in laws based on Sinai can only be due to an uncertainty to the chain of tradition. It makes no sense to argue against a law which one accepts as having emanated from God Himself. Thus disagreement is logically excluded, as long as one trusts the claims of tradition.

Maimonides asserts that there has never been any disagreement regarding the laws for which the authority of Sinai is claimed. However another body of law exists which does allow for disagreement; there is no claim for its emanation from Sinai. It does issue from the application of talmudic rules of hermeneutics which serve as principles by which men can analyze texts and infer laws.[25] Maimonides writes that after the death of Moses, Joshua and his generation developed laws on the basis of halakhic reasoning in areas where there was no Mosaic legislation. Maimonides writes:

And with regard to the issues which they learned [by rules of hermeneutics] there are matters in which there was no disagreement but there was unanimity [*Ijma*], and some cases where there was disagreement between two views, one person arguing with an argument [*Qiyas*] which appeared strongest to him and another with an argument [*Qiyas*] which appeared strongest to him. For in the ways of argumentative reasoning such occurrences will result, and when such a disagreement occurs we follow the majority, as Scripture says, "After the many to follow" (Ex. 23:2).[26]

In this area of Halakhah, disagreement is possible due to the inherent nature of laws which emerge from legal reasoning. Law based on reasoning is not defended by appealing to authority, but to the compelling force of argument. Such laws appeal to human understanding and not to loyalty to authority. Disagreement within this body of law does not imply a lack of loyalty to authority; the logic of the appeal of such laws points to the reasonableness of the argument, not to the status of the person who promulgated the law.

Majority rule is a procedure for resolving disagreement when a verdict is necessary, e.g., when social order requires uniform modes of behavior.[27] It is not a procedure for ascertaining truth, since the rejected position has not been shown to be false. Even when the Talmud declares the law to be as one of the disputants, the rejected opinion is still mentioned in the Talmud.[28] The Halakhah permits a judge to disagree with the decision of the highest court as long as he does not encourage deviant practice which would undermine social stability:[29]

If the Elder is the outstanding member of a court and he dissents from a decision by the Supreme Court, persists in communicating his opinion to others, but does not give it in the form of a practical ruling, he is not liable, for it is said, "and the man that does presumptuously" (Deut. 17:12), that is, not who says presumptuously but who instructs others to act upon his opinion or acts upon it himself.[30]

Maimonides in his *Commentary to the Mishnah* claims, however, that this distinction between disagreeing and rendering a decision does not apply to fundamental principles of Judaism or norms grounded in the authority of Sinai.[31] To question a norm based on Sinai or a fundamental belief is to question that which is not subject to disagreement. However, in matters of law based on the thirteen hermeneutic principles, disagreement by the judge does not imply disloyalty to the authority of tradition, but is instead a legitimate response to laws which allow for reasoned disagreement.

The failure to discriminate between the logic of different types of laws led many people to attribute legal disagreements in the Talmud to the lack of attentiveness of students to their teachers. Ibn Daud, in his *Book of Tradition*, writes:

> Now should anyone infected with heresy attempt to mislead you, saying: "It is because the Rabbis differed on a number of issues that I doubt their words," you should retort bluntly and inform him that he is a "rebel against the decision of the Court"; and that our Rabbis, of blessed memory, never differed with respect to a commandment in principle, but only with respect to its details; for they had heard the principle from their teachers, but had not inquired as to its details, since they had not waited upon their masters sufficiently.[32]

Maimonides would disagree with this method of protecting the rabbinic tradition from the attack of Karaites.[33] To Maimonides disagreement is not the result of a lack of attentiveness to details, a lack which in principle could have been avoided, but is the natural outcome of developing a law based on reasoning:

> But the opinion of one who thought that also the laws wherein there is disagreement are received from Moses, and that disagreement took place due to an error in receiving the tradition [*kabbalah*] or due to forgetfulness, i.e., that one [disputant] is correct in his tradition and the second errs in his tradition, or he forgot or he did not hear from his teacher all that he should have; and he [who holds this opinion] offers as evidence for this what they said, "When the disciples [of Shammai and Hillel] who had insufficiently studied, increased in number, disputes multiplied in Israel and the Torah became as two Torot" (T.B. Sanhedrin 88b). Behold this, as God knows, is a despicable and very strange position, and it is an incorrect matter and not compatible to principles. And he [who holds this position] suspects people from whom we received the Torah and all this is idle. What brought

them to this deficient view is the limitation of their knowledge of the words of the Sages in the Talmud, since they found the category "laws received from Moses" [*perush mekubal mi-Moshe*] and it is correct according to the principles discussed earlier, but they did not distinguish between received principles and new matters that were learned by ways of analysis.[34]

To Maimonides, Hillel and Shammai, as opposed to their students, were in agreement not because they possessed a common tradition, but because they had a similar method of reasoning. Their agreement was not necessary but was the contingent outcome of their similar approaches to law. The logical possibility always existed that Hillel and Shammai would disagree. In fact, Maimonides shows that in specific cases they did disagree:

But as for their saying that when the disciples [of Hillel and Shammai] who had insufficiently studied, increased, dispute increased, this matter is very clear, for when two people are identical in understanding and in study and knowledge of the principles [*Usul*] from which they learn, there will not occur at all between them disagreement in what they learn by one of the hermeneutic principles, and if there will be disagreements they will be few, just as we have never found disagreements between Hillel and Shammai other than in a few laws, for their methods of study in all that they would learn by one of the principles were similar to one another, and also the correct general principles which were held by one were held by the other.[35]

Only in the domain of law based on Sinai was there no possibility for disagreement. By not distinguishing between tradition-based law and reason-based law, men such as Ibn Daud must relegate the arguments in the Talmud to minute details which in principle could have been avoided had the students "waited upon their masters sufficiently." Maimonides does not censure the students of Hillel and Shammai because he believes that their disagreements stem from their differing mental capacities and methods of interpretation. The similarity of approach of their masters, Hillel and Shammai, was lost by the students:

And when the study of their students became less and the methods of argument became weakened for them in comparison to Shammai and Hillel, their teachers, disagreement befell them during the give-and-take on many issues, because each one of them reasoned according to the power of his intellect and according to the principles known to him. And one should not blame them for this, for we cannot compel two people who are arguing to argue according to the level of the intellects of Joshua and Pinḥas. Also we are not permitted to have doubts regarding that about which they differed insofar as they are not as Shammai and Hillel or above them, for God Almighty did not obligate us to do so; but He obligated us to listen to the wise men, wise men of any generation whatsoever, as He said, "[you shall] appear before the levitical priests, or the magistrate in charge at the time, and present your problem" (Deut. 17:9). And in this manner befell disagreement, not that they erred in their receiving of tradition and one's tradition is true and the other's false. And how clear are these matters to one who reflects on them, and how great is this fundamental principle in the Torah.[36]

The rabbis of the tradition could be trusted as transmitters of the tradition, despite the occurrence of disagreement in the Talmud, because they understood when they were appealing to reason and when to authoritative tradition. No disagreement ever occurred regarding laws based on authority. But, given the epistemological features of laws emerging from reasoning, disagreement was entirely legitimate. The text which Maimonides uses to justify the existence within Halakhah of laws developed by human reasoning is the same text which removed the prophet from participating as a prophet in halakhic debates and judgments. The appeal of the prophet to the authority of God is incompatible with the logic of legal deliberation. The prophet offers no room for disagreement. The appeal to the authority of God allows either for acceptance or for rejection, based upon whether one is either loyal or disloyal. To affirm loyalty to God, yet also to disagree with what the prophet proclaims, makes no sense.

At stake in Maimonides' position is the logical status of legal reasoning. To Maimonides, legal rationality differs both from demonstrative proof and authoritative dictates. In authoritative appeals, only one position is valid: The authority—God—either said or did not say what the prophet claims. Similarly, in demonstrative proof, only one position is acceptable. The conclusion of a demonstrative inference whose premises are true, must also be true; whatever conclusions contradict this demonstrated conclusion must be false. One who disagrees with a demonstrated conclusion is either obstinate or irrational. Maimonides writes in the *Guide:*

For in all things whose reality is known through demonstration there is no tug-of-war and no refusal to accept a thing proven— unless indeed such refusal comes from an ignoramus who offers a resistance that is called resistance to demonstration.[37]

In legal reasoning, however, when one is not simply transmitting a law based on authority, arguments are involved which support conclusions outside of strict entailment.[38] Legal arguments make a position reasonable, sometimes even more reasonable than a rival position. They do not demonstrate that the contradictory is impossible. A judge may issue a verdict on the basis of arguments presented to him, yet he may still feel the weight of counter-arguments which could justify a future appeal of his decision. Since legal argumentation lacks the logical status of demonstrative proof, the procedure of deciding legal issues on the

basis of majority rule is rationally comprehensible. In arguments based on demonstrative inference or on questions
of fact, such procedure is unjustified and clearly absurd.

Maimonides, the master of legal rabbinic thought, understood the logical status of legal argumentation. He was
well aware of those conditions under which it would make
sense to speak of rational disagreement. Only one conclusion is valid when the appeal is to the authority of tradition
or to demonstrative reason. The text, "And [you shall]
appear before the levitical priests or the magistrate in
charge at the time," is the paradigm-text. By declaring the
legitimacy of laws grounded in human reasoning, it prevents the prophet from appearing among scholars of the
Halakhah and arguing from a base of prophetic authority.
In the house of learning where scholars debate legal matters, one must follow the procedure of legal adjudication
to decide which opinion shall prevail:

> . . . even if one-thousand Prophets who are as Elijah and Elisha
> would interpret any interpretation, and one-thousand-and-one
> wise men interpret the opposite of that interpretation, "After
> the many to follow" (Ex. 23:2) and we follow the position of the
> one-thousand-and-one wise men, not the position of the one-
> thousand outstanding Prophets. And thus the Sages say, "By God!
> Even if Joshua, the son of Nun, had told it to me by his own
> mouth I should not have obeyed it and not have accepted it!"[39]

Maimonides' position excludes prophecy from a key
portion of halakhic law and maintains that rabbinic argumentation is independent of appeals to divine authority
and is thus subject to disagreement. In addition to the
certainties of Mosaic prophecy and traditions from Sinai,
Maimonides offers the Jew norms developed by men who
rationally struggle to resolve problems about which they
often disagree, and who never demonstrate that alternate

approaches to the law are invalid. It is not surprising to find a strong trend within Judaism opposed to this position.[40] In a legal system based upon revelation, it is natural to expect that individuals would prefer the certainties of prophetic pronouncements and law based on traditions from Sinai rather than laws based on legal reasoning. Tradition-based law, which mediates the content of revelation to man, speaks with unquestioned authority. It offers individuals the security and certainty of knowing precisely what God wills. By eliminating prophets from halakhic argumentation and restricting the scope of tradition-based law, Maimonides weakens the security which results from obedience to traditional authority.

Maimonides was careful to make distinctions which would restrict obedience to authority to certain classes of laws, while legitimizing disagreements based on reason in other classes. Maimonides does not eliminate the appeal to authority in Halakhah. He limits its applicability and is consistently emphatic in excluding it from areas which are not subject to its appeal. These important distinctions have broad spiritual implications. By knowing how to discriminate between the different types of laws, the halakhic Jew avoids an orientation of uncritical obedience to halakhic authority. The keen discernment which Maimonides hopes to encourage is vividly portrayed by him in the following exaggerated, hypothetical situation:

If a Prophet whose claim to prohecy has already been validated by us, as we have explained, tells us—on the Sabbath—to arise, women and men, to set a fire and make in it armaments and girdle ourselves with them and fight against the people of such and such place, today which is the Sabbath, and that we plunder their wealth and conquer their wives, we are obligated—we who are commanded by the Torah of Moses—to arise immediately, without hesitation regarding anything he commands us. And we shall fulfill all that he commands with vivacity and diligence, without hesitation or delay, and we shall believe that all that is done on that day, which is the Sabbath, be it the kindling of fire, the performance of acts of work [melakhot], or engagement in killing and war, is a commandment regarding which we will hope for a reward from God. For we have heeded the command of the Prophet for it is a positive commandment to listen to his words, as God, through Moses, commanded, "him you shall heed" (Deut. 18:15), and we received by tradition, "In all matters, if a prophet tells you to violate the teachings of Torah, listen to him save for idolatry" (T.B. Sanhedrin 90a), for if he tells us worship this day only this form, or offer incense to this star at this time only, behold this prophet is killed, and we do not listen to him.

But [consider] a man who sees himself, according to his imagination, as righteous and just, who is old and of advanced years, and he says to himself, "I am very old, and I am already such and such years old, and I have never violated any of the commandments at all. How can I arise on this day, which is the Sabbath, and violate a prohibition—whose penalty is stoning—and go to war? For I will not add nor detract and there are others to take my place, and many people will fulfill this commandment!"

Behold that man violated the word of God and he deserves death by heavenly decree, for he violated what the Prophet commanded him. And He who commanded that one rest on the Sabbath is He who commanded that one fulfill the words of the Prophet and what he establishes. And whoever violates His commandment deserves what we said. And this is what the Almighty said, "and if anybody fails to heed the words he speaks in My name, I Myself will call him to account" (Deut. 18:19). However, one who ties a permanent knot on this Sabbath day while performing those acts of work and he is not required to tie this knot so as to contribute in any way to what the Prophet commanded, behold this person deserves stoning.

And regarding this prophet himself who commanded whatever he commanded us to do on this day, which is the Sabbath, and whose words we fulfilled, if he [the prophet] says that the Sabbath limit is two thousand less one cubit or two thousand and one cubit and he relates this to [prophetic] inspiration and not to the method of analysis and argument, behold this person is a false prophet and he is killed by strangulation. And by this method shall you judge all that the Prophet commands you.[41]

Maimonides, in his introduction to the *Commentary to the Mishnah,* did not only elaborate upon the limits of prophetic authority through discursive arguments, but found it necessary to dramatize the halakhic Jew's discriminating approach to authority: The prophet arrives. He addresses the community which is absorbed in everyday concerns. He mobilizes it for war. Time, place, and enemy are decided according to the prophet's decree.

The community, Maimonides says, must comply with the prophet. The prophet can compel an entire community to violate one of its most important and symbolic religious events—the Sabbath—as well as to fight, kill, plunder, and, perhaps, die at his bidding. In the context of a community following a prophet to war, Maimonides brings in a seemingly irrelevant detail—the old man. Once the old man is mentioned, one feels compassion for him and is tempted to question Maimonides' fanatic concern that all obey the prophet. After all, what difference does it make if such an old man is not mobilized? What harm would there be if he were permitted to end his life without having disrupted his orderly pattern of piety? Yet Maimonides is adamant and uncompromising in his insistence that all—even such a man—follow the prophet. The situation of the old man accentuates the disruptive features which accompany a critical approach to authority. Habits of religious behavior can numb one's consciousness of the base of one's halakhic behavior. God, who commands one to rest on the Sabbath, can also command one to follow a prophet, thereby violating His established commandment. The authority of God is the ground of religious observance. Lest religious behavior become a self-justifying end, the Jew is constantly aware that his commitment is ultimately to God who, in principle, can disrupt the familiar routine of religious life.

After exhibiting concern that the prophet's authority be accepted and followed at all costs, Maimonides qualifies his opinion by reference to an apparently trivial detail of Halakhah. The community is at war. Because of the command of the prophet, its members are plundering, killing, and being killed. Yet, within this context, Maimonides cautions one not to tie a permanent knot on the Sabbath unless it is necessary, for this act is prohibited by the Halakhah. Concern for this minute detail of religious ritual within the context of war appears absolutely absurd. The concern, however, expresses Maimonides' feeling that obedience to the authority of the prophet must be circumscribed even in situations of stress. Obedience to the political authority of the prophet, under the conditions presented, could become total and lead to the reaction that everything else is permitted. In the situation described, a natural and human response to expect from the community would be the feeling that if some aspects of life are upset, everything, therefore, is permitted. But Maimonides insists that one must never relax one's ability to discriminate. One obeys the prophet only to whatever degree is necessary. Beyond that, other obligations remain intact.

Though the authority given to the prophet is enormous, the prophet is powerless regarding issues not in his domain. His authority ceases when he participates in rational discourse with scholars. As a prophet, he may initiate a war, but he may not decide whether the Sabbath limit is to be one cubit more or less. The juxtaposition of minute details of Halakhah with the life-and-death command to war focuses attention on a crucial principle: Prophecy has a role in Judaism, yet this role is not limitless. Even if the limits of prophetic authority are manifested in seemingly trivial minutiae of Halakhah, one must conscientiously ensure that these limits are not overstepped.

Maimonides insists that the Jew must be aware of the exact scope of obedience to authority. He must not only discriminate among all the grounds of different norms, but he must also act on the basis of his discrimination. The security of routine or of a single type of response to religious norms is absent from the mind of the Halakhic Jew, according to Maimonides. The crux of his response is meticulous selectivity. He approaches Halakhah with principles for discriminating the scope and type of various commandments. Halakhic observance that is grounded in routine and uncritical obedience could not sustain the upsetting changes introduced by the prophet; people either would resist his demands or they would accept his disruptive demands in a manner which would destroy existing values. Only a reflective person could live with change in his religious life and still maintain an approach of discrimination as opposed to the all-or-nothing response of the uncritically obedient.

From Maimonides' first major legal work, we recognize the Jew which he believed emerged from Halakhah. In comparing Halakhic man to philosophic man it is not correct to claim that the former reflects the virtue of unthinking obedience and the latter the value of critical reflection.[42] The Halakhah itself develops a disciplined, discriminating approach. A person who follows the prophet to war yet who refuses to unnecessarily tie a knot on the Sabbath, or who refuses prophetic authority for halakhic laws which are open to human reasoning, is the type of person who critically evaluates the claims of authority. The personality which Halakhah cultivates, according to Maimonides, is the same as that which emerges when the Jew is exposed to philosophy. The same critical discrimination characterizes the Jew's attitude toward beliefs. We can now analyze Maimonides' approach to beliefs and show how the anthropology which emerges from

Halakhah is also manifested in the cognitive claims of Judaism.

As a system which includes the notion of God's revelation in history, Judaism is anchored, at least in part, on authoritarian claims. The belief in divine revelation—as well as numerous other principles which claim divine action in history—cannot be rationally demonstrated.[43] Thus, among the fundamental principles of religion, there are those which must rely on the authority of tradition for their acceptance. Yet, according to Maimonides, other principles—such as God's existence and non-corporeality —are capable of being demonstrated rationally.[44]

In his introduction to *Ḥelek*, Maimonides does not distinguish between the logical status of those principles of Judaism which can be established by reason and those which rest on the authority of tradition. However, Maimonides must account for the acceptance of principles grounded in the authority of tradition if he is to maintain that Aggadah be included within a universal framework of truth. In *The Guide of the Perplexed* Maimonides does clarify the situation by offering definite criteria which justify one's acceptance of beliefs based on the authority of tradition. Simply stated, Maimonides claims that appeals to authority are justified when it can be shown that demonstrative reason is not able to offer certainty. This is the method he uses when he argues with those who claim that the eternity of the world has been demonstrated by Aristotle:

What I myself desire to make clear is that the world's being created in time, according to the opinion of our Law—an opinion that I have already explained—is not impossible and that all those philosophic proofs from which it seems that the matter is different from what we have stated, all those arguments have a certain point through which they may be invalidated and the inference drawn from them against us shown to be incorrect. Now inasmuch as this is true in my opinion and inasmuch as this question—I mean to say that of the eternity of the world or its creation in time—becomes an open question, it should in my opinion be accepted without proof because of prophecy, which explains things to which it is not in the power of speculation to accede. For as we shall make clear, prophecy is not set at naught even in the opinion of those who believe in the eternity of the world.[45]

Truths based upon demonstrative certainty, however, can never be contradicted by an appeal to prophetic authority:

That the Deity is not a body has been demonstrated; from this it follows necessarily that everything that in its external meaning disagrees with this demonstration must be interpreted figuratively, for it is known that such texts are of necessity fit for figurative interpretation. However, the eternity of the world has not been demonstrated. Consequently, in this case, the texts ought not to be rejected and figuratively interpreted in order to make prevail an opinion whose contrary can be made to prevail by means of various sorts of arguments.[46]

Allegiance to community and to its recognized authorities may be the source of man's understanding of the world and of God if it can be shown that tradition-based convictions are never in discord with the proven truths of reason. This procedure makes it possible for the individual to participate in two "communities": With the universal community of rational men, he shares truths which are established through demonstrative reason, while retaining his particular community's beliefs based upon loyalty to its authorities. Acceptance of beliefs based upon communal authority does not entail that one must doubt the capacity of reason to establish truth. The tradition will always agree with reason when the problem is within the domain in which reason is completely competent, e.g., in demonstrating that God is non-corporeal. Demonstrative arguments are never susceptible to refutation by claims based upon authority.

A similar approach to the Halakhah has been established by Maimonides. Just as a prophet cannot argue from his authority in law matters derived from hermeneutic reasoning, so does Maimonides insist that he cannot argue from authority about truths that are based upon demonstrative reason. The prophet must cast off his mantle of authority in both the academies of legal and demonstrative reasoning.

In discussing the first two commandments of the Decalogue, Maimonides writes:

Now with regard to everything that can be known by demonstration, the status of the Prophet and that of everyone else who knows it are equal; there is no superiority of one over the other. Thus these two principles are not known through prophecy alone.[47]

The first two commandments, since they are capable of being demonstrated by reason, are logically independent of the category of authority.[48] All of Israel—in fact all rational men—can, in principle, share with Moses the same certainty regarding the truths of God's unity and non-corporeality.

Another similarity between legal and speculative argumentation is noticeable from statements in the *Mishneh Torah* and the *Guide*. In both cases, disagreement with men of authority need not imply rejection of their authority.

In Halakhah, one may disagree with the statements of an authority without being accused of disloyalty to him if his claim is based upon legal reasoning.

In *Hilkhot Mamrim,* Maimonides stipulates the conditions required for the abrogation of legislation enacted by previous courts. In a case where the legislation was based solely on the authority of the courts, he writes:

> If the Supreme Court instituted a decree, enacted an ordinance, or introduced a custom, which was universally accepted in Israel, and a later Supreme Court wishes to rescind the measure, to abolish the ordinance, decree, or custom, it is not empowered to do so, unless it is superior to the former both in point of wisdom and in point of number. If it is superior in wisdom but not in number, or in number but not in wisdom, it is denied the right to abrogate the measure adopted by its predecessor, even if the reason which prompted the latter to enact the decree or ordinance has lost all force.
>
> But how is it possible for any Supreme Court to exceed another in number, seeing that each Supreme Court consists of seventy-one members? We include in the number the wise men of the age, who agree to and accept without demur the decision of the [contemporaneous] Supreme Court.[49]

When, however, the legislation was derived from the application of the hermeneutic principles, the above requirements for legal charge do not apply:

> If the Great Sanhedrin, by employing one of the hermeneutical principles, deduced a ruling which in its judgment was in consonance with the Law and rendered a decision to that effect, and a later Supreme Court finds a reason for setting aside the ruling, it may do so and act in accordance with its own opinion, as it is said: "[and appear before] the magistrate in charge at the time" (Deut. 17:9); that is, we are bound to follow the directions of the Court of our own generation.[50]

In the former case, abrogation of the law would imply disloyalty to the authority of the previous court since the legislation was grounded solely in its authority to enact new legislation. In the latter case, however, since the enactment of law was based upon reasoned argument, the later court need not be greater in number and wisdom; in disagreeing with the decision of the previous court it was not questioning its superior legal authority.[51] Similarly, about speculative truths, one may disagree with talmudic authorities when their arguments do not emanate from their positions of authority but from reason:

> You should not find it blameworthy that the opinion of Aristotle disagrees with that of the Sages, may their memory be blessed, as to this point. For this opinion, I mean to say the one according to which the heavenly bodies produce sounds, is consequent upon the belief in a fixed sphere and in stars that return. You know, on the other hand, that in these astronomical matters they preferred the opinion of the sages of the nations of the world to their own. For they explicitly say: "The sages of the nations of the world have vanquished." And this is correct. For everyone who argues in speculative matters does this according to the conclusions to which he was led by his speculation. Hence the conclusion whose demonstration is correct is believed.[52]

The categories of loyalty and disloyalty do not enter into disagreements based on reasoned argument.

There is a common logic that unites Aggadah and Halakhah. The methods that the law student uses to understand when reason, in relation to authority, may apply in legal issues are similar to his approach to the speculative claims of his tradition.

The Aggadah of Judaism can be found both in the Talmud and the Bible.[53] The same biblical text that Maimonides uses to reject a fundamentalist approach to rabbinic Aggadah is used to justify a nonliteral understanding of prophetic Aggadah.[54] All Aggadah, both rabbinic and prophetic, must take cognizance of universal criteria of truth. When one studies Aggadah susceptible to demonstrative certainty, loyalty is to reason not to authority. The certainties of demonstrative reason transcend the logic of communal authority.

Maimonides' attempt at reconciling the Aggadah of Judaism with Aristotle's physics is not based upon his loyalty to Athens, but upon his commitment to truth.[55] Once a truth has been established through demonstrative reason, it ceases to have any logically significant relationship to the one who established it. The acceptance of truths based upon demonstrative reason does not in any way reveal the cultural or historical loyalties of an individual. The approach of modern thinkers who view knowledge as being historically and culturally determined should not confuse our understanding of how Maimonides perceived the science of Athens. Not only in the *Guide* but also in the *Mishneh Torah,* Maimonides expresses this:

As regards the logic for all these calculations—why we have to add a particular figure or deduct it, how all these rules originated, and how they were discovered and proved—all this is part of the sciences of astronomy and mathematics, about which many books have been composed by Greek sages—books that are still available to the scholars of our time. But the books which had been composed by the Sages of Israel, of the tribe of Issachar, who lived in the time of the Prophets, have not come down to us. But since all these rules have been established by sound and clear proofs, free from any flaw and irrefutable, we need not be concerned about the identity of their authors, whether they be Hebrew Prophets or Gentile sages. For when we have to do with rules and propositions which have been demonstrated by good reasons and have been verified to be true by sound and flawless proofs, we rely upon the author who has discovered them or transmitted them only because of his demonstrated proofs and verified reasoning.[56]

Just as there is no "Jewish" astronomy so there is no "Greek" physics. Demonstrative truths claim assent on the basis of their content, and not by the appeal of their author. In his attempt at reconciling the science of his day with Torah, Maimonides did not see himself as attempting to merge two cultural loyalties. He was loyal to the Jewish tradition; he did not believe that this demanded the denial of universal truths. Maimonides was loyal to the authority of Moses and Abraham; he was intellectually open to the rational arguments of Aristotle and al-Farabi.[57] From the perspective of his general position that demonstrative truths are not subject to arguments from authority, we can understand Maimonides' astonishing claim that there always was an oral tradition of philosophic knowledge in Judaism:

> Know that the many sciences devoted to establishing the truth regarding these matters that have existed in our religious community have perished because of the length of the time that has passed, because of our being dominated by the pagan nations, and because, as we have made clear, it is not permitted to divulge these matters to all people. . . . Now if there was insistence that the legalistic science of law should not, in view of the harm that will be caused by such a procedure, be perpetuated in a written compilation accessible to all the people, all the more could none of the "mysteries of the Torah" have been set down in writing and be made accessible to the people. On the contrary, they were transmitted by a few men belonging to the elite to a few of the same kind, just as I made clear to you from their sayings: "The mysteries of the Torah may only be transmitted to a counselor, wise in crafts, and so on." This was the cause that necessitated the disappearance of these great roots of knowledge from the nation.[58]

Maimonides is showing his student, who is concerned about the conflict of reason with authority, that just as there is—in Judaism—an oral legal tradition which claims his assent on the basis of authority, so, too, there is an oral tradition—in philosophy—which claims his assent on the basis of demonstrative argument. What appears as an exaggerated, provincialistic claim actually states that Judaism always recognized that philosophic truths transcended loyalty to authority. One shows allegiance to the tradition by refusing to allow for the possibility of a contradiction between teachings based upon authority, and demonstrative truths. By maintaining that Judaism from Sinai onward contained both a legal and philosophical oral tradition, Maimonides enables the student of the *Guide* to realize that one remains a traditional Jew by joining loyalty to the oral law with loyalty to reason. The unity of Halakhah and Aggadah, within the tradition, makes it possible for an individual to unite allegiance to community with respect for truth regardless of the source of the truth.[59] Maimonides' philosophic explanation of prophetic Aggadah is a traditional mode of explanation since the tradition always recognized the difference between arguments from authority and arguments from reason.[60] Biblical Aggadah is not misinterpreted if it is understood from the perspective of universal criteria of knowledge: The Bible never intended to speak from authority when demonstrative reason was capable of establishing truth.[61]

The task of the Jewish philosopher, as understood by Maimonides, is to provide the believing Jew with epistemological guidelines which enable him to identify those beliefs which his community accepts on the basis of authority, and those beliefs his community shares with the universal community of rational men. The Jewish philosopher makes it possible for the Jew to believe that it can be compatible to be both a philosopher and a traditional Jew.[62] To do this, he must establish and justify the legitimate place occupied by beliefs based on authority. Beliefs accepted on the basis of authority become legitimate when one realizes that the human intellect has limitations and that demonstrative reason alone is not a sufficient source of knowledge:[63]

Do not think that what we have said with regard to the insufficiency of the human intellect and its having a limit at which it stops is a statement made in order to conform to Law. For it is something that has already been said and truly grasped by the philosophers without their having concern for a particular doctrine or opinion. And it is a true thing that cannot be doubted except by an individual ignorant of what has already been demonstrated.[64]

The recognition of this limitation, which can be established by rational arguments, makes it possible for one to fully embrace both the task of being a philosopher and of being a loyal Jew:

The utmost power of one who adheres to a law and who has acquired knowledge of true reality consists, in my opinion, in his refuting the proofs of the philosophers bearing on the eternity of the world. How sublime a thing it is when the ability is there to do it! And everyone who engages in speculation, who is perceptive, and who has acquired true knowledge of reality and does not deceive himself, knows that with regard to this question —namely the eternity of the world or its temporal creation—no cogent demonstration can be reached and that it is a point before which the intellect stops.[65]

The acceptance of the doctrine of creation, on the basis of tradition, is made possible by a knowledge of epistemology. He who knows both the scope and the limits of demonstrative reason realizes that claims based upon authority have a legitimate place in the philosophical mind. Even Aristotle, according to Maimonides, appealed to the authority of consensus to establish belief in the eternity of the universe.[66]

The condition for embracing philosophy and Judaism is one's ability to discern the epistemological status of different types of statements. Regarding the talmudic statement that ascribes the following virtue to the wise man, "He questions according to the subject and replies according to the rule" (T.B. Avot 5:7), Maimonides comments:

He would question what is necessary to question relative to that matter; he would neither request a mathematical demonstration in the science of physics, nor an argument from physics in the mathematical sciences and matters of the like. If he were the one who were questioned, he would also answer in accordance with the subject of the question. [That is], if he would be questioned in subjects which by their nature require a proof, he will answer in accordance with the subject of the questioner with a proof. If he could be questioned in that which is beneath this [i.e., which does not require a proof], he will answer according to that which is his opinion and [according to] its [i.e., the subject's] nature. Moreover, he would not be asked for the material cause to which he will offer the formal cause, or be asked for the formal cause to which he will offer the material cause. Rather, he will reply from the standpoint of the object [of the question], as it was said, "He questions according to the subject and replies according to the rule." This will come to pass only after extraordinary wisdom.[67]

The "extraordinary wisdom" which is required to discern appropriate criteria of knowledge is especially important for the Jew who embraces philosophy. The key to intellectually harmonizing philosophy with Judaism is knowledge of epistemology, insofar as this prevents one from confusing claims based upon authority with claims based upon reason. To confuse the two is to experience conflict and perplexity where they do not exist. The consequences of a limited knowledge of logic can lead not only to perplexity, but ultimately to apostasy. It is from this perspective that Maimonides interprets the talmudic parable dealing with the apostasy of Elisha ben Abuya:

Four men entered *pardes* and they were: Ben Azzai, Ben Zoma, Elisha Aher and Rabbi Akiva . . . Ben Azzai gazed and died . . . Ben Zoma gazed and went mad . . . Elisha Aher cut the roots . . . Rabbi Akiva entered in peace and departed in peace.[68]

Maimonides identified *pardes* with the philosophical disciplines of physics and metaphysics. His interpretation of the reason that Rabbi Akiva was able to sustain his commitment to Judaism within *pardes*, whereas Elisha was not, is:

For if you stay your progress because of a dubious point; if you do not deceive yourself into believing that there is a demonstration with regard to matters that have not been demonstrated; if you do not hasten to reject and categorically to pronounce false any assertions whose contradictories have not been demonstrated; if, finally, you do not aspire to apprehend that which you are unable to apprehend—you will have achieved human perfection and attained the rank of Rabbi Akiva, peace be on him, who "entered in peace and went out in peace" when engaged in the theoretical study of these metaphysical matters. If, on the other hand, you aspire to apprehend things that are beyond your apprehension; or if you hasten to pronounce false, assertions the contradictories of which have not been demonstrated or that are possible, though very remotely so—you will have joined Elisha Aḥer.[69]

Elisha Aḥer, the celebrated apostate of the Talmud, was led to apostasy due to his deficient knowledge of logic. Maimonides knew that when engaged in philosophical speculation, inability to analyze the logical status of different types of arguments would destroy one's loyalty to tradition. If one forgets the distinction between speculative arguments, which are logically subject to appeals to authority, and demonstrative arguments (where such appeals are illegitimate), it will be impossible to maintain belief in Torah.[70] To accept the Torah, one must believe in the doctrine of creation:

Know that with a belief in the creation of the world in time, all the miracles become possible and the Law becomes possible, and all questions that may be asked on this subject, vanish.[71]

Were one to mistakenly accept the philosophers' speculative arguments for the eternity of the universe as having the same force as a demonstrative proof, he would be compelled to abandon his allegiance to Torah. Belief in eternal necessity makes belief in revelation at Sinai logically impossible:

> ... if the philosophers would succeed in demonstrating eternity as Aristotle understands it, the Law as a whole would become void, and a shift to other opinions would take place.[72]

This is where Elisha erred. He thought that the speculative arguments for eternity had the status of demonstrative proofs. He therefore found it impossible to remain within a tradition based upon a false belief in creation. Maimonides attempts to prevent such lapses as Elisha's apostasy by offering the *Guide* as an epistemological map which leads the student along a route that integrates the claims of authority and reason.[73]

The religious significance of the study of logic as a means of integrating an independent spiritual aspiration with a commitment to community is evident from Maimonides' treatment of the difference between Akiva and Aḥer. It is also possible to respond to the perplexity which philosophical study creates for the halakhic Jew by rejecting the way of Athens rather than of Jerusalem. Maimonides does not educate toward an unquestioning acceptance of Aggadah. He therefore outlines his epistemological map for the general community of halakhic Jews. In "The Letter on Astrology" to the rabbis of Marseilles, Maimonides presents a clear demarcation between the domains of reason and traditional authority:

> Know, my masters, that it is not proper for a man to accept as trustworthy anything other than one of these three things. The first is a thing for which there is a clear proof deriving from man's reasoning—such as arithmetic, geometry, and astronomy. The second is a thing that a man perceives through one of the five

senses—such as when he knows with certainty that this is red and this is black and the like through the sight of his eye; or as when he tastes that this is bitter and this is sweet; or as when he feels that this is hot and this is cold; or as when he hears that this sound is clear and this sound is indistinct; or as when he smells that this is a pleasing smell and this is a displeasing smell and the like. The third is a thing that a man receives from the Prophets or from the righteous. Every reasonable man ought to distinguish in his mind and thought all the things that he accepts as trustworthy, and say: "This I accept as trustworthy because of tradition, and this because of sense perception, and this on the grounds of reason."[74]

After the rabbis are made to understand these three distinct criteria of knowledge, they are then introduced to an understanding of rabbinic Aggadah:

I know that you may search and find sayings of some individual Sages in the Talmud and *midrashot* whose words appear to maintain that at the moment of man's birth the stars will cause such and such to happen to him. Do not regard this as a difficulty, for it is not fitting for a man to abandon the prevailing law and raise once again the counterarguments and replies [that preceded its enactment]. Similarly it is not proper to abandon matters of reason that have already been verified by proofs, shake loose of them, and depend on the words of a single one of the Sages from whom possibly the matter was hidden. . . . A man should never cast his reason behind him, for the eyes are set in front, not in back. "Now I have told you all my heart" on this subject.[75]

Maimonides explains to the rabbis of Marseilles that talmudic authorities cannot make a spurious science, i.e., astrology, into a genuine science. The criteria of what is to count as legitimate, scientific truth is established by the canons of reason:

The position of the astrologers is given the lie by reason, for correct reasoning has already refuted, by means of lucid proofs, all those follies that they have maintained.[76]

The rabbis are told to rely on the philosophers when they evaluate the claims of their rabbinic authorities. Throughout this important letter, which is addressed to students of the law, Maimonides does not hide his love for philosophy. He goes so far as to identify "the remnant . . . whom the Lord shall call" (Joel 3:5) with those philosophers who are able to provide criteria for distinguishing between the genuine science of astronomy and the spurious science of astrology.[77]

The rabbis of Marseilles are shown how to use philosophic reason to support or supplement the teachings of Judaism. They are taught to recognize which principles of Judaism rest upon agreement with philosophic reason and which principles in Judaism rest upon the authority of tradition. Astrology is not only proven to be false on the basis of philosophy, but, as Maimonides writes:

It also is regarded as a falsehood by us because of the religious tradition, for if the matter stood thus, of what utility would the Torah and the commandment and the Talmud be to a particular individual? For in that event, every single individual would lack the power to do anything he set his mind to, since something else draws him on—against his will—to be this and not to be that; of what use then is the command or the Talmud? The roots of the religion of Moses, our Master, we find, refute the position of these stupid ones—in addition to reason's doing so with all those proofs that the philosophers maintain to refute the position of the Chasdeans and the Chaldeans and their associates.[78]

However when Maimonides deals with belief in individual providence which is based solely on the authority of the Torah and not on demonstrative reason, he writes:

The position of the philosophers who maintain that these things are due to chance is also regarded as a falsehood by us because of the religious tradition.[79]

In contrast to astrology, which is rejected both by the claims of reason and of tradition, individual providence is accepted solely on the basis of tradition.

We have discussed "The Letter on Astrology" to indicate that Maimonides exposed his legal students and associates to the same epistemological principles which he established in the *Guide*. All of Maimonides' students are encouraged to develop their rational faculties without fear of being contradicted by traditional authorities. Because Maimonides carefully and clearly differentiates the three types of criteria upon which one can base one's knowledge, the student of Torah knows when he must demonstrate allegiance to his tradition and when he is free to follow independent reason. The integrity of man's intellect will never be violated by the tradition since, according to Maimonides, the tradition distinguishes knowledge based upon sense, upon reason, and upon authority.

A factor in Maimonides' anger with the Mutakallimun is that he viewed their method as a violation of the integrity of reason:

Now when I considered this method of thought, my soul felt a very strong aversion to it and had every right to do so. For every argument deemed to be a demonstration of the temporal creation of the world is accompanied by doubts and is not a cogent demonstration except among those who do not know the difference between demonstration, dialectics, and sophistic argument.[80]

The Mutakallimun disregarded the important distinction between arguments from authority and from reason.[81] The Mutakallimun claimed to have demonstrated the existence of God yet the premises upon which they based their demonstrations were, at best, only probable. They spoke as if they were offering demonstrative proof, but actually they were appealing from authority.

The consequences of using the mask of demonstrative reason to cover claims from authority can be disastrous. When one believes that his truth is self-evident, or that the impossibility of the contrary is demonstrated, and when no such demonstration exists, the reactions of those who disagree with him are interpreted as obstinacy or personal rebukes. In such situations, Maimonides recognizes that man would resort to violence to discourage the doubt caused by a faulty demonstration:

> . . . we would claim that we have a demonstration of the creation of the world in time and we would use the sword to prove it so that we should claim to know God by means of a demonstration.[82]

Violence would be justified by the necessity to change the stubborn will of one who refuses to accept that which is believed to be self-evident and demonstratively certain. Where reason is faulty and is not recognized as such, power will be used to compensate for the failures. Political leaders will respond with an unlimited abuse of power if they do not recognize the logical basis for their claims. Arguments from authority—which appear in the guise of demonstrative reason—are strong obstacles to the development of a world view which attempts to develop individual spiritual excellence—based upon reason—within a traditional religious society. It is against this background that one should understand Maimonides' meticulous concern for explaining the epistemological grounds of his statements.[83]

Maimonides' approach to beliefs and halakhic behavior opens the way for the integration of philosophy and Torah. The person whose spiritual life is nurtured by reason can fully embrace the spiritual life of his community. His intellect is never compromised when he acts within the framework of Torah. Had the Jewish tradition demanded the acceptance of beliefs which reason establishes as false, such a person would be compelled to suppress his intellect, or to reject his tradition, or to accept tradition for political expediency. Maimonides' epistemology eliminates the need to choose one of these options. The individual who has found his way to God by reason can accept communal forms of spirituality, i.e., Halakhah, as a whole man; he need not sever his political and social life from his individual aspirations. He knows that Judaism never allows authority to overstep the limits of its legitimate competence and to invade domains where reason is master.

———⋯◦≪∞≫◦⋯———

FOUR

THE PHILOSOPHIC
RELIGIOUS SENSIBILITY

The preceding chapter on Maimonides' epistemology indicated the extent to which he went to make the community aware of the universality of demonstrative truth. As Shlomo Pines wrote, "[Maimonides] evidently considered that philosophy transcended religious or national distinction."[1] It is this understanding of the universality and importance of philosophy which led to Maimonides' attempt to integrate philosophic knowledge with his own tradition. Maimonides was convinced that his own tradition recognized the possibility of an approach to God which was not exclusive to Jews. His demonstration of the existence, unity, and noncorporeality of God on the basis of premises which do not presuppose creation can be viewed as an expression of this fundamental conviction. By proving the reality of God independent of premises which are the presuppositions of the Jewish world view, Maimonides was not simply fortifying the certainty of specific theological claims. He was also implying that there is a way to God independent of the particular traditions of community.[2]

Given this understanding of God, we should recognize that the major spiritual problem facing the believing Jew is how simultaneously to accept the halakhic way to

God specific to his community while believing in the possibility of a spiritual way that does not presuppose membership in Israel.[3] What makes Maimonidean philosophy perennially significant is his attempt to explain Jewish particularity in the light of his acceptance of the universal way of reason.[4]

Membership within the covenant-community is fundamental to the spiritual life of a believing Jew. His daily relationship to God is structured by the religious forms of the community. Heresy not only involves denying God's existence, but is expressed as well by the individual's willful separation from the historical and political realities of his community. The wicked son of the Passover liturgy is considered a heretic because he dissociates himself from the historical experience of the community in Egypt.[5] The three pilgrimage festivals—Passover, Shavuot, and Sukkot—are all based on the relationship of God to a particular people.

The yearning for atonement, which one would assume to be the expression of an individual's relationship to God, also has a significant connection with community. Maimonides writes in the *Mishneh Torah:*

Although repentance and supplication are always good, they are particularly so and are immediately accepted during the ten days intervening between the New Year and the Day of Atonement, as it is said, "Seek you the Lord while He may be found" (Is. 55:6). This only applies, however, to an individual. But as for a community, whenever its members repent and offer supplications with sincere hearts, they are answered, as it is said, "For what great nation is there that has a god so close at hand, as is the Lord our God whenever we call upon Him" (Deut. 4:7).[6]

It should therefore be clear why Maimonides, in his *Iggeret Hashmad,* places the importance of community above that of the prophets, and why, in *Iggeret Teman,* he endangers his life for the welfare of community.[7]

Attempts to explain Maimonides' attachment to Judaism solely on the accident of heredity are contradicted both by what he wrote and by the way he lived.[8] Professor Pines writes of the significance of community for Maimonides' political thought:

It is even more significant that he propounded a perhaps at least partly original theoretical legitimation for the actvity of the legislator and the statesman by regarding it as a kind of imitation of God. (In this he possibly went beyond the Plato of the *Republic,* who required the philosopher to return to the "cave," but did not attempt to mitigate the regret that they must feel at being torn from the pure contemplation of the eternal truths and obliged to govern the polis.)[9]

This feature of Maimonides' philosophy is understandable if we remember the significance that the God of Israel has for Jewish spirituality. Within the framework of Plato and Aristotle to which the philosopher is drawn by the contemplative ideal, or within the framework of religious traditions which remove God from relatedness to a specific political community, there exists the ground for a detachment of the individual from community.[10] The concept of Israel, however, does not merely refer to a collectivity of faithful individuals, but involves the notion of community—a convert to Judaism must identify himself with the political destiny of the people of Israel and not only with its god.[11] Before one can stand at Sinai with the covenant-community, he must participate with pagan slaves in their political struggle for freedom in Egypt.[12]

Because of these essential and characteristic features of Judaism, we believe that the way of integration is the most appropriate model for understanding Maimonides. Since community defined his spiritual consciousness so deeply, it is mistaken to presume that he separated his individual quest for God from communal forms of spirituality.[13] The crux of Maimonides' approach is how the individual rethinks the communal way based upon tradition after he has discovered the universal way of reason.

Gershom Scholem in his work *Major Trends in Jewish Mysticism* interprets Maimonides' historical approach to biblical law as supporting a position opposed to our own understanding of Maimonides. He writes:

The whole world of religious law remained outside the orbit of philosophical inquiry, which means of course, too, that it was not subjected to philosophical criticism. It is not as if the philosopher denied or defied this world. He, too, lived in it and bowed to it, but it never became part and parcel of his work as a philosopher. It furnished no material for his thoughts. This fact, which is indeed undeniable, is particularly glaring in the case of thinkers like Maimonides and Saadia in whom the converging streams meet. They fail entirely to establish a true synthesis of the two elements, Halakhah and philosophy, a fact which has already been pointed out by Samuel David Luzzatto. Maimonides, for instance, begins the *Mishneh Torah*, his great codification of the Halakhah, with a philosophical chapter which has no relation whatever to the Halakhah itself. The synthesis of the spheres remains sterile, and the genius of the man whose spirit molded them into a semblance of union cannot obscure their intrinsic disparity.

For a purely historical understanding of religion, Maimonides' analysis of the origin of the *mitzvot*, the religious commandments, is of great importance, but he would be a bold man who would maintain that his theory of the *mitzvot* was likely to increase the enthusiasm of the faithful for their actual practice, likely to augment their immediate appeal to religious feeling. If the prohibition against seething a kid in its mother's milk and many similar irrational commandments are explicable as polemics against long-forgotten pagan rites, if the offering of sacrifice is a concession to the primitive mind, if other *mitzvot* carry with them antiquated moral and philosophical ideas—how can one expect the community to remain faithful to practices of which the antecedents have long since disappeared or of which the aims can be attained directly through philosophical reasoning? To the philosopher, the Halakhah either had no significance at all, or one that was calculated to diminish rather than to enhance its prestige in his eyes.[14]

Regarding Scholem's initial criticism, the connection between the introductory chapters of the *Mishneh Torah*
and the subsequent chapters on Halakhah has already
been discussed. The philosophic chapters prevent the
Halakhah from becoming a system insulated from universal criteria of truth. They show that Jewish particularity
must not block one from understanding the spiritual way
to God independent of community, and that disinterested
love, which is the goal of Halakhah, is made possible by a
philosophic understanding of nature. These points clearly
show the integral place which the philosophic chapters
occupy in the *Mishneh Torah*. It has also been shown how
the halakhic distinctions between *din* and *lifnim mi-
shurat ha-din* are important for Maimonides' philosophic
understanding of the relationship of the individual to community, within the tradition.

What remains as a challenge to our approach, and
possibly suggests that the Halakhah had no significance for
Maimonides as a philosopher, is his historical understanding of revelation. Maimonides' approach to revelation appears to support the view that his two major works reflect
two opposing points of view and are addressed to two
distinct and incompatible audiences. How else can one
compare his codification of the eternal law of Judaism in
the *Mishneh Torah* with his time-bound, situational, understanding of the law in the *Guide*? Regarding the categories we have employed so far, does this not suggest that,
as a philosopher, Maimonides is spiritually removed from
the Halakhah of the community?

Rather we argue that the way Maimonides understands the law in the *Guide* has the opposite effect—it
provides grounds for a philosophically trained Jew to take
Halakhah seriously. What lays at the bottom of his situational understanding of the *mitzvot* is the attempt to
achieve a unified understanding of nature and Torah reve-

lation and it is this unification which would elict the philosophic Jew's serious interest in Halakhah.

In order to appreciate both the problem and the audience to which Maimonides addresses himself in his historical approach to the commandments, it is important to examine his attempt to develop a religious personality whose relationship to God would be grounded in reason. Different religious types emerge as a result of how one understands the manifestation of the will of God within Torah and nature. Only if the religious sensibility Maimonides attempts to cultivate is understood, will his approach to revelation of the law in the *Guide* make sense.

As shown earlier, Maimonides, by referring to the following biblical text, established that Judaism recognized universal criteria of truth:

Observe them faithfully, for that will be proof of your wisdom and discernment to other peoples, who on hearing all these laws will say, "Surely, that is a great nation of wise and discerning people" (Deut. 4:6).

On closer examination, one discovers that this text deals primarily with the laws of Judaism. Thus, if one were to accept Maimonides' understanding of the text, he would expect that not only Jewish cognitive claims but also the *mitzvot* should be understood and appreciated by all men:[15] the Torah way of life must be intelligible within universal categories of evaluation.

By refusing to allow for the possibility that the tradition would make claims which contradict reason's understanding of nature, Maimonides was negating an approach which understood revelation as revealing a new order of truth. If this latter view of revelation were accepted, it would suggest, that outside of the historical revelation of

God to the community, there is no independent reality which is revelatory of God. The consequence of negating this point of view is that man's approach to religious bodies of knowledge need not be one of unconditional allegiance to authority. Although one might accept this approach regarding questions of truth, one might switch to the posture of unconditional obedience in the observance of the commandments. If we accept Maimonides' proof-text, we should oppose any split between the way of cognition and the way of action in terms of the role given to critical reason.

The anthropology which emerges within a system which values independent reflection differs from that cultivated by a system which exclusively emphasizes obedience to the legal authority of God. The previous chapter showed how the anthropology cultivated by reason was supported by the existence, within Halakhah, of a method for developing law based on specific rules of legal inference. The ability to discriminate between laws grounded on authority and laws evolved by human reasoning prevented the halakhic Jew from adopting obedience to authority as his sole posture toward the legal tradition. Yet, aside from the issue of legal authority and methods for developing law, there still remains the question of the content of laws. Maimonides believed that reason was capable of developing norms of action based on a conception of human nature.[16] If reason is to be a factor in the Jew's mode of action, the content of Jewish laws must conform to reason's understanding of the nature of man.

In chapter six of his *Eight Chapters*, Maimonides discusses this problem:

Philosophers maintain that though the man of self-restraint performs moral and praiseworthy deeds, yet he does them desiring and craving all the while for immoral deeds, but, subduing his passions and actively fighting against a longing to do those things to which his faculties, his desires, and his psychic disposition excite him, succeeds, though with constant vexation and irritation, in acting morally. The saintly man, however, is guided in his actions by that to which his inclination and disposition prompt him, in consequence of which he acts morally from innate longing and desire. Philosophers unanimously agree that the latter is superior to, and more perfect than, the one who has to curb his passions, although they add that it is possible for such a one to equal the saintly man in many regards. In general, however, he must necessarily be ranked lower in the scale of virtue, because there lurks within him the desire to do evil, and, though he does not do it, yet because his inclinations are all in that direction, it denotes the presence of an immoral psychic disposition. . . . When, however, we consult the Rabbis on this subject, it would seem that they consider him who desires iniquity, and craves for it [but does not do it], more praiseworthy and perfect than the one who feels no torment at refraining from evil; and they even go so far as to maintain that the more praiseworthy and perfect a man is, the greater is his desire to commit an iniquity, and the more irritation does he feel at having to desist from it.[17]

The rabbis' insistence on the necessity to subdue one's natural impulses in obeying Halakhah suggests that the laws of Torah are not in harmony with the nature of man. If this is so, then the anthropology which Maimonides developed regarding cognitive aspects of the tradition would be subverted by the legal norms of Judaism by which submission to authority would exclusively characterize halakhic behavior.[18]

Maimonides counters this potential conflict by restricting the scope of commandments which must be obeyed through willful self-repression.

At first blush, by a superficial comparison of the sayings of the philosophers and the Rabbis, one might be inclined to say that they contradict one another. Such, however, is not the case. Both are correct and, moreover, are not in disagreement in the least, as the evils which the philosophers term such—and of which they say that he who has no longing for them is more to be praised than he who desires them but conquers his passion—are things which all people commonly agree are evils, such as the shedding of blood, theft, robbery, fraud, injury to one who has done no harm, ingratitude, contempt for parents, and the like. The prescriptions against these are called "commandments" *[mitzvot]*, about which the Rabbis said, "If they had not already been written in the Law, it would be proper to add them." Some of our later Sages, who were infected with the unsound principles of the Mutakallimun, called these "rational laws." There is no doubt that a soul which has the desire for, and lusts after, the above-mentioned misdeeds, is imperfect, that a noble soul has absolutely no desire for any such crimes and experiences no struggle in refraining from them. When, however, the Rabbis maintain that he who overcomes his desire has more merit and a greater reward [than he who has no temptation], they say so only in reference to laws that are ceremonial prohibitions. This is quite true, since, were it not for the Law, they would not at all be considered transgressions.[19]

Although there remains a realm of halakhic observance, *ḥukkim*, which has no connection with the nature of man and thus requires a highly developed sense of obedience to authority, one must recognize that many laws of the Torah (*mitzvot*—termed *mishpatim* elsewhere) reflect and express the nature of man. Maimonides' analysis of Jewish laws in his *Eight Chapters*, in terms of *ḥukkim* and *mishpatim*, indicates his need to counter the religious orientation which focuses exclusively on the nonintelligibility of norms and the consequent individual who solely values obedience to tradition.

Mishpatim express Jewish particularity as it embodies universal understanding of the nature of man. *Ḥukkim* reflect Jewish particularity in isolation from reason. There is an interesting parallelism between this approach to law and Judaism's understanding of nature. To Maimonides, Judaism accepts *mishpatim* and those laws of nature which reason discovers. In both these areas, Judaism par-

ticipates in a common universe of discourse with all rational men. Yet there still remains the belief in the independent will of God which is not identical with the horizontal
structure of being. Miracles reflect the autonomous will of
God which cannot be understood or predicted by human
reason.[20] To the believing Jew, miracles can symbolize
God's singling out of the Jewish community and therefore
can reflect its unique relationship to God. The community's unique status in history is confirmed, as well, by
a way of life which includes *hukkim*, i.e., norms which are
binding exclusively on the recipients of divine revelation.

Maimonides' legal works give expression to a conception of Jewish spirituality which contains a balanced attitude to universality and particularity. The religious sensibility that Maimonides was attempting to heal is the one
that focuses primarily on the miraculous events in nature
and the laws of Torah which suggest Israel's particular
relationship to God.[21] This type of sensibility experiences
the immediacy of God in those events and laws in which
only Israel participates.

In his *Treatise on Resurrection*, Maimonides writes of
many committed Jews whose most beloved activity is to
bifurcate Torah and reason by emphasizing miraculous
features of Torah which openly contradict the order of
nature.[22] As opposed to this group, Maimonides states that
his efforts were directed at making Torah compatible with
the order of nature. Only when such an approach would
do violence to the explicit sense of certain biblical statements does Maimonides feel compelled to admit the occurrence of a miracle.[23] Maimonides did not believe that
horizontal explanations, i.e., explanations which conform
to criteria of objectivity as understood by all rational men,
would weaken the personal immediacy of the relationship
with God. Wherever possible, he tried to understand de-

scriptions of God's relationship to Israel within a context of universal intelligibility.

Regarding the talmudic statement in Sotah, "By the standard with which a man measures, with it shall he be measured," which suggests that God intervenes in history by rewarding or punishing men in accordance with the nature of their deeds, Maimonides writes:

This is a matter that is apparent to the inner eye in every time, in every period, and in every place—that everyone who will do evil and devise forms of wrongdoing and vices, he himself will be injured by those evil deeds themselves which he devised, for he taught the art which will do harm to him and to someone else. Thus, whoever teaches virtue which brings into being any manner of good act, he will attain the benefit of that act, for he taught the matter which will do good to him and to someone else. The words of Scripture pertaining to this are excellent, he said, "The work of a man will He requite unto him (and according to the way of a man will He cause him to find)."[24]

The language of reward and punishment need not imply divine miraculous intervention. An understanding of the social consequences of human action is one way Maimonides tries to have his reader understand the language of reward and punishment.

Maimonides constantly attempts to interpret the seemingly miraculous in natural terms. Vertical actions of God are not understood in isolation from the ordinary structure of nature or human action. Biblical descriptions of divine actions in history, which appear to suggest that divine working is independent of human action, are understood by Maimonides in a manner making God similar to a perceptive prognosticator of human events:

But is it not written in the Torah, "And they shall be enslaved and oppressed" (Gen. 15:13)? Did not then the Almighty decree that the Egyptians should do evil? It is also written, "This people

will thereupon go astray after the alien gods in their midst (Deut.
31:16). Did He not decree that Israel should worship idols? Why
then did He punish them? [The answer is] that He did not decree
concerning any particular individual that that individual should
be the one to go astray. Any one of those who went astray and
worshiped idols, had he not desired to commit idolatry, need not
have done so. The Creator only instructed Moses as to what the
future course of history would be, as one might say, "This people
will have among them righteous and wicked persons." A wicked
man has no right, on that account, to say that it had been decreed
that he should be wicked, because the Almighty had informed
Moses that among Israel there would be wicked men, just as the
text, "For there will never cease to be needy ones in your land"
(Deut. 15:11) does not imply that any particular individual is
destined to be poor.[25]

Man in history is not a lifeless tool in the hands of an
omnipotent will. The biblical description of God harden-
ing Pharaoh's heart suggests that God removed freedom
from man and thus allows for a conception of history
wherein men are lacking in will and are God's puppets.
Maimonides, however, interprets these verses in a way
which protects human freedom from the nonrational intrusion of the vertical will of God:

To sum up, God did not decree that Pharaoh should ill-treat
Israel, or Sihon sin in his land, or that the Canaanites should
commit abominations, or that Israel should worship idols. All of
them sinned by their own volition; and all accordingly incurred
the penalty that repentance should be withheld from them.[26]

Maimonides writes of prayers for grace:

What is meant by David's utterance, "Good and upright is the
Lord; therefore does He instruct sinners in the way. He guides
the humble in justice; and He teaches the humble His way"
(Ps. 25:8, 9)? It refers to the fact that God sent them Prophets to
teach them the ways of the Lord and bring them back in repentance; furthermore, that He endowed them with the capacity of
learning and understanding. For it is characteristic of every hu-

man being that, when his interest is engaged in the ways of wisdom and righteousness, he longs for these ways and is eager to follow them. Thus the Sages say, "Whoever comes to purify himself receives aid"; that is, he will find himself helped in his endeavor.[27]

Petitional prayers for divine guidance can be understood within the horizontal structure of reality.[28] One can understand God's response to man's petitional prayers for divine guidance by understanding how human reason is a manifestation of divine governance.[29] This nonmiraculous understanding of divine grace finds similar expression in Maimonides' approach to historical redemption. Redemption in history is not initiated by the autonomous will and power of God, but by human repentance (*teshuvah*):

All the Prophets charged the people concerning repentance. Only through repentance will Israel be redeemed, and the Torah already offered the assurance that Israel will, in the closing period of his exile, finally repent, and thereupon be immediately redeemed.[30]

The biblical promise of redemption does not refer to God's miraculous intervention in history, but is based upon the conviction that a change in man's moral life will ultimately affect a change in man's political conditions. Just as God answers man's prayer for guidance by providing him with an intellect, so too does He answer man's longing for redemption by giving the community a Torah which implants in the believing Jew the conviction that his historical condition is affected by his moral actions. Both intellect and Torah can be perceived by religious man as immediate divine response to his longing for divine guidance. Torah and creation can be perceived by the religious Jew as continuous manifestations of divine activity and love. The "promise" in the Torah that Israel will ultimately

repent is based upon the fact that Torah creates the impetus for a permanent need for *teshuvah*:

In the same way the commandment given to us to call upon Him,
may He be exalted, in every calamity—I mean its dictum, "You
shall sound short blasts on the trumpets"—likewise belongs to
this class. For it is an action through which the correct opinion
is firmly established that He, may He be exalted, apprehends our
situations and that it depends upon Him to improve them, if we
obey, and to make them ruinous, if we disobey; we should not
believe that such things are fortuitous and happen by chance.
This is the meaning of its dictum, "But if, despite this, you disobey Me and remain hostile to Me," by which it means: If you
consider that the calamities with which I cause you to be stricken
are to be borne as a mere chance, I shall add for you unto this
supposed chance its most grievous and cruel portion. This is the
meaning of its dictum: "[But if, despite this,] you disobey Me and
remain hostile to Me, I will act against you in wrathful hostility
. . ." For their belief that this is chance contributes to necessitat-
ing their persistence in their corrupt opinions and unrighteous
actions, so that they do not turn away from them; thus it says:
"You have stricken them, but they were not affected." For this
reason we have been commanded to invoke Him, may He be
exalted, and to turn rapidly toward Him, and call out to Him in
every misfortune.[31]

Torah trains the believing Jew to recognize the power of
teshuvah to alter his political and economic condition by
constantly reminding him that his political and material
life is determined by his relationship to God. It is this
training which can explain the prophet's certainty that
Israel will repent.

Maimonides knew of those who maintained that grace
and redemption imply acts of God which are independent
of human action.[32] His rejection of the preoccupation with
miracles expresses itself in his making knowledge of God
a necessary—and perhaps sufficient—condition for historical redemption:[33]

These great evils that come about between the human individuals who inflict them upon one another because of purposes, desires, opinions, and beliefs, are all of them likewise consequent upon privation. For all of them derive from ignorance, I mean from a privation of knowledge. Just as a blind man, because of absence of sight, does not cease stumbling, being wounded, and also wounding others, because he has nobody to guide him on his way, the various sects of men—every individual according to the extent of his ignorance—does to himself and to others great evils from which individuals of the species suffer. If there were knowledge, whose relation to the human form is like that of the faculty of sight to the eye, they would refrain from doing any harm to themselves and to others. For through cognition of the truth, enmity and hatred are removed and the inflicting of harm by people on one another is abolished. It holds out this promise, saying: "And the wolf shall dwell with the lamb, and the leopard shall lie down with the kid, and so on. And the cow and the bear shall feed, and so on. And the sucking child shall play, and so on." Then it gives the reason for this, saying that the cause of the abolition of these enmities, these discords and these tyrannies, will be the knowledge that men will then have concerning the true reality of the Deity. For it says: "They shall not hurt nor destroy in all My holy mountain; for the earth shall be full of the knowledge of the Lord, as the waters cover the sea." Know this.[34]

In Maimonides' description of the actions of the Messiah, it is a slow process of education—and not miracles—which brings about a redeemed world:[35]

For in those days, knowledge, wisdom, and truth will increase, as it is said "For the earth shall be full of the knowledge of the Lord" (Is. 11:9), and it is said, "They shall teach no more every man his neighbor, and every man his brother (Jer. 31:34), and further, "I will remove the heart of stone from your flesh" (Ezek. 36:26). Because the king who will arise from the seed of David will possess more wisdom than Solomon and will be a great Prophet, approaching Moses, our Teacher, he will teach the whole of the Jewish people and instruct them in the way of God; and all nations will come to hear him, as it is said, "And in the end of days it shall come to pass that the mountain of the Lord's house shall be established as the top of the mountains" (Mic. 4:1; Is. 2:2).[36]

Messianism does not bring about a qualitative change in history or nature.[37] Man's nature is not transformed in the messianic age; Torah which guides and educates man, will be as necessary then as it is now.[38]

Even the universal acceptance of Judaism by the nations of the world is not described by Maimonides as being the result of a miraculous act of God.[39] From the perspective of the medieval world, the universal triumph of Judaism was not so inconceivable an occurrence as it would be today. Christianity and Islam had spread the teachings of the Bible, so that all that was necessary was the correction of the false claim that Judaism had been superseded by the Christian and Islamic revelations. For a thinker, living in a political reality permeated by biblical categories, it was not inconceivable to expect an ideological change among all believers. Once they witnessed the national rebirth of Israel, the claim that Israel was the rejected people of God would be proven false.[40]

The foregoing examples from the *Mishneh Torah* illustrate Maimonides' attempt to provide a method of translating the religious passion of immediacy (which is nurtured by belief in the power of the divine will to affect history), in a way which could be understood within the horizontal framework of being. Prophetic descriptions of God's direct relationship with history can be understood, according to Maimonides, within the context of causality:

It is very clear that everything that is produced in time must necessarily have a proximate cause which has produced it. In its turn, that cause has a cause and so forth till finally one comes to the First Cause of all things, I mean God's will and free choice. For this reason all those intermediate causes are sometimes omitted in the dicta of the Prophets, and an individual act produced in time is ascribed to God, it being said that He, may He be exalted, has done it. All this is known. We and other men from among those who study true reality have spoken about it, and this is the opinion of all the people adhering to our Law.[41]

Maimonides' understanding of divine action presupposes one's ability to recognize how the horizontal world of cause and effect, within the structure of both human and natural history, points ultimately to God. To retain religious immediacy from the perspective of philosophy, one must go beyond proximate causal explanations of phenomena to discover the ultimate causal source in God.[42]

If human behavior is explained in terms of human reason, and we ignore the fact that the human intellect has its source in the active intellect which, in turn, has its ultimate source in God, then God is not recognized as the guide when man reflects:

In the same way the remaining portion of this verse, "In Your light do we see light," has the selfsame meaning—namely, that through the overflow of the intellect that has overflowed from You, we intellectually cognize, and consequently we receive correct guidance, we draw inferences, and we apprehend the intellect. Understand this.[43]

Only by grasping the whole chain of causality can one recognize the divine presence in the immediately given. For those who lack this understanding of the extended chain of causality, God's immediacy can only be understood by the notion of an all-powerful will which performs miracles.[44] The religious man in quest of a direct relationship with God would react to Maimonides' natural explanations of phenomena as robbing him of the intimacy with God for which he longs.

While recognizing that not all would be prepared to accept his approach, Maimonides attempts to provide his readers with an understanding of the intimacy and immediacy with God within causal explanations of phenomena. Both in his legal and philosophic writings, Maimonides maintains that the halakhic way to God need not negate the concept of nature.[45] The fact that Jews accept creation, and philosophers generally accept eternity, need not imply that the Jew's sense of religious immediacy must be based on miracles. In opposing those who explain nature only in terms of the will of God, Maimonides writes:

For there is no incongruity in our saying that the existence and nonexistence of all these acts are consequent upon His wisdom, may He be exalted; we, however, are ignorant of many of the ways in which wisdom is found in His works. It is upon this opinion that the whole of "the Torah of Moses, our Master" is founded; it opens with it: "And God saw all that He had made, and found it very good." And it concludes with it: "The Rock!— His deeds are perfect, and so on." Know this. If you consider this opinion and the philosophic opinion, reflecting upon all the preceeding chapters in this treatise that are connected with this notion, you will not find any difference between them regarding any of the particulars of everything that exists. You will find no difference other than that which we have explained: namely, that they regard the world as eternal and we regard it as produced in time. Understand this.[46]

Maimonides' fundamental argument with the Mutakallimun (see chapter three) is based on his rejection of their understanding of the relationship of nature to God. In his first legal work, Maimonides writes:

As regards the theory generally accepted by people, and likewise found in rabbinic and prophetic writings, that man's sitting and rising, and in fact all of his movements, are governed by the will and desire of God, it may be said that this is true only in one respect. Thus, for instance, when a stone is thrown into the air and falls to the ground, it is correct to say that the stone fell in accordance with the will of God, for it is true that God decreed that the earth and all that goes to make it up should be the center of attraction, so that when any part of it is thrown into the air, it is attracted back to the center. Similarly, all the particles of fire ascend according to God's will which preordained that fire should go upward. But it is wrong to suppose that when a certain part of the earth is thrown upward, God wills at that very moment that it should fall. The Mutakallimun are, however, of a different opinion in this regard for I have heard them say that the Divine Will is constantly at work, decreeing everything from time to time. We do not agree with them, but believe that the Divine Will ordained everything at Creation, and that all things, at all times, are regulated by the laws of nature, and run their natural course, in accordance with what Solomon said, "As it was, so it will ever be, as it was made so it continues, and there is nothing new under the sun."[47]

In the *Guide*, Maimonides argues that the proofs offered by the Mutakallimun for God's existence involve premises which run counter to the established nature of existence and rely on the presupposition that nothing has an established nature:

The proofs of the Mutakallimun, on the other hand, are derived from premises that run counter to the nature of existence that is perceived so that they resort to the affirmation that nothing has a nature in any respect. In this treatise, when speaking of the creation of the world in time, I shall devote for your benefit a chapter explaining to you some proof for the creation of the world in time. For I reach the goal that every Mutakallim desires, without abolishing the nature of existence and without disagreeing with Aristotle with regard to any point he has demonstrated. For whereas the proof, with the aid of which some Mutakallimun proved by inference the creation of the world in time and which is their most powerful proof, is not consolidated for them until they abolish the nature of all existence and disagree with everything that the philosophers have made clear, I reach a similar proof without running counter to the nature of existence and without having recourse to violating that which is perceived by the senses.[48]

What Maimonides meant when he said that he reached the same goal as the Mutakallimun without abolishing the nature of existence is not simply that he had established a proof for the existence of God without negating Aristotelian physics. What is involved is his having secured a religious world view which does not negate the concept of nature in order to establish immediacy with God.[49]

The crucial difference between Maimonidean man who seeks God in nature and one who requires miracles to confirm religious immediacy, above all, is a difference of religious sensibilities.[50] Once an individual admits that miracles are possible, as Maimonides does by accepting the doctrine of creation, then, from a strictly logical perspective, it makes no difference whether he admits one or one thousand miracles.[51] Once eternal necessity is rejected, the approach to miracles will be determined by what is considered the most significant way of understanding God's relationship to man.[52]

The difference between religious sensibilities is discussed by Maimonides with reference to various descriptions of the development of the human fetus:

How great is the blindness of ignorance and how harmful! If you told a man who is one of those who deemed themselves "the Sages of Israel" that the Deity sends an angel, who enters the womb of a woman and forms the fetus there, he would be pleased with this assertion and would accept it and would regard it as a manifestation of greatness and power on the part of the Deity, and also of His wisdom, may He be exalted. Nevertheless he would also believe at the same time that the "angel" is a body formed of burning fire and that his size is equal to that of a third part of the whole world. He would regard all this as possible with respect to God. But if you tell him that God has placed in the sperm a formative force shaping the limbs and giving them their configuration and that this force is the "angel," or that all the forms derive from the act of the Active Intellect and that the latter is the "angel" and the "prince of the world" constantly mentioned by the "Sages," the man would shrink from this opinion. For he does not understand the notion of the true greatness and power that consists in the bringing into existence of forces active in a thing, forces that cannot be apprehended by any sense.[53]

This description presents us with the two opposing spiritual sensibilities which Maimonides discussed in his *Treatise on Resurrection.*[54] It is not only the unlearned masses who adopt this approach; it is also the supposed sages of Israel, the talmudists of the *Treatise on Resurrection,* who separate the revelation of Torah from the world of reason. Their only way of relating to God is by submitting to His will. They understand Aggadah literally, they are exclusively involved with details of law, and they thrive on miracles and unintelligible norms as a confirmation of God's unique relationship with Israel. This orientation reflects the absence of the concept of independent reason and nature within one's spiritual life.

Maimonides' *Guide* was addressed to those who could not sever their understanding of nature from their relationship to God.[55] Their religious sensibilities were nurtured by intelligibility and the capacity to understand Judaism through universal criteria of truth. To accept the claim that Jewish spirituality does not isolate them from the universal community of rational men, such individuals must be shown that nothing in Judaism violates that religious sensibility they acquired from Maimonides' insistence that physics and metaphysics are part of Talmud. They cannot be satisfied with Maimonides' explanation of *ḥukkim* in the *Eight Chapters.* As readers of the *Guide,* they know that as long as *ḥukkim* convey the same form of immediacy as miracles, they are blocked from approaching Torah through reason. They cannot locate the God of being within Torah as long as they confront norms which appear to suggest that God desires unconditional obedience rather than understanding. These students may not be repelled logically by appeals to the will of God to explain commandments since creation allows for the possibility of the unintelligible. However, their religious sensibilities would force them to look elsewhere for guidance in their spiritual lives.

Maimonides cannot separate the world of Halakhah from its relationship to God. In order, therefore, for one to relate to the Halakhah, he must first be drawn to the God of Halakhah. One who has been nurtured by the spiritual way of reason will find his individual way within the system of Torah law only if the God who is the ground of Halakhah draws men on the basis of reason. It is to this person that Maimonides addresses his chapters on the commandments in *The Guide of the Perplexed.* The central thrust of the Maimonidean theory of commandments is to show how the laws of the Torah reflect a rational lawgiver and not simply the will of a God who is primarily interested in submission and obedience. Maimonides' method of revealing the wisdom of the lawgiver of the Torah, in part, is to explain the historical conditions at the time of the giving of Torah. Maimonides is not simply engaged in historically oriented biblical scholarship; many aspects of Torah law become intelligible in light of those conditions.

In chapter two, it was shown that a key feature of Maimonides' understanding of Halakhah revolves around his approach to levels of worship. The talmudic teachers and the divine lawgiver were cognizant of the various spiritual capacities which were prevalent in the community. This awareness enabled them to issue norms and statements which led from a lower to a higher level of worship. Maimonides applies the same orientation which he discovered in the Talmud's approach to levels of worship to his understanding of biblical law. He begins the chapter in the *Guide* which attempts to show the relationship between history and revelation with a description of teleological patterns in nature:

If you consider the Divine actions—I mean to say the natural actions—the Deity's wily graciousness and wisdom, as shown in the creation of living beings, in the gradation of the motions of the limbs, and the proximity of some of the latter to others, will through them become clear to you. . . . Similarly the Deity made a wily and gracious arrangement with regard to all the individuals of the living beings that suck. For when born, such individuals are extremely soft and cannot feed on dry food. Accordingly breasts were prepared for them so that they should produce milk with a view to their receiving humid food, which is similar to the composition of their bodies, until their limbs gradually and little by little become dry and solid. Many things in our Law are due to something similar to this very governance on the part of Him who governs, may He be glorified and exalted. For a sudden transition from one opposite to another is impossible. And therefore man, according to his nature, is not capable of abandoning suddenly all to which he was accustomed. . . . and as at that time the way of life generally accepted and customary in the whole world and the universal service upon which we were brought up consisted in offering various species of living beings in the temples in which images were set up, in worshiping the latter, and in burning incense before them—the pious ones and the ascetics being at that time, as we have explained, the people who were devoted to the service of the temples consecrated to the stars— His wisdom, may He be exalted, and His gracious ruse, which is manifest in regard to all His creatures, did not require that He give us a Law prescribing the rejection, abandonment, and abolition of all these kinds of worship. For one could not then conceive the acceptance of [such a Law], considering the nature of man, which always likes that to which it is accustomed. At that time this would have been similar to the appearance of a Prophet in these times who, calling upon the people to worship God, would say: "God has given you a Law forbidding you to pray to Him, to fast, to call upon Him for help in misfortune. Your worship should consist solely in meditation without any works at all."[56]

This statement reveals Maimonides' attempt to indicate parallel structures within Torah and nature. The teleological patterns of nature are never far from the mind of the philosophic Jew who is seeking to understand the God of the Law. Just as the God of nature provides a nursing breast for the newborn child until it is able to digest heavier forms of food, so too does God in the Torah wean man from idolatry by allowing him to partake of those forms of worship (digestable food) which he could assimilate at his early stage of development.[57]

Maimonides supports his understanding of sacrifices by showing how the Bible gave expression to different levels of religious worship:

I return to my subject and say that, as this kind of worship—I mean the "sacrifices"—pertain to a second intention, whereas invocation, prayer, and similar practices and modes of worship come closer to the first intention and are necessary for its achievement, a great difference has been made between the two kinds. For one kind of worship—I mean the offering of sacrifices—even though it was done in His name, may He be exalted, was not prescribed to us in the way it existed at first; I mean to say in such a way that sacrifices could be offered in every place and at every time. Nor could a temple be set up in any fortuitous place, nor could any fortuitous man offer the sacrifice: "Whosoever would, he consecrated him." On the contrary, He forbade all this and established one single house [as the temple], "to the site that the Lord will choose," so that sacrifices should not be offered elsewhere: "Take care not to sacrifice your burnt offerings in any place you like." Also only the offspring of one particular family can be "priests." All this was intended to restrict this kind of worship, so that only the portion of it should subsist whose abolition is not required by His Wisdom. On the other hand, invocation and prayers are made in every place and by anyone whoever he may be.[58]

The Bible weaned man from his attachment to idolatry by restricting the first form of worship—sacrifices—to the specific location of the temple and to specific persons—the priests. Along with communal worship by animal sacrifices there also existed verbal prayer practiced by individuals able to transcend pagan forms of worship. Since the restrictions of place and persons only applied to sacrifices and not to verbal prayer, Maimonides inferred that at the time of the Bible verbal prayer represented a higher form of worship.

Maimonides states in the *Mishneh Torah* that verbal prayer was individualistic and spontaneous during the biblical period. It lacked the formal structure of fixed times and texts which would have enabled verbal prayer to become a communal form of worship.[59] After the exile of the community from its land, verbal prayer became formalized and emerged as the system of worship for community. The same relationship between communal and individual forms of worship which was present in the biblical period is present also when verbal prayer becomes the dominant mode of communal worship. In the *Guide*, Maimonides only claims that it would be as difficult for the prophet, in his time, to demand of the members of community that they serve God in contemplative prayer as it would have been for the prophet, during the biblical period, to insist on verbal prayer. At this stage in history, Maimonides suggests, the individual who can transcend the communal form of worship gives expression to his spiritual capacities through silent, contemplative prayer. Such silent, contemplative prayer at the time of exile reflects the same capacity of unique individuals to transcend the influence of their social environment as did verbal prayer at a time when the community was habituated to offer sacrifices.

Maimonides' description of communal prayer in the *Mishneh Torah* suggests that the core element of verbal prayer is petitional:

The first three blessings consist of praises of God, the last three of thanksgiving to Him. The intermediate benedictions are petitions for the things which may stand as categories of all the desires of the individual and the needs of the community.[60]

The thirteen petitional blessings reflect the needs of community and the outpourings of the Jew who turns to God out of crises. The important concern of the rabbinic period was to sustain the community's relationship to God in spite of political exile and suffering; petitional prayer reinforces rabbinic refusal to interpret Jewish history from the secular perspective of brute power. *Teshuvah* and petitional prayer give expression to the belief that God has not abandoned Israel and that He is responsive to its suffering.

During the rabbinic period, silent prayer expresses the level of those individuals who need not turn to God exclusively because of crises but can worship God for His own sake. Silent prayer is a form of worship for one who, even under conditions of exile, can appreciate the joy of contemplating God's perfection.[61] The form of worship for the majority of the community who cannot transcend the historical conditions of exile is petitional prayer. In chapter thirty-one of the *Guide,* Maimonides attempts to show how historical conditions influence the community's understanding of religious worship. Once the community would be liberated from its condition of suffering and abuse, it too would be capable of aspiring toward disinterested forms of worship. Under conditions of messianism, contemplative prayer would not be rejected as absurd by members of the community.

Maimonides' analysis of the three forms of worship reflects his understanding of the relationship between the individual and the community within Jewish spirituality. The three forms of worship—sacrifices, verbal petitional prayer, and silent contemplative prayer—symbolize three stages of Jewish history, i.e., the biblical, rabbinic, and messianic. Whereas the prime concern of the biblical period was to uproot idolatry, the rabbinic period focused on strengthening the community's ability to withstand the cynicism which the sufferings of exile could bring about.[62] Messianic prayer (contemplative prayer), reflects the worship of a community not burdened by the political conditions of oppression.

Maimonides' distinction in the *Guide* between petitional and contemplative prayer does not indicate, that as a philosopher, he had negated the halakhic modes of worship of his tradition. The Halakhah, according to Maimonides, defines prayer as *avodah shebelev*, worship of the heart. The form taken by this worship of the heart depends upon the religious understanding and spiritual capacities of the individual.[63] One need not necessarily look to Avicenna to account for Maimonides' approach to contemplative prayer, for it reflects his deeply Jewish attitude to the meaning of disinterested love of God.[64] Just as he distinguished between *olam ha-ba* and messianism, so too does Maimonides distinguish between contemplative and petitional prayer.

The different regulations which apply to verbal prayer and to sacrifices in the Bible reflect the wisdom of the divine lawgiver in His attempt to lead the community from a lower level of spirituality to the highest level of human development, the love of God. The Torah provides a way in which both the community and its singular individuals can find expression for their spiritual capacities. Just as God, in the Bible, complements sacrifices with verbal prayer, so too does Maimonides, in the *Guide*, complement petitional prayer with silent, contemplative prayer.

As a religious thinker, Maimonides understood different historical periods from the perspective of stages in man's worship of God. Maimonides was not simply a cultural anthropologist or a sociologist doing work in comparative religion. That his work is of interest to later studies in comparative religion should not confuse us into thinking that this was his intention.[65] The impetus to look at the Bible from a historical perspective has its source in the tradition's developmental approach to worship. Just as the rabbis proclaimed that in the rabbinic period the community had overcome the biblical Jews' passion for idolatry, so too did Maimonides claim that messianism would enable the community to aspire toward higher forms of worship.[66] The tradition, as understood by Maimonides, was cognizant of a development in worship from the biblical to the rabbinic and, ultimately, to the messianic period of history. To view the Bible, therefore, as representing the first stage of worship is within the tradition's concept of religious history.[67] Maimonides' understanding of biblical history is derived from his study of Sabeanism; his historical approach to the Bible is rooted in his understanding of talmudic Judaism.

Thus far it has been shown that Maimonides' description of the relationship of petitional to contemplative prayer, and his explanation of sacrifices in terms of the biblical struggle against idolatry, reflect the consistent approach in his legal works regarding the relationship between the individual and community within Halakhah. Let us continue the analysis of how Maimonides led the philosophic Jew to understand how Torah and nature reflect the same God. The chapters in the *Guide* which deal with Maimonides' historical approach to commandments are preceded by a number of chapters which indicate that Maimonides' theory of commandments must be understood together with the broader religious concerns which we have discussed until now.

Chapters twenty-five and twenty-six of the *Guide* argue that there is a common approach which many people adopt in their understanding of both nature and the law.

Those who refuse to recognize causality in nature approach the law as solely embodying the will of God:

> Just as there is disagreement among the men of speculation among the adherents of Law whether His works, may He be exalted, are consequent upon wisdom or upon the will alone without being intended toward any end at all, there is also the same disagreement among them regarding our Laws, which He has given to us. Thus there are people who do not seek for them any cause at all, saying that all Laws are consequent upon the will alone. There are also people who say that every commandment and prohibition in these Laws is consequent upon wisdom and aims at some end and that all Laws have causes and were given in view of some utility.[68]

Maimonides accepted the view which sought to discover wisdom in the commandments. The qualitative difference between *mishpatim* and *ḥukkim* which Maimonides set down in his *Eight Chapters* is now presented as a difference between laws which are manifestly useful and laws whose usefulness can be discovered only after greater analysis and study:

> In the case of some of them, it is clear to us in what way they are useful—as in the case of the prohibition of killing and stealing. In the case of others, their utility is not clear—as in the case of the interdiction of the "first products" [of trees] and of [sowing] "the vineyard with diverse seeds." Those commandments whose utility is clear to the multitude are called *mishpatim* [judgments], and those whose utility is not clear to the multitude are called *ḥukkim* [statutes].[69]

Before Maimonides explains how *ḥukkim* can be viewed as being useful, he suggests that further knowledge is necessary if the reader is to understand his explanations.

In chapter twenty-seven of the *Guide* Maimonides reiterates a theme that appears throughout his legal works, i.e., the two perfections of man: that of the soul and that of the body. The perfection of the soul is made possible by knowledge; the perfection of the body by the abolition of wrongdoing and the acquisition of moral qualities:

> Know that as between these two aims, one is indubitably greater in nobility, namely, the welfare of the soul—I mean the procuring of correct opinions—while the second aim—I mean the welfare of the body—is prior in nature and time. The latter aim consists in the governance of the city and the well-being of the states of all its people according to their capacity. This second aim is the more certain one, and it is the one regarding which every effort has been made precisely to expound it and all its particulars. For the first aim can only be achieved after achieving this second one.[70]

There is an interesting similarity between the above statement and the end of the fourth chapter of *Hilkhot Yesodei ha-Torah* in the *Mishneh Torah*. The law was precise and detailed not because Judaism was solely concerned with the historical well-being of community but, rather, because it realized that a healthy body politic is necessary for the unfolding of higher human capacities. In other words, messianism is a condition for *olam ha-ba*:

> The true Law then, which as we have already made clear, is unique—namely, the Law of "Moses, our Master"—has come to bring us both perfections. I mean the welfare of the states of people in their relations with one another through the abolition of reciprocal wrongdoing and through the acquisition of a noble and excellent character. In this way the preservation of the population of the country and their permanent existence in the same order become possible, so that every one of them achieves his first perfection; I mean also the soundness of the beliefs and the giving of correct opinions through which ultimate perfection is achieved.[71]

The two perfections of man find expression in the different theological beliefs of the Torah. In chapter twenty-eight, Maimonides distinguishes between those theological concepts which have a direct bearing upon the political and economic needs of man, and those which reflect man's disinterested love of God:

In some cases a "commandment" communicates a correct belief, which is the one and only thing aimed at—as, for instance, the belief in the unity and eternity of the Deity and in His not being a body. In other cases the belief is necessary for the abolition of reciprocal wrongdoing or for the acquisition of a noble moral quality—as, for instance, the belief that He, may He be exalted, has a violent anger against those who do injustice, according to what is said: "And My anger shall blaze forth and I will put you to the sword, and so on," and as the belief that He, may He be exalted, responds instantaneously to the prayer of someone wronged or deceived: "Therefore, if he cries out to Me, I will pay heed, for I am compassionate.⁷²

Those beliefs which are central to man's disinterested love of God do not touch upon the idea of God's responsiveness to man. An individual who has transcended the problems of physical survival will primarily be interested in—and inspired by—beliefs which point to the independent reality and perfection of God. Under conditions of suffering, most men long to know that they are not alone: "Therefore, if he cries out to Me, I will pay heed, for I am compassionate." The functions of different descriptions of God can be grasped if one recognizes how they organize and guide the individual in his relationship with God. One's emphasis upon and understanding of political and philosophical beliefs will depend on one's level of worship.

The reader of the *Guide* who has followed Maimonides through his legal works perceives in the two perfections of man and in the different descriptions of God an indication of the tradition's awareness of different levels of worship. He knows that the tradition wants to raise man from an anthropocentric to a theocentric concept of religious life. Chapters twenty-seven and twenty-eight establish the logic of stages of worship within Jewish tradition. Given this perspective, the reader, in chapter twenty-nine, is shown how the Bible itself, through its struggle against idolatry, reflects this logic.

Chapter twenty-nine of the *Guide* introduces the reader to an understanding of the idolatrous beliefs which influenced Jews of the biblical period. The reader must not think that the prevalent belief in monotheism reflects what always was the case. He must not believe that idolatry disappeared because of the necessary progress, in history, from superstition to rationality. Idolatry was overcome as a result of the efforts of the two great fighters against idol worship: Abraham and Moses. Regarding Abraham's influence on history, Maimonides writes:

And in point of fact his activity has resulted, as we see today, in the consensus of the greater part of the population of the earth in glorifying him and considering themselves as blessed through his memory, so that even those who do not belong to his progeny pretend to descend from him.[73]

During the period of the Bible the struggle against idolatry was the predominant concern. Before the community could be exposed to the deeper aspirations of Judaism—love and fear of God—it was necessary to divert it from the powerful attraction of Sabean idolatry:

Consequently all the "commandments" that are concerned with the prohibition against "idolatry" and everything that is connected with it or leads toward it or may be ascribed to it, are of manifest utility, for all of them are meant to bring about the deliverance from these unhealthy opinions that turn one's attention away from all that is useful with regard to the two perfections toward the crazy notions in which our fathers and forefathers were brought up: "Your fathers dwelt of old time beyond the River, even Terah, the father of Abraham and the father of Naḥor; and they served other gods."[74]

The purpose of chapter twenty-nine is to emphasize the centrality of the struggle against idolatry and to explain that the rejection of idolatry is a cardinal principle of the tradition:

For the foundation of the whole of our Law and the pivot around which it turns, consists in the effacement of these opinions from the minds and of these monuments from existence.[75]

The rabbis of the Talmud confirm for Maimonides that the rejection of idolatry is one of the fundamentals of Judaism:

For they say: "Herefrom you may learn that every one who professes idolatry, disbelieves in the Torah in its entirety; whereas he who disbelieves in idolatry, professes the Torah in its entirety." Understand this.[76]

In stressing the importance of the struggle against idolatry, Maimonides provides his reader with an insight into many aspects of biblical law. A lack of appreciation for the attraction that idolatry held for the biblical Jew could result in the assumption that God legislated laws which have no useful human purpose. It is understandable that a community which was no longer attracted to Sabean idolatry would have great difficulty comprehending the purpose of much biblical law. Maimonides' description of Sabeanism is an attempt to recreate the forgotten historical context of biblical legislation. In the *Eight Chapters*, where the reader presumably does not yet possess this knowledge, *mishpatim* alone were seen as being connected with a concept of human nature. In the *Guide*, however, Maimonides shows how many *ḥukkim* are connected not to man's permanent character, but to one that is historically conditioned. *Mishpatim* reflect the constant in human nature; *ḥukkim* reflect it under the influence of Sabean idolatry. Nothing in biblical law necessarily reflects the non-rational intrusion of the divine will in human history.

Maimonides was aware that even though many of his readers would recognize that idolatry was a major threat to biblical Jews, they would nonetheless object to his explanations of the commandments because of their religious sensibilities. Before an explanation of the historical conditions which influenced divine legislation could be accepted, one would have to overcome the spiritual "sickness" which compels insistence on the insulation of Jewish particularity from universal intelligibility. In chapter thirty-one of the *Guide* Maimonides describes the approach to the law which, in chapter twenty-six, he rejects as a spiritual disease:

There is a group of human beings who consider it a grievous thing that causes should be given for any Law; what would please them most is that the intellect would not find a meaning for the commandments and prohibitions. What compels them to feel thus is a sickness that they find in their souls, a sickness to which they are unable to give utterance and of which they cannot furnish a satisfactory account. For they think that if those Laws were useful in this existence and had been given to us for this or that reason, it would be as if they derived from the reflection and the understanding of some intelligent being. If, however, there is a thing for which the intellect could not find any meaning at all and that does not lead to something useful, it indubitably derives from God; for the reflection of man would not lead to such a thing. It is as if, according to these people of weak intellects, man were more perfect than his Maker; for man speaks and acts in a manner that leads to some intended end, whereas a deity does not act thus, but commands us to do things that are not useful to us and forbids us to do things that are not harmful to us.[77]

These individuals do not actually consider humans more rational than God; rather, their approach is characterized by a refusal to understand God's reasons for commandments in terms of what men consider to be useful.[78] For these individuals, God must be completely other than man, both in His essence and in that which He prescribes for man to obey. God's revelation of the law must express His utter transcendence and unintelligibility. Israel's uniqueness in history is exhibited by its capacity to live by what God considers necessary, not by what man considers useful and valuable. The more remote God and the law are from human intelligibility, the more inflamed does the passion become for God. Maimonides considers this a profound sickness of the soul.

Maimonides counters this approach to God and Jewish particularity in the domain of law with the same text he uses to negate this approach to particularity in the domain of knowledge:

And it says: "Who on hearing of all these laws [*ḥukkim*] will say, Surely, that great nation is a wise and discerning people." Thus it states explicitly that even all the laws [*ḥukkim*] will show to all the nations that they have been given with "wisdom and discernment." Now if there is a thing for which no reason is known and that does not either procure something useful or ward off something harmful, why should one say of one who believes in it or practices it that he is "wise and discerning" and of great worth? And why should the religious communities think it a wonder?[79]

The biblical text (Deut. 4:6) establishes the compatibility of both the cognitive and legal claims of Judaism with universal criteria of evaluation. To Maimonides, one who understands nature from the perspective of independent reason will insist on understanding Halakhah from the same perspective. Once one believes that independent reason can provide an understanding of God, an insulated approach to Jewish spirituality can no longer be tolerated.

The theory of history, outlined in chapter thirty-two of the *Guide*, provides a model for understanding Torah and divine action in history which does not require an appeal to miracles or to non-rational laws to make sense of God's relationship to Israel:

"God did not lead them by way of the land of the Philistines, although it was nearer, and so on. But God led the people round-about, by the way of the wilderness at the Red Sea [Sea of Reeds]." Just as God perplexed them in anticipation of what their bodies were naturally incapable of bearing—turning them away from the high road toward which they had been going, toward another road so that the first intention should be achieved—so did He in anticipation of what the soul is naturally incapable of receiving, prescribe the Laws that we have mentioned so that the first intention should be achieved: namely, the apprehension of Him, may He be exalted, and the rejection of idolatry.

Just as it is not in the nature of man that, after having been brought up in slavish service occupied with clay, bricks, and similar things, he should all of a sudden wash the dirt deriving from them from his hands and proceed immediately to fight against "the children of Anak," so is it also not in his nature that, after having been brought up upon very many modes of worship and of customary practices—which the souls find so agreeable that they become as it were a primary notion—he should aban-don them all of a sudden. And just as the Deity used a gracious ruse in causing them to wander perplexedly in the desert until their souls became courageous—it being well known that life in the desert and lack of comforts for the body necessarily develop courage, whereas the opposite circumstances necessarily de-velop cowardice—and until, moreover, people were born who were not accustomed to humiliation and servitude—all this hav-ing been brought about by Moses, our Master, by means of Di-vine commandments: "On a sign from the Lord they made camp and on a sign from the Lord they broke camp; they observed the Lord's mandate at the Lord's bidding through Moses"—so did this group of Laws derive from a Divine Grace, so that they should be left with the kind of practices to which they were accustomed and so that consequently the belief, which consti-tutes the first intention, should be validated in them.[80]

Maimonides' aversion to miracles derives not only from his perception of nature, but also from his perception of Torah. The model of God which emerges from the Bible is that of an educator who acts in response to the capacities of his students. If God does not work within structures of nature, i.e., if He functions by the power of His independent will alone, why then does He not will man into perfection? The fact that God gives man a Torah which attempts to change man through a behavioral process of education is an indication that God works through—and not independently of—man. The giving of Torah and the sending of prophets would be superfluous if supernatural grace were the way God brings man to perfection:

For if it were His will that the nature of any human individual should be changed because of what He, may He be exalted, wills from that individual, sending of Prophets and all giving of a Law would have been useless.[81]

The application of the teleological principle in nature to explain Torah is not a Hellenization of Judaism but is a clear articulation of the implicit dynamic of a tradition that feels God's love for man through His giving of the law.[82] Although the event of Sinai may be classified as a miracle, the particular way of life which emerges from Sinai can only be understood if we abandon the category of miracle as the defining feature of Jewish spirituality. The ongoing process of a Torah way of life is in harmony, therefore, with reason's understanding of nature.[83]

The purpose of Maimonides' treatment of commandments in the *Guide* is to convince his reader that "Indeed, all things proceed from one Deity and one Agent and 'have been given from one Shepherd.' "[84] By establishing orderly patterns within Torah law, by showing parallel structures between Torah and nature, and by explaining the rational purpose of many *ḥukkim*, Maimonides eliminates the obstacle which prevents the philosophically trained Jew from being spiritually at home within Halakhah.[85] The awareness that the God of the Bible took into account the historical nature of this community when He issued norms and guided the community in the desert, reconfirms the philosophic Jew's love for a God who appeals to man's understanding. The philosophically trained Jew need not put on an obedience-cap when he meets the God of Israel. The God of the Halakhah, the God mediated by the community of Israel, can therefore be loved with the same passion as the God of being.

It can be argued that what has been shown about Maimonides' historical approach to commandments obscures the most important danger it creates for the halakhic Jew. Does not Maimonides destroy his own attempt to eliminate an obedience-orientation to Halakhah by explaining the reasons for many laws in terms of the attraction to idolatry which existed at a specific period in the past? Does not his codification of these laws create an obedient personality insofar as he demands that Jews live by laws that have outlived their usefulness?[86] This inconsistency can lead to the claim that Maimonides the philosopher, who understands the laws from the context of the struggle against idolatry, cannot be identified with Maimonides the judge, who codifies animal sacrifices and *ḥukkim* for Jews to obey at all times—even during the messianic era.[87] Various responses can be offered to this problem of inconsistency.

Regarding the claim that a historical interpretation of the commandments implies that these commandments ought to become void under different historical conditions, one must realize that change is a complex procedure within the context of a legal system. Maimonides believed that the legal system as a whole would be weakened if laws were to be altered every time historical conditions changed:

> In view of this consideration, it also will not be possible that the laws be dependent on changes in the circumstances of the individuals and of the times, as is the case with regard to medical treatment, which is particularized for every individual in conformity with his present temperament. On the contrary, governance of the Law ought to be absolute and universal, including everyone, even if it is suitable only for certain individuals and not suitable for others; for if it were made to fit individuals, the whole would be corrupted and "you would make out of it something that varies." For this reason, matters that are primarily intended in the Law ought not to be dependent on time or place; but the decrees ought to be absolute and universal, according to what He, may He be exalted, says "There shall be one law [*ḥukkah*] for you. . . ."[88]

The fact that sacrifices do not lose their normative quality as a result of changed social conditions can be justified by Maimonides' interest in maintaining the integrity of the Jewish legal system.[89]

Although Judaism allows for legal change and innovation, these changes must conform to a prescribed legal procedure to maintain continuity within the process of change:

> I shall say: Inasmuch as God, may He be exalted, knew that the commandments of this Law will need in every time and place— as far as some of them are concerned—to be added to or subtracted from according to the diversity of places, happenings, and conjunctures of circumstances, He forbade adding to them or subtracting from them, saying: "Neither add to it nor take away from it" for this might have led to the corruption of the rules of the Law and to the belief that the latter did not come from God.
>   Withal He permitted the men of knowledge of every period —I refer to the "Great Court of Law"—to take precautions with

a view to consolidating the ordinances of the Law by means of regulations in which they innovate with a view to repairing fissures and to perpetuate these precautionary measures according to what has been said by [the Sages]: "Build a hedge for the Torah."

Similarly they were permitted in certain circumstances, or with a view to certain events, to abolish certain actions prescribed by the Law or to permit some of the things forbidden by it; but these measures may not be perpetuated, as we have explained in the Introduction to *The Commentary on the Mishnah* in speaking of "temporary decisions." Through this kind of governance the Law remains one, and one is governed in every time and with a view to every happening in accordance with that happening. If, however, every man of knowledge had been permitted to engage in this speculation concerning particulars, the people would have perished because of the multiplicity of the differences of opinion and the subdivisions of doctrines. Consequently He, may He be exalted, has forbidden all the men of knowledge with the single exception of the "Great Court of Law" to undertake this, and has those who disagree with [this Court] killed. For if it could be opposed by everyone who engages in speculation, the intended purpose would be annulled and the usefulness of these regulations abolished.[90]

As cited in chapter three, in another context, even regarding rabbinically ordained law, Maimonides writes:

If the Supreme Court instituted a decree, enacted an ordinance, or introduced a custom, which was universally accepted in Israel, and a later Supreme Court wishes to rescind the measure, to abolish the ordinance, decree, or custom, it is not empowered to do so, unless it is superior to the former both in point of wisdom and in point of number. If it is superior in wisdom but not in number, or in number but not in wisdom, it is denied the right to abrogate the measure adopted by its predecessor, even if the reason which prompted the latter to enact the decree or ordinance has lost all force.[91]

It is evident that if lower courts cannot abrogate the enactments of higher courts, even if the original reasons for the legislation are no longer valid, laws that are attributed to the supreme authority within this system—God—can never be abrogated by any human court.

The refusal to change Torah laws, therefore, has a rational basis in terms of Maimonides' understanding of the orderly functioning of a legal system grounded in divine authority. One who adheres to laws whose reasons for enactment are no longer relevant, and who does so out of his commitment to the legal integrity of the Halakhah, does not manifest the same type of obedience as one who maintains that God issues irrational laws. Maimonides judged it important to show that the promulgation of Torah law was not based on the arbitrary will of God.

If the entire system of Jewish law would have outlived its usefulness, it would be difficult to justify commitment to Halakhah by appealing to the need for legal continuity. There were, according to Maimonides, many laws whose purpose remained relevant and significant to his contemporaries. Thus, Maimonides' efforts to maintain the integrity of the legal system, as a justification for maintaining laws related to a specific historical context, is compatible with an overall conception which emphasizes the fundamental rationality of Halakhah.

The preceding argument is based on the assumption that laws which were once intended to draw man away from idolatry but which have lost that significance should still be obeyed because there is a need for legal stability.

Up to this point, we have attempted to reconstruct the actual patterns of Maimonidean thought; we will now present our own validation for sacrifices. Although this explanation is built upon Maimonidean categories of thought, we do not intend to argue that it was actually considered by Maimonides as a reason for the continued observance of sacrifices. Yet we allow ourselves the liberty of this digression, for we believe that the profundity of a thinker can often be measured by the new insights his thought makes available. Thus, let us carefully examine the *Guide* and the *Mishneh Torah*, and see if these laws possess a permanent meaning even when the impulse to idolatry has disappeared.

Maimonides did not believe in the necessary progress of man. Although he recognized human changes within history (changes which he sketched in his characterization of the biblical, rabbinic, and messianic periods), he did not believe that such changes brought about qualitative transformations of human nature. After describing the Sabean way of life, Maimonides writes:

For these were the religious beliefs upon which they were brought up. If the belief in the existence of the Deity were not generally accepted at present to such an extent in the religious communities, our days in these times would be even darker than that epoch. However, their darkness is of different kinds.[92]

This parenthetical remark reminds the reader that man's move away from paganism does not indicate a change in human nature. For Maimonides, human nature is constant, as we see from his description of messianism. The same training and education that Torah offers to men under conditions of exile will also be necessary during the messianic period.[93] Messianism simply provides the political and economic conditions that make it possible for the members of a community to achieve intellectual understanding of Torah and of God.

Maimonides rejected any romantic conception of human history. One is never secure from human weakness simply because of the era in which he lives. Given this understanding of human nature, we should be sensitive to the importance of those rituals that allow us to appreciate and to respect our own vulnerability to corruption.[94] In his discussion of *teshuvah*, Maimonides suggests the same point regarding the individual's approach to his sinful past. One of the requirements of repentance, according to the Halakhah, is confession of sins.[95] Maimonides accepts the viewpoint of Rabbi Eliezer ben Yaacov when he codifies the following law:

Transgressions confessed on one Day of Atonement are again confessed on the next Day of Atonement, even if one has continued penitent, as it is said, "For I know my transgressions; and my sin is ever before me" (Ps. 51:5).[96]

The person who has done *teshuvah* must not live with the illusion that he has transcended the capacity to repeat his sin. By refusing to allow the individual to block past errors from his consciousness, the Halakhah prevents him from deluding himself with the belief that his human nature has changed.[97]

The same halakhic principle which maintains that an individual must reenact the confession of his past sin, even though at present he is not guilty of this act, can also be applied to the community. One who knows the inner experience of Judaism is aware of the profound importance historical memory plays in Jewish ritual: "In every generation a man is bound to regard himself as though he personally had gone forth from Egypt."[98] Through its rituals Torah inculcates a collective memory in each Jew. The Halakhah unites all generations into one organic unit; the strong identification of every generation of Jews with the founding events of Judaism characterizes many features of Halakhah. If there is a dimension of mystic union in Jewish experience it is not necessarily with God, but with the entire historical drama of the people of Israel. It is correct to say that within the life-pattern of the observant Jew past, present, and future merge into a personal drama leading from Egypt to messianism. Therefore it is understandable when Maimonides uses the same principle to explain the confessions of both individual and community.

In explaining why sin-offerings consist of he-goats *(se'irim)*, Maimonides writes:

However the Sages, may their memory be blessed, consider that the reason for which the congregation is constantly atoned for by means of *se'irim* is that the whole congregation of Israel committed their first act of disobedience with the help of a kid [*se'ir*] of goats. They refer to the sale of Joseph, the righteous, in whose story it is said: ". . . slaughtered a kid, and so on." Do not regard this reason as feeble. For the end of all these actions is to establish firmly in the soul of every disobedient individual the constant need for remembering and making mention of his sin—as it is said: "And my sin is ever before me"—and that he, his descendants, and the descendants of his descendants, must seek forgiveness for the sin by an act of obedience belonging to the same species as the act of disobedience.[99]

The same text, "And my sin is ever before me," which supports the requirement that an individual remember his personal past is also used to explain the need for the community of Israel to remember the sins of its forefathers.

The same reason which explains the choice of specific animals for sacrifices can also be applied to explain the continuity of sacrifices as a form of religious worship. Just as the community must ever remain aware of man's potential for cruelty by recalling the sale of Joseph by his brothers, so too must the community of Israel remember that its forefathers were subject to the attractions of paganism. "In the beginning, our forefathers were pagans" is an important memory that Jews retain as they grow in their relationship to God.[100] Jews must not succumb to the illusion that they have transcended the need for a Halakhah

—for a structure of behavior which supports their understanding of God. It was the law which weaned men away from paganism, but this "weaning" is not a necessary process in history. By maintaining the laws of sacrifices, the Jew might be reminded of his human vulnerability to paganism. Thus, ample room exists for legitimatizing halakhic practices whose legislative rationale is no longer operative.[101]

The preceding arguments attempt to show that Maimonides' codification of sacrifices in the *Mishneh Torah* does not necessarily negate the approach to God which he later develops in the *Guide*. Maimonides, the judge, is still the philosopher when he codifies the Halakhah for the entire community.

Within this discussion, note must be taken of Gershom Scholem's statement that the specific historical reasons Maimonides gives for the law, in the *Guide*, show that "to the philosopher, the Halakhah either had no significance at all, or one that was calculated to diminish rather than to enhance its prestige in his eyes." However this is not the only conclusion one must reach after studying Maimonides' reasons for the commandments.[102] One must remember that, in the *Guide*, Maimonides' purpose in offering reasons for commandments is not to make them relevant to his contemporaries. Scholem overlooks this when he writes, "he would be a bold man who would maintain that this theory of the *mitzvot* was likely to increase the enthusiasm of the faithful for their actual practice."

We must distinguish between the question, "What meaning can commandments have for an individual with a particular spiritual outlook?" and the theological question, "Do the laws in the Torah reveal a God who acts by reasons which are intelligible to man?" The first question deals with the different meanings one can give to commandments. One need not claim that what one considers a pertinent explanation of a commandment is in fact what the divine lawgiver intended. The second question is more concerned with the purpose of commandments at the actual time of biblical legislation; the ground of this inquiry is to discover if nature and the Bible reveal compatible or incompatible models of God. Maimonides was pursuing the second form of inquiry in the *Guide,* but he recognized the significance of the former approach:

As for the "four species that constitute a *lulav,*" the Sages, may their memory be blessed, have set forth some reason for this in the manner of midrashim whose method is well known by all those who understand their discourses. For these [namely, the midrashim] have, in their opinion, the status of poetical conceits; they are not meant to bring out the meaning of the text in question. . . . What seems to me regarding the "four species that constitute a *lulav"* is that they are indicative of the joy and gladness [felt by the Children of Israel] when they left the desert —which was "a place with no grain or figs or vines or pomegranates . . . There is not even water to drink"—for places in which there were fruit-bearing trees and rivers. For the purpose of commemoration, the finest fruit of these places was taken and the one that was most fragrant, as well as their finest leaves and finest verdure, I mean the willows of the brook. Three things are found in common in these four species. The first one is that at that time they were plentiful in the Land of Israel so that everyone could procure them. The second one is that they are beautiful to look at and full of freshness; and some of them, namely the citron and the myrtle have an excellent fragrance, while the branches of the palm tree and the willow have neither a good nor an offensive smell. The third one is that they keep fresh for seven days, which is not the case with peaches, pomegranates, asparagus, pears, and the like.[103]

As for the prohibition against hewing the stones of the altar, you know the reason [the Sages] have given for this in their dictum: "It is not fitting for that which shortens [human life] to be lifted up against that which prolongs it." This is excellent in the manner of the midrashim, as we have mentioned. However, the reason for this is manifest, for the idolators used to build altars with hewn stones.[104]

Maimonides recognized the subjective freedom which the talmudic rabbis allowed themselves in their attempt to make Torah significant for their generation. For the religious Jew, Torah was not the product of a culture of the past, but was renewed again and again in each generation. Regarding the biblical text, "Take to heart these instructions with which I charge you this day," the Sifre states: "They should not be in your eyes as an antiquated royal command to which no one looks with respect, but as one newly given which all run to welcome."[105] Although Maimonides accepted and valued this approach to Torah, he was insistent that one should not use the teachings which midrashic writers themselves *derive* from the text as a basis for understanding the intention of the Author of the Bible.

Maimonides was explicit in maintaining that he was not attempting to explain the meaning of Torah as it was practiced in his time:

And he who has deprived someone of a member, shall be deprived of a similar member: "The injury he inflicted on another shall be inflicted on him." You should not engage in cogitation concerning the fact that in such a case we punish by imposing a fine. For at present my purpose is to give reasons for the [biblical] texts and not for the pronouncements of the legal science.[106]

His primary concern in the *Guide* was not with the law as practiced by his community, but with the law as a reflection of the nature of its Author. He was not attempting to inspire one to observe commandments, but to convince his reader that nature and Torah reveal the same God. In order that the philosophically trained Jew be convinced that his love for the God of being need not be compromised by his embracing of Torah, he must be shown that the God of revelation gave men laws which were useful.

For the philosophic Jew drawn to a conception of God revealed by reason, Maimonides provides a concept of the God of Israel which can be understood and appreciated by all rational men. Maimonides does this with both the beliefs and the norms of tradition. Once the philosophic Jew accepts that "Indeed, all things proceed from one Deity and one Agent and 'have been given from one Shepherd,' " he is prepared to listen to how the Halakhah, in fact, can give expression to his theocentric passion.

FIVE

MORALITY AND THE
PASSIONATE LOVE FOR GOD

Leo Strauss understands the difference between the *Mishneh Torah* and the *Guide*, as well as the internal structure of the *Guide*, in terms of the fundamental distinction between thought and action:

> To sum up, according to Maimonides the *Mishneh Torah* is devoted to *fiqh*, the essence of which is to deal with actions; while the *Guide* deals with the secrets of the Torah, i.e., primarily opinions or beliefs, which it treats demonstratively, or at least as demonstratively as possible. Demonstrated opinions or beliefs are, according to Maimonides, absolutely superior in dignity to good actions or to their exact determination. In other words, the chief subject of the *Guide* is *Ma'aseh Merkavah*, which is "a great thing," while the chief subject of the *Mishneh Torah* is the precepts, which are "a small thing." Consequently the subject of the *Guide* is, according to Maimonides, absolutely superior in dignity to the subject of the *Mishneh Torah*. Since the dignity of a book, *caeteris paribus*, corresponds to the dignity of its subject, and since, as is shown by a comparison of Maimonides' own introductory remarks to the two books, he wrote the *Guide* with no less skill and care than his *Code*, we must conclude that he considered the *Guide* as absolutely superior in dignity.[1]

The distinction between theoretical and practical virtue, however, is an inadequate model with which to explain a philosopher rooted in a tradition in which man's relationship to God is mediated both by community and by a revealed law. The difference between thought and action (the one defining the spiritual life of the philosophic Jew, the other outlining the halakhic life of the community) does not do justice to Maimonides' conception of spirituality. The distinction between different levels of religious worship, suggested in preceding chapters, cuts across the distinction between thought and action. The analysis of Maimonides' legal writings indicates that the difference between individual excellence and community is expressed not only in the way one understands God, but also in the way one acts. *Din* was seen as the practice of a community that understands God on the basis of legal authority; *lifnim mi-shurat ha-din* as the practice of those individuals whose understanding of God is based upon the study of physics and metaphysics. This approach to law and community, apparent in Maimonides' legal writings, is also evident in the concluding chapters of *The Guide of the Perplexed.*

Maimonides recognizes an important difference between knowledge which serves the ideal of self-realization and knowledge which serves as a condition for man's passionate love of God.[2] For Maimonides, mastery of the disciplines contained in *Ma'aseh Merkavah* does not mean that one has attained the highest level of human development.

If, however, you have understood the natural things, you have entered the habitation and are walking in the antechambers. If, however, you have achieved perfection in the natural things and have understood Divine science, you have entered in the ruler's palace "into the inner court," and are with him in one habitation. This is the rank of the men of science; they, however, are of different grades of perfection.[3]

In his parable of the palace of the king, Maimonides explicitly indicates that this stage of perfection—of having mastered the natural and divine sciences—must not be accepted as the end of the individual's aspirations:

But their having come into the inner part of the habitation does not mean that they see the ruler or speak to him. For after their coming into the inner part of the habitation, it is indispensable that they should make another effort; then they will be in the presence of the ruler, see him from afar or from nearby, or hear the ruler's speech or speak to him.[4]

The additional effort that one must make refers to the levels of worship to which one aspires after knowledge is attained. Without knowledge man cannot truly worship God; without knowledge he fails to grasp His true reality:[5]

As for someone who thinks and frequently mentions God, without knowledge, following a mere imagining or following a belief adopted because of his reliance on the authority of somebody else, he is to my mind outside the habitation and far away from it and does not in true reality mention or think about God. For that thing which is in his imagination and which he mentions in his speech does not correspond to any being at all and has merely been invented by his imagination, as we have explained in our discourse concerning the attributes.[6]

If one's conception of God is defined by imagination without knowledge, one's religious life revolves around a belief in that which does not exist. Yet knowledge of metaphysics is a necessary but not sufficient condition for true religious worship:

If, however, you have apprehended God and His acts in accordance with what is required by the intellect, you should afterward engage in totally devoting yourself to Him, endeavor to come closer to Him, and strengthen the bond between you and Him —that is the intellect. Thus it says; "It has been clearly demonstrated to you that the Lord alone is God, and so on"; and it says: "Know therefore this day and keep in mind, and so on"; and it says: "Know you that the Lord He is God." The Torah has made it clear that this last worship to which we have drawn attention in this chapter can only be engaged in after apprehension has been achieved. It says: "Loving the Lord your God and serving Him with all your heart and soul." Now we have made it clear several times that love is proportionate to apprehension. After love comes this worship to which attention has been drawn by [the Sages], may their memory be blessed, who said: "This is the worship in the heart." In my opinion it consists in setting thought to work on the first intelligible and in devoting oneself exclusively to this as far as this is within one's capacity. Therefore you will find that David exhorted Solomon and fortified him in these two things, I mean his endeavor to apprehend Him and his endeavor to worship Him after apprehension has been achieved. He said: "And you, Solomon my son, know you the God of your father and serve Him, and so on. If you seek Him, He will be found of you, and so on." The exhortation always refers to intellectual apprehensions not to imagination; for thought concerning imaginings is not called "knowledge" but that which comes into your mind. Thus it is clear that after apprehension, total devotion to Him and the employment of intellectual thought in constantly loving Him should be aimed at.[7]

At the end of the "Book of Knowledge" of the *Mishneh Torah*, and in the *Guide*, Maimonides interpreted the Song of Songs as an expression of the all-consuming passion of love which claims the lover's attention to the exclusion of every other concern.[8] The religious philosopher is not content to know that were he asked he could demonstrate God's existence. For Maimonides, knowledge of God is not a static fund of information, it is an activity wherein one actively reflects on God.

Those philosophers who aspire to worship God know that "The more they think of Him and of being with Him, the more their worship increases."[9] The religious philosopher's goal is not to achieve intellectual expertise in the manner of the skillful scribe who spends only a part of his time actually writing.[10] To describe the goal of individual excellence in Maimonides' thought as "intellectual virtue" is to miss the passionate love characterizing the religious philosopher's relationship to the object of his knowledge.[11] To Maimonides, the importance of philosophy is that it enables one to become a passionate lover of God. Maimonides interprets Psalm 91 as referring to the philosopher's level of worship of God:

"Because he has set his love upon Me, therefore I will deliver him; I will set him on high because he has known My name." We have already explained in preceding chapters that the meaning of "knowledge of the name" is: apprehension of Him. It is as if [the psalm] said that this individual is protected because he has known Me and then passionately loved Me. You know the difference between the terms "one who loves [*oheb*]" and "one who loves passionately [*hoshek*]"; an excess of love [*mahabbah*], so that no thought remains that is directed toward a thing other than the beloved, is passionate love [*ishq*].[12]

The intoxicated lover of God represents the philosopher who strives to eliminate any distraction from the joy of intellectual love of God.[13]

In Maimonides' description of the lover's yearning for solitude one can sense the terrible emptiness the lover feels upon being separated from his beloved:

Thus it is clear that after apprehension, total devotion to Him and the employment of intellectual thought in constantly loving Him should be aimed at. Mostly this is achieved in solitude and isolation. Hence every excellent man stays frequently in solitude and does not meet anyone unless it is necessary.[14]

The religious passion which the intellect makes possible leads one to view ordinary social interactions as a burden:

When, however, you are alone with yourself and no one else is there and while you lie awake upon your bed you should take great care during these precious times not to set your thought to work on anything other than that intellectual worship consisting

in nearness to God and being in His presence in that true reality
that I have made known to you and not by way of affections of
the imagination.[15]

Once one recognizes that the highest spiritual ideal,
according to Maimonides, is *ḥoshek*, the passionate activity of joyful contemplation of God, one must consider how
the aspiration toward this ideal affects one's total way of
life.

The way of life of the philosophic lover of God, as it
is expressed in the descent to the everyday world, is different from the way of life of one who aspires to knowledge
of God. In preparing himself to "enter into the chambers
of the king," the philosopher has no difficulty accepting
the physical needs entailed in living as a human being; the
ascent is characterized by the attempt to limit the satisfaction of those needs only to necessities.[16] In preparing for
the ascent, the struggle is within the individual. Will excessive hungers draw him to a life of unrestrained pleasure-
seeking, or will the intellect define his needs and his
desires? Once intellectual love of God is the defining feature of one's life, the problem is the elimination of any
human involvement which impinges upon one's active
love of God. There is no difficulty in satisfying minimal
physical needs when attempting to materialize intellectual capacities. But when one strives to reach the passion
of intellectual love, even attending to human necessities
becomes a burden:

Know that even if you were the man who knew most the true
reality of the Divine science, you would cut that bond existing
between you and God if you would empty your thought of God
and busy yourself totally in eating the necessary or in occupying
yourself with the necessary. You would not be with Him then,
nor He with you. For that relation between you and Him is
actually broken off at that time. It is for this reason that excellent

men begrudge the times in which they are turned away from Him by other occupations and warn against this, saying: "Do not let God be absent from your thought."[17]

According to Maimonides, a person's attitude to his physical needs changes when he becomes capable of intellectual love of God. It is important, therefore, when evaluating Maimonides' writings, to ascertain whether he is discussing the necessary conditions for achieving intellectual understanding, or whether he is describing the life pattern of one who seeks to be actively engaged in passionate love for God *(ḥoshek)*.

An analysis of Maimonides' statements about Halakhah at the end of the *Guide* will indicate that the ascent-descent background is operative in Maimonides' understanding and appreciation of the law. In the context of ascent, the Halakhah guides and educates the community toward knowledge of God. The law aims to eliminate idolatry and social wrongdoing and also to structure a communal way of life which would make possible the individual's ascent toward intellectual love of God. The Torah leads the community toward love of God by cultivating moral habits, by abolishing wrongdoing in society, and by communicating correct opinions—God's existence, unity, and eternity.[18]

As distinct from this training, the Halakhah of the descent—after knowledge of God has been acquired, is a discipline which trains the philosopher to empty his thoughts of everything except God:

From here on I will begin to give you guidance with regard to the form of this training so that you should achieve this great end. The first thing that you should cause your soul to hold fast onto is that, while reciting the *Shema*, you should empty your mind of everything and pray thus. You should not content yourself with "being intent" while "reciting the first verse of *Shema*" and saying "the first benediction." When this has been carried out correctly and has been practiced consistently for years, cause your soul, whenever you read or listen to the Torah, to be constantly directed—the whole of you and your thought—toward reflection on what you are listening to or reading. When this too has been practiced consistently for a certain time, cause your soul to be in such a way that your thought is always quite free of distraction and gives heed to all that you are reading of the other discourses of the Prophets and even when you read all the benedictions, so that you aim at meditating on what you are uttering and at considering its meaning. If, however, while performing these acts of worship you are free from distraction and not engaged in thinking upon any of the things pertaining to this world, cause your soul—after this has been achieved—to occupy your thought with things necessary for you or superfluous in your life, and in general with "worldly things," while you eat or drink or bathe or talk with your wife and your small children or while you talk with the common run of people. Thus I have provided you with many and long stretches of time in which you can think all that needs thinking regarding property, the governance of the household, and the welfare of the body. On the other hand, while performing the actions imposed by the Law, you should occupy your thought only with what you are doing, just as we have explained.[19]

Although the Halakhah, as stated in the *Mishneh Torah*, only requires that one have *kavvanah* (intent) during the first verse of the *Shema* and the first benediction of the *Amidah*, the philosophic Jew of the *Guide* is not satisfied with this minimal standard.[20] The *Shema* is one of those commandments which, Maimonides claims, teaches the community correct opinions.[21] For the man who has acquired demonstrative knowledge, the *Shema* is no longer purposeful in communicating correct opinions; rather it provides a discipline that trains the individual to focus all of his attention on God.

The philosopher appreciates Halakhah not only for

political reasons, but also for its personal guidance in his quest for intellectual love of God. If the significance of Halakhah to the philosopher were solely its capacity to establish an orderly religious society, the philosopher would be satisfied with the minimal requirements the Halakhah establishes for all members of the community. If for Maimonides, the philosopher, the way of Halakhah is unimportant, why then does Maimonides insist that Halakhah be understood and observed differently by the Jew who has achieved philosophic excellence? By emphasizing that the observance of and perspective on Halakhah changes for the philosophic Jew, Maimonides clearly indicates that he does not adopt the way of dualism regarding tradition.

In addition to training the philosopher to empty his thought of everything but God, the Halakhah also serves to provide him with a discipline that can encompass both passionate love of God and the inevitable demands of human existence.

The Halakhah, according to Maimonides, is addressed to humans and not to disembodied intelligences;[22] we remain corporeal creatures in spite of our intellectual capacities. Within Jewish tradition, Solomon is the archetype of one who was deceived into believing, that by virtue of his intellectual capacities, he transcended the problems of the body and therefore had no need for specific halakhot.[23] The Torah never allows us to forget that our bodies must be ordered properly if we are to achieve the goal for which the intellect hungers.[24] The philosophic Jew appreciates the Halakhah because he knows, in all humility, that:

it is by all the particulars of the actions and through their repetition that some excellent men obtain such training that they achieve human perfection, so that they fear, and are in dread and in awe of, God, may He be exalted, and know who it is that is with them and as a result act subsequently as they ought to.[25]

Maimonides knew that living continuously with intellectual love of God was possible only for Moses and the patriarchs,[26] who symbolize the possibility of retaining such a passion regardless of the problems and claims of human life.[27] Yet, Maimonides writes, "This rank is not a rank that, with a view to the attainment of which, someone like myself may aspire for guidance. But one may aspire to attain that rank which was mentioned before this one through the training that we described."[28] Humans who are distracted by the pressures and pains of existence require a disciplined mode and defined time for the expression of their passion for God.[29] The philosopher needs a way of life which respects both the all-consuming yearning for intellectual love of God and the inescapable claims of normal human existence. Halakhah addressed itself to the human dilemma of being both intellect and body. The God of creation, who endowed man with the capacity for passionate intellectual love, provided him, at Sinai, with a way of life which makes this love humanly possible.[30] The Halakhah makes it possible for the philosophic Jew to live within the human world while aspiring toward a passionate love for God.

Thus far, the analysis of Maimonides' approach to the philosophic Jew's understanding of Halakhah has been restricted to those halakhot that relate directly to the individual's worship of God and allow him to develop and to give expression to his passionate love of God.[31] Since the philosophic Jew is primarily concerned with the theocentric passion, it would appear that concern for community is not related to his quest for love of God. What remains to be explored, then, is the question of Maimonides' attitude to community.

In order to understand the Maimonidean conception of the importance of community in the life of the philosophic Jew, one must remember the ascent-descent framework when analyzing different statements on this subject in the *Guide.*

In his discussion of the preconditions for becoming a prophet, Maimonides advises the aspiring prophet to view the community as a herd of cattle:

He should rather regard all people according to their various states with respect to which they are indubitably either like domestic animals or like beasts of prey. If the perfect man who lives in solitude thinks of them at all, he does so only with a view to saving himself from the harm that may be caused by those among them who are harmful if he happens to associate with them, or to obtaining an advantage that may be obtained from them if he is forced to it by some of his needs.[32]

Taken out of context this statement suggests that both the prophet and, by implication, the philosophic Jew are essentially removed from community and that the community has no personal spiritual significance for them.[33] The statement, however, is presented within the context of the training of individuals who wish to ascend to prophetic excellence. It is immediately preceded by:

It is likewise necessary for the thought of that individual should be detached from the spurious kinds of rulership and that his desire for them should be abolished—I mean the wish to dominate or to be held great by the common people and to obtain from them honor and obedience for its own sake.[34]

Maimonides is discussing the necessity to transcend the level of those political leaders who hunger for power and dominion and whose dignity and self-worth are defined exclusively by their political status. The aspiring prophet must transcend this egocentric dependency on society, so that his assumption of political leadership will not be grounded in the longing for power.[35] The disdain for the community, then, is the condition of the prophet during his ascent, i.e., when he is struggling to transcend the political leader's dependency on the community.

If one understands this condition as a permanent attitude on the part of the prophet, how is one to make sense of Maimonides' statement in the next paragraph, ". . . prophetic revelation did not come to Moses, peace be on him, after the disastrous incident of the spies and until the whole generation of the desert perished, in the way that revelation used to come before, because—seeing the enormity of their crime—he suffered greatly because of this matter"?[36] Why should Moses suffer for the mistakes of the community if, to the prophet, other human beings are like domestic animals or beasts of prey? The source of Moses' suffering is his love for the community. Disdain for the community characterized the prophet during his ascent; in exact contrast, love for the community becomes his characteristic quality during his descent.

The prophet's involvement with the community results from the overflow of his individual perfection.[37] The prophet typifies the political leader who does not view political activity as a means to gratify egocentric needs. Similarly, the community which the prophet establishes is not based solely on the self-interest needs which social order satisfies. The law which the prophet brings to men is concerned not only with political well-being but:

Accordingly if you find a Law the whole end of which and the whole purpose of the chief thereof, who determined the actions required by it, are directed exclusively toward the ordering of the city and of its circumstances and the abolition in it of injustice and oppression; and if in that Law attention is not at all directed toward speculative matters, no heed is given to the perfecting of the rational faculty, and no regard is accorded to opinions being correct or faulty—the whole purpose of that Law being, on the contrary, the arrangement in whatever way this may be brought about, of the circumstances of people in their relations with one another and provision for their obtaining, in accordance with the opinion of that chief, a certain something deemed to be happiness—you must know that that Law is a *nomos* and that the man who laid it down belongs, as we have mentioned, to the third class, I mean to say to those who are perfect only in their imaginative faculty.

If, on the other hand, you find a Law all of whose ordinances are due to attention being paid, as we stated before, to the soundness of the circumstances pertaining to the body and also to the soundness of belief—a Law that takes pains to inculcate correct opinions with regard to God, may He be exalted in the first place, and with regard to the angels, and that desires to make man wise, to give him understanding, and to awaken his attention, so that he should know the whole of that which exists in its true form —you must know that this guidance comes from Him, may He be exalted, and that this Law is Divine.[38]

The community, to the prophet, is not only a political framework whose sole function is to satisfy man's social and physical needs, but a structure which aims at creating those economic and political conditions within which men can aspire to realizing their highest human end—knowledge of God.

The impetus to establish such a community flows from the basic nature of prophetic perfection. The Jewish prophet believes that God is related to history. Moses' attachment to the community is inseparable from his intellectual love for a God who is the creator of the universe and the lord of history. Although the perfection of the philosopher finds its fullest expression in writing books, prophetic perfection finds its consummation in perfecting the community:

It has already become clear to you that, were it not for this additional perfection, sciences would not be set forth in books and Prophets would not call upon the people to obtain knowledge of the truth. For a man endowed with knowledge does not set anything down for himself in order to teach himself what he already knows. But the nature of that intellect is such that it always overflows and is transmitted from one who receives that overflow to another one who receives it after him until it reaches an individual beyond whom this overflow cannot go and whom it merely renders perfect, as we have set out in a parable in one of the chapters of this treatise. The nature of this matter makes it necessary for someone to whom this additional measure of over-flow has come, to address a call to people, regardless of whether that call is listened to or not, and even if he as a result thereof is harmed in his body. We even find that Prophets addressed the call to people until they were killed—this Divine overflow moving them and by no means letting them rest and be quiet, even if they met with great misfortunes.[39]

This analysis of the prophet's commitment to the community is connected with one of the most difficult problems of the *Guide*—the relationship of morality to man's ultimate perfection. The last chapter of the *Guide* appears to present a paradoxical understanding of the place morality occupies in the perfection of man. In his last chapter, Maimonides examines the various perfections which men consider valuable. The first, "the perfection of possessions," and the second, "the perfection of the bodily constitution and shape," are rejected because they do not relate to the perfection of man as man. The third, the perfection of moral virtues, is also rejected as the highest perfection of man, because:

. . . this species of perfection is likewise a preparation for something else and not an end in itself. For all moral habits are concerned with what occurs between a human individual and someone else.[40]

The highest perfection of man is identified, by Maimonides, with theoretical virtue:

The fourth species is the true human perfection; it consists in the acquisition of the rational virtues—I refer to the conception of intelligibles, which teach true opinions concerning the Divine things. This is in true reality the ultimate end; this is what gives the individual true perfection, a perfection belonging to him alone; and it gives him permanent perdurance; through it man is man.[41]

Maimonides supports his evaluation of the various perfections by appealing to the prophets:

The Prophets too have explained to us and interpreted to us the selfsame notions—just as the philosophers have interpreted them—clearly stating to us that neither the perfection of possession nor the perfection of health nor the perfection of moral habits is a perfection of which one should be proud or that one should desire; the perfection of which one should be proud and that one should desire is knowledge of Him, may He be exalted, which is the true science. Jeremiah says concerning these four perfections: "Thus spoke the Lord: Let not the wise man glory in his wisdom, neither let the mighty man glory in his might, let not the rich man glory in his riches; but let him that glories glory in this, that he understands and knows Me."[42]

After explaining the order of perfections, however, Maimonides appears to contradict what he has just established when he writes:

As we have mentioned this verse and the wondrous notions contained in it, and as we have mentioned the saying of the Sages, may their memory be blessed, about it, we will complete the exposition of what it includes. For when explaining in this verse the noblest ends, he does not limit them only to the apprehension of Him, may He be exalted. For if this were his purpose, he would have said: "But let him that glories glory in this, that he understands and knows Me," and have stopped there; or he would have said: "that he understands and knows Me that I am one"; or he would have said: "that I have no figure," or "that there is none like Me," or something similar. But he says that one should glory in the apprehension of Myself and in the knowledge of My attributes, by which he means His actions, as we have made clear with reference to its dictum; "let me know Your ways, and so on." In this verse he makes it clear to us that those actions that ought to be known and imitated are "lovingkindness, judgment, and righteousness."[43]

Previously, morality was presented as inferior to intellectual perfection; now morality appears as the end of knowledge of God and thus the highest perfection. Intellectual perfection, as distinct from moral perfection, does not require that one live in society or interact in any way with other men. To act with lovingkindness, judgment, and righteousness, however, one must be a part of society and act among others. Crucial to Maimonides' paradoxical evaluation is the problem of whether community is an essential feature of human perfection.[44]

Guttmann resolves this apparent paradox by suggesting that the morality "grounded in the knowledge of God is completely distinct from the morality which is prior to knowledge."[45] Although one may accept this distinction, one must disagree with Guttmann when he writes that, to Maimonides, "Ethics, though previously subordinate to knowledge, has now become the ultimate meaning and purpose of the knowledge of God."[46] This approach can be questioned in the light of Maimonides' constant emphasis on intellectual worship of God and in the light of his claims, repeated throughout his legal writings, that *olam ha-ba* represents the ultimate telos of Judaism. If the meaning and purpose of knowledge of God is ethics, why guide an individual toward a yearning for God that is consummated in a non-historical reality? Maimonides' passion for *olam ha-ba* does not express the yearning of one who longs solely for moral perfection.[47] According to Maimonides, man feels intellectually inadequate in comparison to cosmic intelligences whose knowledge has no ethical significance. This felt inadequacy would be unintelligible if the only meaning and purpose of knowledge of God was ethics.[48] One must therefore, agree with Shlomo Pines, that knowledge of God is not primarily moral knowledge.[49]

The difference between Maimonides' two evaluations of morality is to be understood in the same way that one understands his description of the prophet's attitude to the community. One who attempts to transcend the anthropocentric view of life understands the significance of morality as a means to the higher goal of the theocentric love of God. In this context, the yearning for God is of greater significance than moral actions. In the attempt to become a passionate lover of God, everything valued by human beings—possessions, physical strengths, and moral virtues—is insignificant in comparison to the yearning to be with God:

This ultimate perfection, however, pertains to you alone, no one else being associated in it with you in any way: "Let them be only your own, and so on." Therefore you ought to desire to achieve this thing, which will remain permanently with you, and not weary and trouble yourself for the sake of others, O you who neglect your own soul so that its whiteness has turned into blackness through the corporeal faculties having gained dominion over it—as is said in the beginning of the poetic parables that have been coined for these notions; it says: "My mother's sons were incensed against me; they made me keeper of the vineyards; but my own vineyard have I not kept." It says on this very same subject: "Lest you give your vigor to others, and your years to the cruel."[50]

Maimonides' understanding of Jeremiah's statement appears to support placing his first evaluation of morality within the context of guiding an individual away from what people ordinarily consider to be valuable:

Consider how he mentioned them according to the order given them in the opinion of the multitude. For the greatest perfection in their opinion is that of "the rich man in his riches," below him "the mighty man in his might," and below him "the wise man in his wisdom." [By the expression "the wise man in his wisdom,"] he means him who possesses the moral virtues; for such an individual is also held in high esteem by the multitude, to whom the discourse in question is addressed.[51]

Although the multitude lacks an appreciation for theoretical knowledge of God it is still able to value moral virtue. Men who value possessions and physical strength also can understand the social value of morality.

However, once one has acquired knowledge of God, morality assumes a different meaning:

It is clear that the perfection of man that may truly be gloried in is the one acquired by him who has achieved, in a measure corresponding to his capacity, apprehension of Him, may He be exalted, and who knows His providence extending over His creatures as manifested in the act of bringing them into being and in their governance as it is. The way of life of such an individual, after he has achieved this apprehension, will always have in view lovingkindness, righteousness, and judgment, through assimilation to His actions, may He be exalted, just as we have explained several times in this treatise.[52]

When Maimonides describes morality as an imitation of God's actions he is describing a morality which has its roots in an intellectual understanding of God. The ground of this morality is neither specific rules nor principles but, rather, the actions of God as they are manifest in nature. The key difference between the morality of the multitude and the morality of the religious philosopher is that the former is rule-dominated and based in the juridical authority of God, the latter an imitation of the God of creation.[53] Knowledge of God based on the study of nature reveals lovingkindness, righteousness, and judgment as constant features of being.[54] The constancy of God's *ḥesed*, reflected in being, guides the religious philosopher to act with *ḥesed* toward men even though they have no claim on him.

Maimonides ends the *Guide* exactly as he began his earliest legal work. By distinguishing between morality before and after knowledge of God, Maimonides is expressing a key theme of his philosophy: theoretical knowledge of God affects practice.

This essay began by showing that in his first legal work, Maimonides claimed that without the theoretical knowledge of God derived from the study of nature one cannot become a *ḥasid*. It continued with an explanation of how different orientations to Halakhah are a function of different conceptions of God. Knowledge of God derived from the study of physics and metaphysics is necessary in order to transcend the motive of self-interest and to become a person whose actions reflect the principle of *lifnim mi-shurat ha-din*.

To Maimonides, practice is affected not only by moral knowledge. Practice also changes when one adopts a different orientation to life.[55] "Man does not sit, move, and occupy himself when he is alone in his house, as he sits, moves, and occupies himself when he is in the presence of a great king."[56] It is not that a person who is alone is ignorant of or violates moral rules of behavior, but that intellectual worship of God and the awareness of being in His presence provide man with a different orientation to the significance of practice. The framework of life within which one locates oneself—anthropocentric or theocentric—will influence one's characteristic patterns of behavior. The practice of the *ḥasid* results from a perspective on life where *olam ha-ba* is the telos of human history and of human existence. The *ḥasid* severs his attachment to what people ordinarily consider valuable, e.g., possessions and physical pleasures, as a direct result of his understanding of the purpose of life. *Lifnim mi-shurat ha-din* becomes the characteristic response of one who defines himself by the theocentric perspective. Anyone, at any given time, may perform an action that is beyond the strict requirement of Halakhah. Yet, to the *ḥasid*, such acts are not isolated moments of religious fervor; they derive from the nature of his intellectual love of God.

Maimonides' description of the relationship of philosophy to Halakhah has its roots in his understanding of the structure of Torah. Torah does not begin with the account of Sinai but with God's relationship to the universe.[57] For Maimonides the juridical moment of Sinai is only fully internalized by individuals who interpret Sinai from the perspective of creation:

God, may His mention be exalted, wished us to be perfected and the state of our societies to be improved by His laws regarding actions. Now this can come about only after the adoption of intellectual beliefs, the first of which being His apprehension, may He be exalted, according to our capacity. This, in its turn, cannot come about except through Divine science, and this Divine science cannot become actual except after a study of natural science. This is so since natural science borders on Divine science, and its study precedes that of Divine science in time as has been made clear to whoever has engaged in speculation on these matters. Hence God, may He be exalted, caused His book to open with the "Account of the Beginning," which as we have made clear, is natural science.[58]

In order to understand fully the relationship of the individual to community, or of philosophy to Halakhah in Maimonidean thought, it is important that we appreciate how Maimonides led the halakhic Jew from Sinai to creation and then back to Sinai.

The philosophic Jew, according to Maimonides, need not lose his particular halakhic identity when he appropriates the universal disciplines of the philosophers. The philosophic Jew appropriates the particular forms of his community from the perspective of his rational understanding of the universal God of being. The concrete forms of expression are particular to his tradition; the intellectual passion which infuses these forms is universal. The Halakhah, which is mediated by his membership in the covenant community, provides him with concrete forms for expressing his understanding of the universal God of being.

This integration of the universal (nature) and the particular (Halakhah) is observed in the way Maimonides, in the *Guide*, provides a Jewish expression for the universal experience of fear of God. In the first book of the *Mishneh Torah*, chapters two and four, Maimonides writes:

And what is the way that will lead to the love of Him and the fear of Him? When a person contemplates His great and wondrous works and creatures and from them obtains a glimpse of His wisdom which is incomparable and infinite, he will straightaway love Him, praise Him, glorify Him, and long with an exceeding longing to know His great Name; even as David said "My soul thirsted for God, for the living God" (Ps. 42:3). And when he ponders these matters, he will recoil affrighted, and realize that he is a small creature, lowly and obscure, endowed with slight and slender intelligence, standing in the presence of Him who is perfect in knowledge. And so David said "When I behold Your heavens, the work of Your fingers, . . . what is man, that You are mindful of him?" (Ps. 8:4–5).[59]

When a man reflects on these things, studies all these created beings, from the angels and spheres down to human beings and so on, and realizes the Divine Wisdom manifested in them all, his love for God will increase, his soul will thirst, his very flesh will yearn, to love God. He will be filled with fear and trembling, as he becomes conscious of his own lowly condition, poverty, and insignificance, and compares himself with any of the great and holy bodies; still more when he compares himself with any one of the pure forms that are incorporeal and have never had association with corporeal substance. He will then realize that he is a vessel full of shame, dishonor, and reproach, empty and deficient.[60]

This description of *yirah* reflects the tension characterizing the human experience of love of God. Human reason, the image of God in man, leads to the theocentric world of non-human lovers of God. The intellect of man, however, is tied to his body. The awareness of being human and the inability, even during sublime moments of intellectual love, to transcend the human condition constitutes this experience of *yirah*.[61]

For Maimonides, intellectual love of God does not lead to a condition of mystic union in which man transcends the awareness of his humanity.[62] *Yirah* implies that man is conscious of himself as a creature even during moments of intellectual communion. This experience of *yirah*, which is available to all men and which is an outgrowth of knowledge of God, is interpreted by Maimonides, in the *Guide*, as describing the way in which the philosophic Jew understands Halakhah:[63]

This purpose to which I have drawn your attention is the purpose of all the actions prescribed by the Law. . . . He, may He be exalted, has explained that the end of the actions prescribed by the whole Law, is to bring about the passion of which it is correct that it be brought about, as we have demonstrated in this chapter for the benefit of those who know the true realities. I refer to the fear of Him, may He be exalted, and the awe before His command. It says: "If you fail to observe faithfully all the terms of this Teaching that are written in this book, to reverence this honored and awesome Name, the Lord your God."[64]

The philosophic Jew understands Halakhah as providing a life-form for that which is present to all men only during moments of intellection.[65] The awe and humility felt by the philosopher when he encounters God's majesty results from reflection on God's wisdom as manifest in nature. For the philosopher who lives by Halakhah, the consciousness of being a creature who lives in the presence of God results from the discipline of the *mitzvot*. Halakhah continuously sets God before the philosopher.

This essay has attempted to make the reader aware of the mutual interaction of philosophy and Halakhah in Maimonidean thought. The discussion of Maimonides' treatment of *yirah* pointed to the influence of philosophy on one's understanding of Halakhah. At the end of the *Guide*, Maimonides also suggests that the halakhic consciousness influences the philosophic ideal of intellectual love of God. The concept of *teshuvah*, which has its source in the Halakhah and which occupies a central place in the *Mishneh Torah*, defines the philosophic Jew's response to suffering.

Because of Sinai, the halakhic Jew understands his historical condition through obedience or disobedience to the will of God. Physical suffering is interpreted as a message from God calling one to examine his relationship to Torah:

A positive Scriptural commandment prescribes prayer and the sounding of an alarm with trumpets whenever trouble befalls the community. For when Scripture says, "against an aggressor who attacks you, you shall sound short blasts on the trumpets" (Num. 10:9), the meaning is: Cry out in prayer and sound an alarm against whatsoever is oppressing you, be it famine, pestilence, locusts, or the like.

This procedure is one of the roads to repentance, for as the community cries out in prayer and sounds an alarm when overtaken by trouble, everyone is bound to realize that evil has come upon him as a consequence of his own evil deeds, as it is written, "Your iniquities have turned away these things, and your sins have withheld good from you" (Jer. 5:25), and that his repentance will cause the trouble to be removed.

If, on the other hand, the people do not cry out in prayer and do not sound an alarm, but merely say that it is the way of the world for such a thing to happen to them, and that their trouble is a matter of pure chance, they have chosen a cruel path which will cause them to persevere in their evil deeds and thus bring additional troubles upon them. For when Scripture says, "if you disobey Me and remain hostile to Me, I will act against you in wrathful hostility" (Lev. 26:27–28), the meaning is: If, when I bring trouble upon you in order to cause you to repent, you say that the trouble is purely accidental, then I will add to your trouble the fury appropriate to such an "accident."[66]

No suffering is perceived as accidental; God's will addresses man through what is normally perceived as being accidental. According to Maimonides, this understanding of the relationship of suffering to *teshuvah* is implied by the convenantal election of Israel.[67] The philosophic Jew brings this covenantal consciousness into his quest for intellectual communion with the God of being.

In the end of the *Guide,* Maimonides suggests that the philosophic-halakhic Jew should understand his suffering as resulting from his failure to fulfill the *mitzvah* of intellectual love of God:

The providence of God, may He be exalted, is constantly watching over those who have obtained this overflow, which is permitted to everyone who makes efforts with a view to obtaining it. If a man's thought is free from distraction, if he apprehends Him, may He be exalted, in the right way and rejoices in what he apprehends, that individual can never be afflicted with evil of any kind. For he is with God and God is with him. When, however, he abandons Him, may He be exalted, and is thus separated from God and God separated from him, he becomes in consequence of this a target for every evil that may happen to befall him. For the thing that necessarily brings about providence and deliverance from the sea of chance consists in that intellectual overflow. Yet an impediment may prevent for some time its reaching the excellent and good man in question, or again it was not obtained at all by such and such imperfect and wicked man, and therefore the chance occurrences that befell them happened.

To my mind this belief is also shown as true by a text of the Torah; He, may He be exalted, says "And I will abandon them and hide My countenance from them. They shall be ready prey; and many evils and troubles shall befall them. And they shall say on that day, 'Surely it is because our God is not in our midst that these evils have befallen us.' " It is clear that we are the cause of this "hiding of the countenance," and we are the agents who produce this separation. This is the meaning of His saying: "Yet I will keep My countenance hidden on that day, because of all the evil they have done." There is no doubt that what is true of one is true of a community. Thus it has become clear to you that the reason for a human individual's being abandoned to chance so that he is permitted to be devoured like the beasts is his being separated from God.[68]

Both the halakhic Jew lacking knowledge of philosophy and the halakhic Jew possessing such knowledge recognize that "there is no suffering without transgression" and "if a man sees that painful sufferings visit him, let him examine his conduct." The difference between them, however, is that the former understands his failure solely within the rubric of halakhic practice whereas the latter perceives his sin as the absence of intellectual love of God. These two approaches to what constitutes the cause of suffering are mirrored, respectively, in the yearnings for messianism and for *olam ha-ba*.

The *Mishneh Torah,* which strives primarily to guide the community toward halakhic practice, ends with a description of the ideal political condition for a Halakhic community—messianism. Messianism gives expression to the hopes of a halakhic community which understands *teshuvah* as its failure to fulfill halakhic norms. However the individual who follows the path to intellectual love of God delineated in *The Guide of the Perplexed,* expresses his longing for *teshuvah* by a passionate yearning for freedom from the limitations of human existence. He longs for *olam ha-ba*:

Yet in the measure in which the faculties of the body are weakened and the fire of the desires is quenched, the intellect is strengthened, its lights achieve a wider extension, its apprehension is purified, and it rejoices in what it apprehends. The result is that when a perfect man is stricken with years and approaches death, this apprehension increases very powerfully, joy over this apprehension and a great love for the object of apprehension become stronger, until the soul is separated from the body at that moment in this state of pleasure. Because of this the Sages have indicated with reference to the deaths of Moses, Aaron, and Miriam that "the three of them died by a kiss." . . . Their purpose was to indicate that the three of them died in the pleasure of this apprehension due to the intensity of passionate love. In this dictum the Sages, may their memory be blessed, followed the generally accepted poetical way of expression that calls the apprehension that is achieved in a state of intense and passionate love for Him, may He be exalted, "a kiss," in accordance with its dictum: "Let him kiss me with the kisses of his mouth, and so on." [The Sages], may their memory be blessed, mention the occurrence of this kind of death, which in true reality is salvation from death, only with regard to "Moses, Aaron, and Miriam."

The other Prophets and excellent men are beneath this degree; but it holds good for all of them that the apprehension of their intellects becomes stronger at the separation, just as it is said: "And your righteousness shall go before you; the glory of the Lord shall be at your back." After having reached this condition of enduring permanence, that intellect remains in one and the same state, the impediment that sometimes screened him off having been removed. And he will remain permanently in that state of intense pleasure, which does not belong to the genus of bodily pleasures, as we have explained in our compilations and as others have explained before us.[69]

Our analysis of the concluding chapters of the *Guide* clearly indicates how Maimonides attempted to integrate the philosophic and halakhic sensibilities. The halakhic imperative "And you shall love the Lord your God" merged into love based on the philosophic knowledge of God.

There were individuals who were outraged at Maimonides' claim that competent talmudic authorities who lacked philosophic knowledge of God were outside the chamber of the king:

Those who have come up to the habitation and walk around it
are the jurists who believe true opinions on the basis of traditional authority and study the Law concerning the practices of
Divine service, but do not engage in speculation concerning the
fundamental principles of religion and make no inquiry whatever regarding the rectification of belief.[70]

Many individuals refused to believe that Maimonides actually wrote this; some suggested that it be removed from
the text of the *Guide*.[71] Their shock and alarm is incom-
prehensible if it is considered to be directed solely at the
Guide, for this simile is no more radical than the approach
Maimonides adopted in his legal works. In the *Mishneh
Torah* Maimonides makes competence in philosophic disciplines a condition for prophecy and love for God. Great
talmudic teachers of the tradition were described in that
work as engaging in the disciplines of *pardes* knowledge
—physics and metaphysics. Maimonides began his codification of Jewish law with a description of the God of being,
to indicate that the particular way of Israel must not re-
volve around the false assumption that God is only accessible to members of the covenant.[72]

Interpreters of Maimonides can be differentiated by
where they locate the "true" Maimonides. Halakhists who
primarily study his brilliant legal works cannot imagine
that Maimonides, the Rambam, was deeply concerned
with philosophy. On the other hand, those who understand his philosophic interests do not consider his meticulous concern with details of Halakhah philosophically significant. Both approaches are correct in what they affirm,
but are incorrect in what they deny. There are many students of Maimonides who understand the legal brilliance
of his *Mishneh Torah*. However, they fail to realize that he
wanted his readers to understand his passion for Halakhah
from the perspective of the first four chapters of that work
which describe how the God of being can be understood

and loved by all rational men. There are many who understand the intellectual pathos of the *Guide*. However, they fail to recognize that it is the same pathos of a halakhist who consummated his halakhic creativity with the *Guide of the Perplexed*. The *Mishneh Torah* and the *Guide* reflect the unified approach of a single man. Maimonidean thought is subject to the same misunderstanding that any individual may encounter if he passionately loves his community's way of life but does not claim that this particular way of life exhausts the whole field of spiritual authenticity.

Maimonides, the writer of the *Mishneh Torah* and the *Guide*, remains a lonely figure because he believed that a total commitment to the Jewish way of life—Halakhah—can be maintained by one who recognizes that there exists a path to God independent of the Jewish tradition. Maimonides was a witness to the fact that intense love for a particular way of life need not entail intellectual and spiritual indifference to that which is beyond one's own tradition.[73]

NOTES

The following abbreviations have been used for works and journals which are cited frequently in these notes:
C.M.—*Commentary to the Mishnah*
Guide—*The Guide of the Perplexed*
HTR—*Harvard Theological Review*
HUCA—*Hebrew Union College Annual*
JQR—*Jewish Quarterly Review*
M.T.—*Mishneh Torah*
PAAJR—*Proceedings of the American Academy for Jewish Research*
REJ—*Revue des Études Juives*
T.B.—*Talmud Bavli*

INTRODUCTION
Multiple Responses to the Conflict of Philosophy and Halakhah

1. The description of Jewish experience presented in the introduction is well-known and does not require detailed documentation. For an understanding of the possible conflict between Athens and Jerusalem the description is correct and adequate, although much that is written regarding specific details is subject to important qualifications. For an excellent exposition of rabbinic thought, see E. E. Urbach, *The Sages: Their Concepts and Beliefs* [Hebrew] (Jerusalem: The Magnes Press, 1969). I am greatly indebted to this work for an understanding of the different approaches to God and

Torah which Maimonides may have discovered in rabbinic thought.

2. See W. Jaeger, "The Philosophical Ideal of Life," *Aristotle: Fundamentals of the History of His Development* (London: Oxford University Press, 1948), pp. 426–61; L. Strauss, *Persecution and the Art of Writing* (Glencoe, Illinois: The Free Press, 1952), pp. 1–21 (hereafter cited as *Persecution*).

3. I. Husik, "The Philosophy of Maimonides," *Maimonides Octocentennial Series*, 4 (New York: Maimonides Octocentennial Committee, 1935), p. 4.

4. Ibid., pp. 19–20.

5. Husik, *A History of Medieval Jewish Philosophy* (New York: Meridian Books and Philadelphia: The Jewish Publication Society of America, 1958), p. 300.

6. H. A. Wolfson, "Maimonides and Halevi," *JQR*, II, 3 (January 1912), pp. 314–15. Wolfson's work on Philo suggests that he modified his earlier position on Maimonides. See *The Jewish Expression*, J. Goldin, ed. (New York: Bantam Books, 1970), p. xxiii.

7. Strauss, *Persecution*, pp. 38–94; "Notes on Maimonides' Book of Knowledge," *Studies in Mysticism and Religion Presented to Gershom G. Scholem* (Jerusalem: The Magnes Press, 1967), p. 279 (hereafter cited as "Notes").

8. Strauss, *Persecution*, pp. 19–21.

9. Ibid., pp. 22–37.

10. Ibid., p. 36.

11. Ibid., pp. 81–87; "Notes," pp. 280–83. See also *Persecution*, pp. 95–141, where Strauss writes:

> It is hardly necessary to add that it is precisely this view of the non-categoric character of the rules of social conduct which permits the philosopher to hold that a man who has become a philosopher, may adhere in his deeds and speeches to a religion to which he does not adhere in his thoughts; it is this view, I say, which is underlying the exotericism of the philosophers (p. 139).

This statement should be remembered when evaluating Strauss' understanding of morality and practical beliefs in Maimonidean thought; cf. *Persecution*, p. 43.

12. See "Quelques Remarques sur la Science Politique de Maimonides et de Farabi," *REJ*, 100 (1936), pp. 14, 34 regarding myth of individual providence; "Farabi's *Plato*," *Louis Ginzberg Jubilee Volume* (New York: PAAJR, 1945), pp. 357–93; "Maimonides' Statement on Political Science,"

What Is Political Philosophy and Other Studies (New York: The Free Press of Glencoe, 1959), pp. 155–69. For an understanding of the continuity of Platonism in the Arabic tradition, see R. Klibansky, *The Continuity of the Platonic Tradition During the Middle Ages* (London: Warburg Institute, 1939), pp. 14–18.

13. Strauss, *Persecution*, p. 18.

14. Ibid., p. 35; see pp. 60–78, 84 for an explanation of the difference between "my speech" and "our opinion," "How To Begin To Study *The Guide of the Perplexed,*" *The Guide of the Perplexed*, S. Pines, trans. (Chicago and London: Chicago University Press, 1963), pp. xvii-xxv (hereafter cited as "How To Study *The Guide*").

15. Strauss, *Persecution*, pp. 7–8, 32–37.

16. See Strauss, "Jerusalem and Athens," *The City College Papers*, no. 6; Husik, "Hellenism and Judaism," *Philosophical Essays*, M. C. Nahm and L. Strauss, eds. (Oxford: Blackwell, 1952), pp. 3–14.

17. Strauss, *Persecution*, pp. 19, 40–43. See also "How To Study *The Guide,*" p. civ.

18. It is difficult to grasp what Strauss is suggesting in the statement: "Maimonides' link with the Torah is, to begin with, an iron bond; it gradually becomes a fine thread. But however far what one may call his intellectualization may go, it always remains the intellectualization of the Torah" ("How To Study *The Guide,*" p. xliv). See Strauss, *Persecution*, p. 84, regarding Maimonides' subordination to the tradition.

19. See "Farabi's *Plato,*" pp. 370–71, 375, 381, 386.

ONE
Philosophy in Maimonides' Legal Works

1. *The Guide of the Perplexed*, S. Pines, trans. (Chicago and London: Chicago University Press, 1963), pp. 3–6, 16 (hereafter cited as *Guide*).

2. Introduction to *Commentary to the Mishnah*, J. Kafih, trans. (Jerusalem: Mossad Harav Kook, 1963), p. 48 (hereafter cited as *C.M.*); *The Book of Knowledge: Mishneh Torah*, M. Hyamson, trans. (Jerusalem: Boys' Town, 1965), p. 46 (hereafter cited as *M.T.*); *Treatise on Resurrection*, J. Finkel, ed. (New York: *PAAJR*, 1939), IV, p. 4.

3. Husik, "The Philosophy of Maimonides," p. 4; Strauss, *Persecution*, pp. 86, 94.

4. For a contemporary attempt at discovering a unity between philosophy and law in Maimonides' thought, see I. Twersky, "Some Non-Halakhic Aspects of the *Mishneh Torah,"Jewish Medieval and Renaissance Studies*, A. Altmann, ed. (Cambridge, Mass.: Harvard University Press, 1967), pp. 95–118.

5. S. Lieberman, *Hilkhoth ha-Yerushalmi (The Laws of the Palestinian Talmud of Rabbi Moses Ben Maimon)* (New York: The Jewish Theological Seminary of America, 1947), pp. 6–13; Kafih, introduction to his translation of the *Commentary to the Mishnah, Seder Zera'im.*

6. *C.M.*, pp. 34–35.

7. Ibid., p. 35, translation by E. Yagod and E. Kohlberg.

8. Strauss does not give sufficient weight to Maimonides' evaluation of Aggadah within the Jewish tradition. See *Persecution*, pp. 19–21. For a contemporary discussion of the relationship between Halakhah and Aggadah, see A. J. Heschel, *God in Search of Man* (New York: Farrar, Straus and Cudahy, 1955), pp. 320–48.

9. *C.M.*, *Hagigah*, II, 1.

10. Ibid.; Introduction to *C.M.*, pp. 37–39; *Guide*, I, 34, p. 75.

11. T.B. Yoma 67b, Sifra, Aharei Mot, 13, 10; cf. Urbach, *The Sages*, p. 283.

12. Introduction to *Helek*, J. Abelson, trans. *JQR* (October 1906), pp. 34–35. See S. Rawidowicz, "On Interpretation," *PAAJR*, XXVI (1957), pp. 83–126.

13. All translations from "Book of Knowledge" and "Book of Adoration" of the *Mishneh Torah* are based on Hyamson (Jerusalem: Boys' Town Publishers, 1965).

14. See *Guide*, III, 43, p. 573, for three ways of understanding Midrash. Regarding those who claim that midrashic explanations of the Bible reflect the true meaning of the text, Maimonides writes, "The first class strives and fights with a view to proving, as they deem, the correctness of the midrashim and to defending them, and think that this is the true meaning of the [biblical] text and that the midrashim have the same status as the traditional legal decisions."

15. For a similar use of this text see Bahya ibn Pakuda, *Duties of the Heart*, by Hyamson, trans. (Jerusalem: Boys' Town Publishers, 1962), I, 3, p. 67.

16. See below, Chapter Four.

17. *Helek*, p. 35.

18. Ibid., pp. 35–36.

19. E. Schweid, *Iyyunim be-Shmoneh Perakim le-Rambam* (Jerusalem: Offset Ha'amanim, 1969), p. 112.

20. *Helek*, p. 36.
21. See Saadia Gaon, *The Book of Beliefs and Opinions*, VII, 2; L. Ginzberg, "Allegorical Interpretation of Scripture," *On Jewish Law and Lore* (New York: Meridian Books and Philadelphia: The Jewish Publication Society of America, 1962), pp. 127–50; Wolfson, *Philo*, vol. I (Cambridge, Mass.: Harvard University Press, 1968), pp. 115–38. For a discussion of Averroes' interpretation of Scripture, see introduction to *Averroes: On the Harmony of Religion and Philosophy*, introduction and notes by G. F. Hourani, trans. (London: Luzac and Co., 1967), pp. 22–28 (hereafter cited as *Harmony of Religion*).
22. *Helek*, p. 37.
23. Introduction to *C.M.*, pp. 35–37; cf. *Guide*, I, 34, and introduction to first part of *Guide*, pp. 10–14; for a discussion of this tradition in Greek philosophy, see Wolfson, *Philo*, vol. I, pp. 24–25, and Averroes, *Harmony of Religion*, p. 106, n. 142. *Guide*, I, 17, shows that Maimonides was aware of this tradition.
24. See *Guide*, introduction to first part, p. 11.
25. See *Guide*, II, 40; III, 34, 45; "The democratization of the God-man confrontation was made possible by the centrality of the normative element in prophecy," J. B. Soloveitchik, "The Lonely Man of Faith," *Tradition*, VII, 2 (Summer 1965), p. 40; see C. J. Friedrich, *The Philosophy of Law in Historical Perspective* (Chicago: University of Chicago Press, 1963), p. 10 (hereafter cited as *Philosophy of Law*).
26. Introduction to *C.M.*, p. 36.
27. Husik, *A History of Medieval Jewish Philosophy*, p. 300.
28. Cf. Strauss, *Persecution*, pp. 20–21.
29. Introduction to *C.M.*, p. 39. It is interesting that Maimonides does not mention the patriarchs explicitly but says "Shem and Ever and those after them."
30. Ibid., pp. 39–42; see Aristotle, *Nicomachean Ethics*, I, 7; X, 7–8, W. F. R. Hardie, *Aristotle's Ethical Theory* (London: Oxford University Press, 1968).
31. See Halevi, *Book of Kuzari*, H. Hirschfeld, trans. (New York: Pardes Publishing House, 1946), II, 66, p. 109; Twersky, "Some Non-Halakhic Aspects of the *Mishneh Torah*," pp. 114–15; Wolfson, *Philo*, Vol. I, pp. 138–43, 160–63.
32. Introduction to *C.M.*, p. 42.
33. The need for Halakhah does not have to be justified to the reader of Maimonides' legal works. Since the commitment to Halakhah is not problematic, Maimonides is free to ex-

press the autonomous significance of philosophy. Compare the argument for the unchangeability of Torah in *M.T., Hilkhot Yesodei; ha-Torah*, IX, 1, and *Guide*, II, 39; cf. Strauss, *Spinoza's Critique of Religion* (New York: Schocken Books, 1965), pp. 156–60.

34. Cf. Strauss, *Persecution*, pp. 38–94.
35. *C.M., Berakhot*, p. 92.
36. *Guide*, Epistle Dedicatory, pp. 3–4.
37. Introduction to *C.M.*, p. 35. I am grateful to Prof. E. Schweid for this interpretation. According to Maimonides, knowledge of *Ma'aseh Bereshit* preceded *Ma'aseh Merkavah*. The request, therefore, of the sage who knew *Ma'aseh Merkavah* is an attempt to discover whether those whom he addressed were prepared to understand *Ma'aseh Merkavah*.
38. Introduction to *C.M.*, pp. 42–43.
39. *C.M.*, Avot, V, 6.
40. Introduction to *C.M.*, p. 43.
41. *M.T., Hilkhot Talmud Torah*, I, 12.
42. Deut. 29:9–15. See Soloveitchik, "The Lonely Man of Faith," pp. 33–40.
43. Introduction to *C.M.*, p. 43. The conception of the value of the non-intellectual masses in the introduction is quite shocking, even revolting. It appears that those unequipped with intellectual capacities are mere tools to serve the needs of the intellectually elite. It is no wonder, therefore, that Maimonides preferred the more human explanation of friendship to that which ascribes an economic value to the life of the *am-ha-arez*. Men say strange things when they attempt to justify the ways of God. See *Guide*, III, 17, for the Ash'ariyya and Mu'tazila approaches to divine providence. Maimonides in *Guide*, III, 13, rejects the approach expressed in his introduction to the *C.M.*
44. See *Guide*, I, 34, II, 36, for a discussion of the reasons for the rarity of intellectual excellence and prophecy.
45. The Maimonidean *hasid* who lives by Halakhah has no difficulty understanding and accepting that the way to God of pre-Mosaic man was not based on Halakhah. His knowledge of philosophy enables him to understand how individuals can build spiritual lives not grounded in Halakhah. See *M.T., Laws of the Sabbatical Year and the Jubilee*, XIII, 12–13.
46. Strauss, *Persecution*, p. 84.
47. See Twersky, "Some Non-Halakhic Aspects of the *Mishneh Torah*."
48. *M.T.*, Book I, *Yesodei ha-Torah*, I–IV.

49. Ibid., I, 5, 7. See *Guide*, I, 71, pp. 180–82, for an explanation of Maimonides' method. Compare E. Levinger, *Maimonides' Techniques of Codification* [Hebrew] (Jerusalem: The Magnes Press, 1965), p. 29.
50. *M.T., Yesodei ha-Torah* 1–6. See comments of Kafih and Heller upon the first commandment in their respective editions of the *Book of Commandments* whether the first commandment refers to knowledge or to belief. Compare S. Rawidowicz, "On Maimonides' Sefer ha-Madda," *Essays In Honour of J. H. Hertz* (London: St. Ann's Press, 1942), pp. 331–39.
51. See *Guide*, I, 61, 63. Compare Halevi, *Kuzari*, IV, 1–23; M. Buber, *Moses* (New York: Harper Torch Books, 1958), pp. 51–55 and "The Faith of Judaism," *Israel and the World* (New York: Schocken Books, 1948), p. 23; Strauss, "Jerusalem and Athens," pp. 15–16. Compare Spinoza, *A Theological-Political Treatise*, R. H. M. Elwes, trans. (New York: Dover Publications, 1951), XIII, pp. 176–81. See *Mekilta D'rabbi Ishmael*, H. S. Horovitz, ed. (Jerusalem: Bamberger and Wahrman, 1960) *Yitro*, V, p. 219; comment of Ramban to first commandment in *Book of Commandments*.

Ramban understands the first commandment as establishing the juridical authority of God. In the second commandment in the *Book of Commandments*, Maimonides understands "the acceptance of the kingdom of Heaven" not in a juridical sense, but as a declaration of belief in God's unity. The fundamental, logical difference between a juridical and an ontological understanding of the first commandment of the Decalogue is that the former implies a necessary connection between the meaning of the first and the rest of the commandments, whereas to Maimonides one could understand the meaning of "I am the Lord" independent of further legislation. For the spiritual implications of Maimonides' position see chapter four. Compare Rawidowicz, *Iyyunim be-Mahashevet Yisrael*, B.C.I. Ravid, ed. (Jerusalem: Rubin Mass, 1969), pp. 355–56.
52. Strauss, "Jerusalem and Athens," pp. 8–9.
53. *M.T., Yesodei ha-Torah*, IV, 12.
54. Ibid., IV, 8.
55. Ibid., IV, 8, 9; *Teshuvah*, VIII, 4–6; IX, 3.
56. See *Eight Chapters*, V, where love of God is identified with the single-minded pursuit of knowledge of God. In *Avot*, I, 3, Maimonides is not discussing how one acquires love but only how love and fear find expression in the observance of

the commandments. Similarly in *Hilkhot Lulav,* VIII, 15, he is describing the joy that a lover feels in the performance of the commandments. The only problematic text which appears to suggest that love of God need not be based solely on knowledge of nature is *Book of Commandments,* Positive Commandment III. By "contemplate His commandments," Maimonides may mean to refer to those commandments which teach true opinions. See *Guide,* III, 28; cf. *Kin'at Sofrim.* For a full discussion of Maimonides' understanding of love of God see G. Vajda, *L'amour de Dieu dans la Théologie Juive du Moyen Age* (Paris: Librairie Philosophique J. Vrin, 1957), pp. 118–45; E. Hoffmann, *Die Liebe zu Gott bei Moses ben Maimon* (Breslau: M and H Marcus, 1937).

57. *Guide,* I, 32.
58. *M.T., Yesodei ha-Torah,* IV, 13.
59. See *Kesef Mishneh* and *Avodat ha-Melekh* on *M.T., Hilkhot Yesodei ha-Torah,* IV, 13.
60. When Maimonides is focusing on his community's courage to withstand the abuse and scorn of the experience of exile, he interprets the Song of Songs in the traditional manner— as a parable which describes the relationship of the community of Israel with God. In the non-polemical works of the *Mishneh Torah* and *Guide,* he also understands the Song of Songs to describe the love of one who has acquired knowledge of God. See *Iggeret ha-Shmad,* IV; *Iggeret Teman,* I, II, IV; *M.T., Hilkhot Teshuvah,* VIII, 2; X, 5; *Guide,* III, 51, 54.

For a discussion on the various ways that the Song of Songs was understood in the tradition see Urbach, "The Homiletical Interpretations of the Sages and the Expositions of Origen on Canticles, and the Jewish-Christian Disputation," *Scripta Hierosolymitana (Studies in Aggadah and Folk Literature),* Vol. XXII (1971), pp. 247–75; Lieberman, "Mishnat Shir ha-Shirim," in G.G. Scholem, *Jewish Gnosticism, Merkavah Mysticism, and Talmudic Tradition* (New York: The Jewish Theological Seminary of America, 1960), pp. 118–26.

61. *M.T., Hilkhot Teshuvah,* 10. See Twersky, "Non-Halakhic Aspects of the Torah," p. 103; A. S. Halkin, "Ibn 'Aknin's Commentary on the Song of Songs," *Alexander Marx Jubilee Volume* (New York: The Jewish Theological Seminary of America 1950), pp. 389–424.
62. *M.T., Laws of the Sabbatical Year and the Jubilee,* XIII, 13. Spinoza, Hermann Cohen, and Leo Strauss never refer to this important statement by Maimonides. Their discussions

regarding Maimonides' attitude to the possibility of a spiritual way which is independent of belief in the Sinaitic revelation center around his statement in *The Book of Judges*, "Kings and Wars," VIII, 11. See Spinoza, *A Theologico-Political Treatise*, p. 80; the preface by Strauss to his *Spinoza's Critique of Religion*, p. 23 and p. 273, n. 58.

Maimonides' statement in "Kings and Wars" cannot be understood, I believe, if we ignore 1) the polemical problem of the conflict between Judaism, Christianity, and Islam regarding the eternally binding character of Sinai, and 2) the fact that Maimonides does not mention in "Kings and Wars" that the individual under discussion possesses knowledge of God. In "Kings and Wars" the question is whether there can be a category of *mitzvah* independent of Sinai. See "Kings and Wars," X, 9–10. For a discussion of the source and meaning of Maimonides' statement in "Kings and Wars," see S. S. Schwarzschild, "Do Noachites Have To Believe in Revelation?," *JQR*, LII, 4 (April 1962), pp. 297–365; M. Guttman, "Maimonide sur l'universalité de la morale religieuse," *REJ*, V, 89 (1935), pp. 34–45.

63. See *Hilkhot Teshuvah*, X, 4, 10, 11.
64. See J. Guttmann, *Philosophies of Judaism*, D. W. Silverman, trans. (New York: Anchor Books, 1966), p. 501, n. 125; see Averroes, *Harmony of Religion*, I, pp. 44–45, and compare with *M.T., Hilkhot Mikvot*, XI, 12.
65. *M.T., Hilkhot Avodah Zarah*, I.
66. *Guide*, I, 36.
67. *Guide*, II, 5, pp. 260–61; Deut. 4:19.
68. *Guide*, III, 31.
69. *M.T., Hilkhot Avodah Zarah*, I, 2.
70. Introduction to *C.M.*, p. 44.
71. See Strauss "How To Study *The Guide*," in the *Guide*, pp. xxii–xxiii, for an approach to Maimonides' treatment of idolatry. Strauss claims that to Maimonides, "the true ground of the rejection of 'forbidden worship' is the belief in creation out of nothing." Maimonides in no way suggests this. If this were his conviction, it would be difficult to understand his claim that Torah is compatible with Plato's cosmology (*Guide*, II, 25). If Strauss were correct this would be unintelligible. In the *Guide*, I, 36, Maimonides understands the prohibition against intermediary-worship in terms of the tendency of the multitude to forget the purpose of forms of worship. Mistaken forms of worship must be clearly distinguished from the idolatry which touches upon the denial of

the existence, unity, and non-corporeality of God. See Lieberman, *Hilkhot ha-Yerushalmi*, p. 21, n. 100; Pines, "The
Philosophic Sources of the *Guide of the Perplexed*," pp.
cxxiv, cxxv (hereafter cited as "The Philosophic Sources"); S.
Atlas, "Moses in the Philosophy of Maimonides, Spinoza, and
Solomon Maimon," *HUCA*, XXV (1954), pp. 369–400.
72. Introduction to *C.M.*, p. 6.
73. *M.T.*, *Avodah Zarah*, I, 2–3.
74. See L. Ginzberg, *The Legends of the Jews* (Philadelphia: The
Jewish Publication Society of America, 1968), p. 209, n. 13,
p. 210, n. 16; Urbach, *The Sages*, pp. 281–82, pp. 295–96,
where he distinguishes between earlier and later midrashic
approaches to Abraham. Urbach does not distinguish between knowledge of God and knowledge of the law in his
treatment of rabbinic material on Abraham. It is obvious
that Maimonides made this distinction.
75. See Twersky, *Rabad of Posquières* (Cambridge, Mass.: Harvard University Press, 1962), pp. 268–69, regarding the Rabad's comment on Maimonides. Twersky's interpretation of
the Rabad is unconvincing. The question is not whether or
not the Rabad was opposed to secular knowledge. The remark of the Rabad indicates a total insensitivity and indifference to the intellectual pathos that is present in Maimonides' description of Abraham. Maimonides and the Rabad
differ as to the significance of the way to God based upon
independent reason.
76. *Guide*, II, 15, p. 290.
77. See *Guide*, I, 63; II, 39; III, 29.
78. *M.T.*, *Avodah Zarah*, I, 3.
79. *Guide*, I, 36, p. 84.
80. Ibid.
81. *M.T.*, *Avodah Zarah*, I, 3; Rawidowicz appears to have overlooked Maimonides' description of Abraham's missionary activity in the *M.T.* See *Iyyunim*, pp. 357–58. [Emphasis our
own.]
82. T.B. Kiddushin 82a, Yoma 28b. See remarks of Urbach, *The
Sages*, regarding the problem of heteronomy and autonomy,
pp. 280–301. Compare Ha-Meiri, introduction to his *Commentary to Avot* (New York: Twersky Bros., 1944), pp. 22–
23. See *M.T.*, *Hilkhot Melakhim*, IX, 1, and the comment of
the *Lehem Mishneh*.
83. *C.M.*, *Hullin*, VII, 6, p. 212; see note by Albeck, p. 379 in
Seder Kodshim of *The Six Orders of the Mishnah* (Jerusalem: Mossad Bialik and Dvir Co., 1959). There can be two

approaches to Maimonides' insistence that the patriarchs did not have legislative prophecy. From the context of the *Guide*, II, 39, one could offer a polemical explanation. Our analysis ascribes a philosophical basis to this distinction. For Maimonides, the patriarchs symbolize a way to God not grounded in legislative Halakhah.

84. *M.T., Avodah Zarah*, I, 3.
85. Sifre Be-Ha'alotkha 67; T.B. Yoma 66b.
86. "You know from what I have said that opinions do not last unless they are accompanied by actions that strengthen them, make them generally known, and perpetuate them among the multitude," *Guide*, II, 31, p. 359. This statement should be remembered when reading Maimonides' description of the relationship of Moses to Abraham in III, 29, p. 517.
87. *M.T., Avodah Zarah*, XI, 15, p. 80a; cf. Strauss, "Notes," p. 280.
88. Compare Spinoza, *Tractatus*, IV, V, VII. See the illuminating study of Pines, "Spinoza's *Tractatus Theologico-Politicus*, Maimonides, and Kant," *Scripta Hierosolymitana*, XX (1968), pp. 3–54 (hereafter cited as "Spinoza, Maimonides, Kant").
89. *M.T.*, Book Two, *Laws of the Mezuzah*, VI, 13.
90. Bahya, in his introduction to *Duties of the Heart*, is fully aware of how the concern with legal matters of Halakhah can be divorced from concern with knowledge of God (p. 29). There is a built-in risk of this occurring, given the scope of Halakhah and its concern•with what normally would be considered legal and not religious questions. It is difficult to make sense of the category *mitzvot ein zerikhot kavvanah* within a system which relates normative obligation to God. See Maimonides *M.T., Hilkhot Keriat Shema*, II, 1; *Hilkhot Tefillah*, IV, 14–15; X, 1; and *Hiddushei R. Hayyim Halevi, Tefillah*, IV, 1; *Hilkhot Hametz u'Matzah*, VI, 2; *Hilkhot Shofar*, II, 4, with comments of *Maged Mishneh* and *Kesef Mishneh*. Contrast their approach with Levinger, *Maimonides' Techniques of Codification*, pp. 176–77. See the illuminating distinction of *Rabenu Yonah* in T.B. Berakhot 12a, and the statement of the Rashbah on Berakhot 13b. Their commentaries should be compared with the approach of the Ramban in *Milhemot ha-Shem, Rosh Hashanah 28a*. See Urbach, *The Sages*, pp. 344–45. See the approach of Twersky to the aggadic themes in the *M.T.*, in *A Maimonides Reader*, I. Twersky, ed. (New York: Behrman House,

1972), pp. 18–19, as well as his introductions to the various sections of the *M.T.*
91. *Guide*, I, 35–36; *M.T., Hilkhot Teshuvah*, III, 15.
92. See I. Heinemann, "Maimuni und die Arabischen Einheits-lehrer," *Monatsschrift für Geschichte und Wissenschaft des Judentums*, LXXIX (1935), 102–48, for the possible historical influences on Maimonides' thinking. One need not explain Maimonides' uncompromising approach in terms of the influence of the Almohads. It can stem from his refusal to allow halakhic piety to develop independently of God.

For an explanation of the approach of the Rabad see Twersky, *Rabad of Posquières*, pp. 282–86. For an analysis of the disagreement between the Rabad and Maimonides, see Wolfson, "The Jewish Kalam," *The Seventy-fifth Anniversary Volume of the J.Q.R.*, A. Neuman and S. Zeitlin, eds. (Philadelphia: *JQR*, 1967), pp. 544–73. Maimonides' statement in the *Guide*, I, 35, clearly shows that he refused to operate with double standards in his evaluation of idolatry. He could not reject Gentile paganism and accept halakhic behavior which was based upon a pagan conception of God.

Chapter two will show that Maimonides is tolerant regarding levels of worship, but not regarding a false concept of God—especially since he considers it to be far worse than a mistaken form of worship. One has difficulty understanding the tolerance of Baḥya, Albo, and the Rabad if they agree with Maimonides' notion of God's non-corporeality.

See Wolfson, "Maimonides on the Unity and Incorporeality of God," *JQR*, 56 (1965), pp. 112–36, for an interesting application of the legal categories of *din* and *lifnim mi-shurat ha-din* to belief. The objection may be raised that these categories apply only to actions and not to matters involving truth and falsity.

For the difference between the approaches of Averroes and Maimonides regarding tolerance of belief in corporeality see Pines, introduction to *Guide*, pp. cxviii-cxix and Guttmann, *Philosophies of Judaism*, p. 202. This difference should caution one from claiming that Maimonides, like Averroes, sought only a legal justification for philosophy. Arthur Hyman makes a similar point in refuting the approach that sees only a political significance to Maimonides' "Thirteen Principles." See "Maimonides' 'Thirteen Principles,'" *Jewish Medieval and Renaissance Studies*, (Cambride, Mass.: Harvard University Press, 1967), pp. 137–38; cf. Strauss, *Persecution*, pp. 19–20.

93. *Maimonides' Treatise on Resurrection*, p. 4. See n. 53 in *Iggerot by Moshe Ben Maimon*, Kafiḥ, trans. (Jerusalem: Mossad Harav Kook, 1972), p. 73.
94. Guttmann, *Philosophies of Judaism*, pp. 202–203. For a critique of Guttmann's understanding of Maimonides' formulation of dogmatic beliefs, see II, n. 31.
95. *Treatise on Resurrection*, p. 3.
96. *M.T., Hilkhot Talmud Torah*, I, 12, p. 58a. See Twersky, "Some Non-Halakhic Aspects of the *Mishneh Torah*," pp. 106–18.

TWO
Halakhic and Aggadic Categories and Their Relationship to Philosophic Spirituality

1. Strauss, "How To Study *The Guide*," p. xiv; *Spinoza's Critique of Religion*, pp. 163–64.
2. *Guide*, II, 2, p. 253.
3. See Guttmann, *Philosophies of Judaism*, pp. 16, 36–37, 201.
4. For a radically different understanding of *hasid*, see Scholem, *Major Trends in Jewish Mysticism* (New York: Schocken Books, 1941), p. 91.
5. See C. Perelman, *Justice* (New York: Random House, 1967), pp. 53–110.
6. T.B. Sanhedrin, XI, 90a.
7. Introduction to *Ḥelek*, pp. 29–30. See Averroes, *Harmony of Religion*, pp. 78–78.
8. Lev. 26; Deut. 11, 28.
9. Mishnah Ta'anit, I, 4–7; II, 1. See *M.T., Hilkhot Ta'anit*, I, 1–4; II, for relationship between fasting and repentance.
10. T.B. Bava Meẓia 30b.
11. The accusations that Maimonides did not believe in the resurrection of the dead are evidence of his failure to bring about a different religious orientation. Compare comment of the Rabad to *M.T., Hilkhot Teshuvah*, VIII, 2. One should read Maimonides' *Treatise on Resurrection* as a tragic and angry confession of failure. This treatise reflects the religious implications involved in the confrontation of reason with tradition. To understand the conflict between reason and revelation as pertaining solely to the legitimacy of different sources of knowledge, is to miss completely the spiritual implications of this conflict. See J. Finkel, "Maimonides' *Treatise on Resurrection*: A Comparative Study," in *Essays*

on *Maimonides*, S. W. Baron, ed. (New York: Columbia University Press, 1941), pp. 93–121. For historical studies on the Maimonidean controversy see D. J. Silver, *Maimonidean Criticism and the Maimonidean Controversy 1180–1240* (Leiden: E. J. Brill, 1965), and J. Sarachek, *Faith and Reason* (New York: Hermon Press, 1970).
12. Introduction to *Ḥelek*, pp. 31–32.
13. Because of Maimonides' love for brevity (see *Treatise on Resurrection*, pp. 25–26), we have treated with special seriousness the elaborate dramatic parallels found in the introductions to *Ḥelek* and to the *C.M.*
14. See D. Flusser, "A New Sensitivity in Judaism and the Christian Message," *HTR*, 61 (1968), pp. 107–27.
15. Introduction to *Ḥelek*, pp. 32–33; see Wolfson, *Philo*, vol. II, pp. 279–88, for a discussion of the approach of the rabbis and the Greek philosophers to providence; cf. Urbach, *The Sages*, for different rabbinic views on providence. Central to Urbach's approach is that the rabbis were not attempting to construct a consistent theoretical position, but were motivated by the practical need to inspire religious practice. See pp. 235, 253, and especially his interpretation of Ben Azzai, pp. 239–41 and pp. 389–92, for a discussion of the new understanding of suffering held by Rabbi Akiva. The variety of models for understanding the divine-human relationship in rabbinic thought is important for Maimonides, because this provides a traditional support for the possibility of a shift in theological models depending on one's level of spiritual growth.
16. Ibid., pp. 33–34. See *M.T.*, *Hilkhot Teshuvah*, X, 4. Note that although Maimonides insists that Abraham did not observe the Halakhah, he nevertheless uses Abraham as the model for observance of the commandments out of love. See Urbach, *The Sages*, pp. 348–70, for a discussion on the rabbinic treatment of *ahavah* and *yirah*.
17. See *M.T.*, *Hilkhot Teshuvah*, X, 1, 2.
18. Introduction to *Ḥelek*, p. 34. See Urbach, *The Sages*, pp. 240, 306, 343–47.
19. See *Guide*, I, 33, 34, for the reasons certain teachings are hidden from the masses. What we are suggesting is that it is from this perspective that one should understand the caution that one must take in communicating the idea of pure love of God. See *M.T.*, *Hilkhot Teshuvah*, X, 9. See Averroes, *Harmony of Religion*, in which different cognitive capacities of individuals serve as descriptions of different human types (pp. 50–71 and introduction by Hourani, pp. 32–37).

20. *The Commentary to Mishnah Avot*, translated into English by A. David (New York: Bloch Publishing, 1968), I, 3, p. 4.
21. T.B. Rosh Hashana 4a, Pesaḥim 8b, Bava Batra 10b. See Rashi and Tosafot on Pesaḥim 8b, and compare with Ha-Meiri. Maimonides would never accept Rashi's interpretation.
22. See T.B. Bava Batra 9b, 10.
23. See Strauss, *Persecution*, introduction, pp. 7–21.
24. *M.T.*, *Hilkhot Teshuvah*, 10.
25. Introduction to *Ḥelek*, pp. 37–38.
26. Compare Twersky, *A Maimonides Reader*, p. 401, for a different understanding of Maimonides' discussion of the three approaches to Aggadah.
27. See Y. Kaufmann, *The Religion of Israel*, translated into English by M. Greenberg (Chicago: University of Chicago Press, 1960), pp. 279–80.
28. *M.T.*, *Hilkhot Teshuvah*, VIII, 7, see *Kesef Mishneh* and *Leḥem Mishneh*.
29. Introduction to *Ḥelek*, pp. 39–40. See *M.T.*, *Hilkhot Teshuvah*, 4.
30. Ibid., p. 38. For a striking parallel to Maimonides' statement, see the position of the philosophers which Al-Ghazali discusses in *Incoherence of the Philosophers (Tahafut Al-Falasifah)*, translated into English by S. A. Kamali (Lahore: Pakistan Philosophical Congress, 1958), pp. 229–34.
31. *C.M.*, *Makkot*, III, 17, p. 247. Guttmann's understanding of Maimonides' reason for formulating the thirteen principles of faith is unconvincing; it would make immortality of the soul the function of a mechanical act. Maimonides' love for the community is more evident in his yearning for messianism; this would create the historical conditions in which the community would be able to realize their spiritual capacities. To Guttmann, Maimonides was concerned with providing everyone with passports to *olam ha-ba*. However, *olam ha-ba* is not simply a description of life after death but reflects a different orientation—love—to one's spiritual life. This could not be realized by mere assent to dogmatic principles. See Guttmann, *Philosophies of Judaism*, pp. 202–203. For a confirmation of our approach to Maimonides' treatment of *olam ha-ba*, see Abraham Maimonides [ben Ha-Rambam], *Milḥemot ha-Shem*, R. Margaliyot, ed. (Jerusalem: Mossad Harav Kook, 1953), p. 61.
32. See *Treatise on Resurrection*, 44, 46, pp. 31–32. Maimonides clearly shows the difference between a belief in resurrection which depends upon acceptance of divine miracles and a

belief in *olam ha-ba* which does not. This understanding of *olam ha-ba* is in harmony with what he writes in *Hilkhot Shemitah Ve-Yovel*, XIII, 13; cf. *Hilkhot Isurei Bi'ah*, XIV, 3–5, where the polemical context is evident.

33. It is interesting that anthropomorphism is attributed to the same class of people who worship God out of *yirah*. See *M.T., Hilkhot Teshuvah*, X, 1, 2, and *Guide*, I, 26, 34, 35, 46, 47.

34. *M.T., Hilkhot Yesodei ha-Torah*, IV, 12.

35. There are three approaches by which Maimonides enables one to understand the biblical blessings and curses: psychological, philosophical, and historical. The psychological approach focuses on the need to motivate observance of commandments by appealing to self-interest (*Guide*, III, 32, p. 528).

    The philosophic explanation views material well-being as a necessary condition for intellectual perfection, but material benefits are not concessions to human egocentricity. What will satisfy the material requirements for intellectual development will depend on whether one is considering the material needs of a singular individual or those of a total community (cf. *Hilkhot Melakhim*, XI, XII, with *Guide*, III, 12).

    In the *Guide*, III, 31, 37, and in the *Treatise on Resurrection*, pp. 31–33, Maimonides offers a historical understanding of the biblical period in order to explain the content of biblical descriptions of reward and punishment. In *Ḥelek*, Maimonides provides both a psychological and philosophical explanation of biblical and rabbinic promises of reward and punishment.

36. Introduction to *Ḥelek*, pp. 40–41. See *M.T., Hilkhot Teshuvah*, IX; cf. *Guide*, III, 27, where language of reward and punishment is not used.

37. *M.T.*, "Kings and Wars," *The Book of Judges*, translated from the Hebrew by A. M. Hershman (New Haven: Yale University Press, 1949), p. 242.

38. *Guide*, III, 29, 53.

39. *M.T., Hilkhot Avodah Zarah*, I, 3, p. 67a.

40. See Scholem, "Toward an Understanding of the Messianic Idea in Judaism," *The Messianic Idea in Judaism* (New York: Schocken Books, 1971), p. 25 (hereafter cited as *Messianic Idea*). Scholem recognizes that, in principle, those for whom the *Guide* was written do not require a messianic reality in order to realize the contemplative ideal of Maimonides.

41. *Republic*, VII, 514–21. See Chapter Four, n. 10.

42. See Soloveitchik, "The Lonely Man of Faith," p. 35n.
43. Although messianism is a traditional belief, it is senseless to separate this belief from Maimonides' philosophical view of Judaism. It is difficult to understand what Scholem means when he claims, "Messianism, in fact, is not a postulate of his philosophic thought" (*Messianic Idea*, p. 30). One must clearly distinguish between the belief in resurrection, which Maimonides received from the tradition and which has no essential connection with his philosophic understanding of Judaism, and his acceptance of the messianic idea. His philosophy regarding the relationship of the individual to community is supported by the messianic concept; cf. *Epistle to Yemen*, introduction and notes by A. S. Halkin, ed. (New York: *PAAJR*, 1952), p. xxviii.
44. See Strauss, "Persecution," p. 20; Ginzberg, *On Jewish Law and Lore*, p. 78; Husik, *Philosophic Essays*, p. 7; cf. Sifre 48, 49.
45. T.B. Shabbat 23a. *Book of Commandments*, Positive Commandment 174 and First Principle; *M.T., Hilkhot Mamrim*, I.
46. *M.T., Hilkhot De'ot*, III, 3, p. 50a. See Urbach, *The Sages*, pp. 298–301, for an analysis of the social and psychological conditions which allow for this comprehensive attitude to Halakhah.
47. Compare L. L. Fuller, *The Morality of Law* (New Haven and London: Yale University Press, 1964), where he attempts to establish the difference between the moralities of duty and of aspiration. This neat distinction is not always operative in Halakhah. How would one categorize "You shall be holy, for I, the Lord your God, am holy" (Lev. 19:2)? His distinction between biblical and Greek moralities breaks down when we consider that halakhic morality contains both duty and aspiration, see pp. 3–32. Fuller's distinction also is inadequate concerning Islamic law. See N.J. Coulson, *Conflicts and Tensions in Islamic Jurisprudence* (Chicago: University of Chicago Press, 1969), pp. 77–95 (hereafter cited as *Conflicts and Tensions*).
48. *The Eight Chapters of Maimonides on Ethics*, with introduction and annotations by J. I. Gorfinkle, ed. and trans. (New York: AMS Press, 1966), p. 68.
49. Ibid., pp. 72–73.
50. It is therefore a mistake to view talmudic Judaism purely as an organized, detailed system of norms which spiritually affords one absolute security. Although the Halakhah is an

all-encompassing legal system whose external authority confronts the believer, there still remains, within this system, ample room for the expression of one's spiritual subjectivity. See Urbach, *The Sages*, p. 294.

51. Introduction to *Helek*, p. 45.
52. See Urbach, *The Sages*, pp. 290–94, n. 55, p. 293; M. Silberg, *Principia Talmudica* [Hebrew] (Jerusalem: Mif'al ha-Shichpul, 1964), pp. 97–138. See T.B. Rosh Hashanah 17b and Berakhot 7a where these categories are applied to God.
53. "Laws of Robbery and Lost Property," *The Code of Maimonides*, Book Eleven, *The Book of Torts*, H. Klein, trans. (New Haven: Yale University Press, 1954), XI, 13, 17, pp. 130–31.
54. Ibid., 7, p. 129.
55. Ibid., "Murder and Preservation of Life," XIII, 1, 3, 4, p. 233.
56. *M.T., Hilkhot Yesodei ha-Torah*, V, 11. See Rawidowicz, *Iyyunim*, pp. 430–31, n. 18.
57. *M.T.*, Book Twelve, "Laws of Slaves," IX, 8, from *A Maimonides Reader*, p. 177. Compare *Hilkhot Melakhim*, X, 12, with *Hilkhot Avodah Zarah*, X, 6, 7, where legal formulations of Halakhah are in conflict with the ethics of imitation of God.
58. One should note the paradox within this law. On the one hand, it is God who is the source of the legislation that the non-Jewish slave may be treated harshly. Yet, God Himself is gracious to all creatures. How then is it that the legislative will of God does not give expression to the way He acts? It appears that legal responsibility cannot transcend the boundaries of mutual responsibility and, therefore, cannot contain legal obligations to individuals who do not feel responsible to the law; cf. Spinoza, *Tractatus*, III, IV. See *M.T., Hilkhot Milveh Ve-Loveh*, I, 2, and Ramban's distinction between the prohibitions against interest and robbery, in Deuteronomy 23:20. For an understanding of the relationship between man's socio-political condition and his moral judgments see *M.T., Hilkhot Matnot Aniyim*, X, 2.
59. *Guide*, III, 53, pp. 630–31.
60. Ibid., I, 72, p. 192; II, 12.
61. See Urbach, *The Sages*, p. 291.
62. *M.T., Hilkhot De'ot*, I, 5, p. 47b; *Eight Chapters*, IV, Commentary to Avot, V, 6, 9, 10, 13. See *M.T., Hilkhot Teshuvah*, VII, 3, where this approach is developed regarding the scope of *teshuvah*.
63. *Commentary to Avot*, IV, 4, pp. 65–66.
64. *M.T., Hilkhot De'ot*, II, 3, p. 48b.

65. *M.T., Hilkhot Talmud Torah*, VI, 12, p. 63b.
66. Ibid., VII, 12, p. 65a.
67. *Commentary to Avot*, IV, 4, p. 67; *M.T., Hilkhot De'ot*, II, 3.
68. There are two other *mitzvot*, treated in the *Book of Knowledge*, which bear directly upon this discussion: *kiddush ha-Shem* and *ḥillul ha-Shem*, and *talmud Torah*. If these two commandments are examined carefully, we discover Halakhah has both a communal and a singular meaning. These two commandments are observed differently depending on the individual's level of spiritual growth. Although Maimonides does not use the legal terminology of *din* and *lifnim mishurat ha-din*, *kiddush ha-Shem* and *ḥillul ha-Shem* and *talmud Torah* express the same spirit as these two categories.

When sanctification of God—*kiddush ha-Shem*—is applied to community, it refers to the halakhic obligation of martyrdom. Rather than violation, there are three commandments for which the Jew must choose death: idolatry, murder, and illicit sex relationships. Under specific conditions, such as times of forced conversion, even simple customs assume the same severity as these principles. The text used to support the demand for martyrdom is, "that I may be sanctified in the midst of the Israelite people" (Lev. 22: 32). If any individual fails to demonstrate such loyalty, he desecrates the name of God.

There is, however, another application of *kiddush* and *ḥillul ha-Shem*, which is neither related to martyrdom nor addressed to all the members of the community:

There are other things that are a profanation of the Name of God. When a man, great in the knowledge of the Torah and reputed for his piety, does things which cause people to talk about him, even if the acts are not express violations, he profanes the Name of God. As, for example, if such a person makes a purchase and does not pay promptly, provided that he has means and the creditors ask for payment and he puts them off; or if he indulges immoderately in jesting, eating, or drinking when he is staying with ignorant people or living among them; or if his mode of addressing people is not gentle, or he does not receive people affably, but is quarrelsome and irascible. The greater a man is, the more scrupulous should he be in all such things, and do more than the strict letter of the law requires. And if a man has been scrupulous in his conduct, gentle in his conversation, pleasant toward his fellow creatures, affable in manner when receiving them, not retorting even when affronted, but showing courtesy to all, even to those who treat him with disdain, conducting his commercial affairs with integrity, not readily accepting the hospitality of the ignorant nor frequenting their company, not seen at all times, but devoting himself to the study of the Torah, wrapped in *tallit* and crowned with phylacteries, and doing more than his duty in all things, avoiding, however, extremes and exaggerations—such a man has sanctified God, and concerning him, Scripture says, "And He said to me: 'You are My servant, O Israel, in whom I will be glorified' " (Is. 49:3). (*Hilkhot Yesodei ha-torah*, V, 11.)

The sanctification and profanation of God by the *hasid* is related to the way he conducts his everyday life. It shows itself not only in relationship to the observance or violation of specific halakhot, but also in neutral areas with which Halakhah does not deal. The text used to support this understanding of *kiddush* and *hillul ha-Shem* is, "You are My servant, O Israel, in whom I will be glorified." God is glorified not only by the actions of the community, but also by the life-patterns of singular individuals. Community does not exhaust the divine-human encounter.

It is worth observing that immediately after distinguishing between the way of community and the way of singular individuals in terms of the relationship of philosophic knowledge to halakhic knowledge (chapter four), Maimonides codifies a legal matter which contains the way of community and the way of the singular individual. This is not accidental. The key halakhic support Maimonides seeks so that Judaism can express a philosophic orientation, is that Halakhah allows for both this collective and singular spiritual way.

Scholem and Guttmann each point to the centrality of learning in the tradition as the possible traditional support for Maimonides' contemplative ideal. Although I agree with them, I suggest that here Maimonides also saw how the mitzvah of *talmud Torah* gives expression to the spiritual capacities of the community and of singular individuals. When Maimonides describes the *mitzvah* that is addressed to every individual in the community he writes:

Every Israelite is under an obligation to study Torah, whether he is poor or rich, in sound health or ailing, in the vigor of youth or very old and feeble. Even a man so poor that he is maintained by charity or goes begging from door to door, as also a man with a wife and children to support, are under an obligation to set aside a definite period during the day and at night for the study of the Torah, as it is said "But you shall meditate therein day and night" (Josh. 1:8). (*Hilkhot Talmud Torah*, I, 8.)

When he describes how this *mitzvah* is practiced by singular individuals, he writes:

He whose heart prompts him to fulfill this duty properly, and to be crowned with the crown of Torah, must not allow his mind to be diverted to other objects. He must not aim at acquiring Torah as well as riches and honor at the same time. "This is the way for the study of the Torah. A morsel of bread with salt thou must eat, and water by measure thou must drink; thou must sleep upon the ground and live a life of hardship, the while thou toilest in the Torah" (Avot 6:4). (*Hilkhot Talmud Torah,* III, 6.)

In chapter three of *Hilkhot Talmud Torah,* Maimonides lists all the virtues necessary for individuals who devote their lives to achieve the crown of Torah.

These two commandments show that to understand the tradition simply in terms of its prescribed minimal halakhic standards and to ignore how tradition gives expression to men of higher spiritual talents (whose lives are not solely directed by common legal obligations) is to misunderstand the spiritual life of Halakhah. The distinction that Maimonides establishes between *pardes*-knowledge (which was meant for unique men) and knowledge of the permitted and the forbidden (which was intended for the entire community) expresses a definite spirit of the way of Halakhah. See *Book of Commandments,* Positive Commandment 9, Negative Commandment 63, and *Iggeret Hashmad,* IV; cf, Strauss, "Notes" pp. 274, 278. See Guttmann, *Philosophies of Judaism,* p. 201; Scholem, *Messianic Idea,* p. 25; Urbach, *The Sages,* pp. 308–16.

69. The most important category Maimonides uses in the *Guide* to explain biblical anthropomorphic descriptions of God is the talmudic expression, "The Torah speaks in the language of man" (T.B. Yevamot 71a, Bava Mezia, 31b). See Bacher, *Ha-Rambam Parshan ha-Mikra,* translated into Hebrew by A. Z. Rabinowitz (Tel Aviv: Achdut, 1932), III, n. 2.

70. "As one is commanded to say that which will be obeyed, so is one commanded not to say that which will not be obeyed" (T.B., Yevamot 65b). This statement should be compared with the discussion in T.B. Arakkin 16b. See the attempt of the *Nemukei Yosef* to reconcile both. See Ha-Meiri, Bava Mezia 31a, T.B. Bezah 30a and the comment of the Ran; *M.T., Hilkhot De'ot,* VI, 7, 8 and comment of *Lehem Mishneh; M.T., Shvitat Asor,* I, 7.

71. "And so Moses' motto was: Let the Law cut through the mountain. Aaron, however, loved peace and pursued peace and made peace between man," T.B. Sanhedrin 6b. See Abot, I, 12; T.B. Yevamot 65b.

72. See discussion in T.B. Sanhedrin 6b.

73. See Urbach, *The Sages*, XI, XIII.

74. This perspective on the *Guide* is opposed to one which says that Maimonides wrote this work wholly as a response to the religiously perplexed person who was caught in the conflict between Judaism and philosophy. Maimonides was convinced that love of God and the way of the *ḥasid* can only result from a philosophic understanding of God. Therefore, it is fallacious to interpret the *Guide* as a response to a particular religious crisis within his time; the *Guide* is an integral part of Maimonidean religious philosophy. His total work must be understood within the mode of teachers of Torah who attempt to elevate the level of religious worship of members of their community from *yirah* to *ahavah*. Cf. Strauss, "How To Study *The Guide.*"

THREE
Reason and Traditional Authority within Halakhah and Philosophy

1. If Maimonides' attachment to Judaism is to be explained from a political perspective, one is puzzled by his unpopular legal decision that talmudic scholars are not to receive economic support from the community for their professional religious activities. Maimonides insists that love for God and the desire to imitate His ways must be the sole basis upon which Talmud scholars are to be motivated in their endeavors. This attitude is unintelligible from a political perspective. See *Commentary to Avot*, IV, 5; *M.T., Hilkhot Talmud Torah*, III, 9, 10, 11; *Tur, Yoreh Deah*, 246, and comment of *Bet Yosef*.

2. My use of the term "independent reason" in relation to authority must be understood in the Maimonidean context of a knowledge not based on the authority of revelation and tradition. I do not use the term in the contemporary sense of moral autonomy. The spiritual way of reason for Maimonides has nothing in common with the Kierkegaardean sense of truth as subjectivity nor does it have anything in common with the subjective experiential certainty of the mystic. To Maimonides, Abraham can make his belief in God intelligible and therefore communicate his spiritual way to others. See Kierkegaard, *Fear and Trembling and the Sickness unto Death*, W. Lowrie, trans. (New York: Doubleday-Anchor, 1954), and *Concluding Unscientific Postscript*, D. W. Swen-

son, trans. (Princeton: Princeton University Press, 1941), part 2, chap. 2; Scholem, *Major Trends in Jewish Mysticism,* pp. 1–39; *On the Kabbalah and Its Symbolism* (New York: Schocken Books, 1965), pp. 5–31; *Messianic Idea,* pp. 282–304; *M.T., Hilkhoth Avodah Zarah,* I; *Guide,* I, 63; II, 39; III, 29. For the *Akedah* in Maimonides, see *Guide,* III, 24.

3. P. Winch, "Authority," *Proceedings of the Aristotelian Society* (1958), p. 236; see C. J. Friedrich, *Philosophy of Law,* pp. 200–205.

4. See E. Fromm, *Psychoanalysis and Religion* (New Haven and London: Yale University Press, 1950), III, pp. 21–64; *Man for Himself* (New York: Rinehart and Co., 1947), pp. 14–20, 143–72; *You Shall Be as Gods* (New York: Holt, Rinehart & Winston, 1966), where Fromm applies the categories of the authoritarian and humanistic character types to an understanding of Judaism. For a critique of Fromm's application of these categories to Judaism, see W. Kaufmann, *Critique of Religion and Philosophy* (New York: Anchor Books, 1961), pp. 331–39.

5. See introduction to *C.M.,* p. 29.

6. This was the basic thrust of Spinoza's claim that the "Old Testament" and the total Jewish tradition had no relationship whatsoever with a spiritual life based on philosophic reason. Spinoza, who had no need to defend Judaism and felt no commitment to its continuous spiritual development, was able to polarize the spiritual types emerging from the revealed religion of Judaism and from philosophic speculation. Maimonides, a loyal and committed philosophic Jew, could not tolerate this polarization. See *Tractatus,* II-V, VII, XI-XVIII; Pines, "Spinoza, Maimonides, Kant," for the possible political motives behind Spinoza's distinction between Moses and Jesus; Strauss, "How to Study Spinoza's *Theological-Political Treatise,*" in *Persecution,* pp. 142–201; A. Hyman, "Spinoza's Dogmas of Universal Faith," in *Biblical and Other Studies,* A. Altmann, ed. (Cambridge, Mass.: Harvard University Press, 1963), pp. 183–95; Wolfson, *The Philosophy of Spinoza,* 2 vols. (New York: Meridian Books, 1958), vol. II, pp. 325–30.

7. For the logical status of different forms of argumentation, see Aristotle, *Topica,* I, 1, 100a; *Nicomachean Ethics,* VI; Averroes, *Harmony of Religion,* I, pp. 44–49, and n. 25, p. 85; Maimonides, *Treatise on Logic,* I. Efros, trans. (New York: PAAJR, 1938), VII, VIII, XIV; *Guide,* I, 31, 71; II, 15, 22.

8. See Urbach, "Halakhah u-Nevuah," *Tarbiẓ*, 18 (1946), pp. 1–27.
9. Introduction to *C.M.*, pp. 11–14; see Urbach, "Halakhah u-Nevuah," p. 5, regarding whether the prophetic power to suspend law temporarily has its basis in prophecy or in the legal authority of the prophet.
10. T.B., Sanhedrin 90a; *M.T., Hilkhot Yesodei ha-Torah*, VIII.
11. Introduction to *C.M.*, p. 60.
12. Although Maimonides shows, in the *Guide*, I, 36, that mistaken forms of worship are compatible with demonstrative truth, we can understand the "testimony to reason" to refer to the argument which Abraham used to convince his generation to abandon intermediary worship (*M.T., Hilkhot Avodah Zarah*, I, 3, and our explication in chapter one). One should appreciate the educational significance of Maimonides' statement that the certainty of reason is greater than the certainty of sight; this prepares the reader to interpret the Torah, based upon the certainty of sight (*Guide*, III, 24, and *M.T., Hilkhot Yesodei ha-Torah*, VIII) in harmony with the certainties of reason. Maimonides is leading his reader to value the claims of reason by showing him that reason sustains one's loyalty to the Torah.
13. This distinction, in Maimonides' first work, shows that Maimonides was training the reader of his legal works to recognize the difference between the logical status of beliefs based upon reason and beliefs based upon tradition. Saadia believed that one could appeal to the power of reason to reject attempts to abrogate the moral commandments of the Torah. See the *Book of Beliefs and Opinions*, III, 1, 2, 3, 8 and Maimonides, *Eight Chapters*, VI; *Treatise on Logic*, VIII, XIV; *Guide*, I, 2; III, 8. M. Fox, in his essay "Maimonides and Aquinas on Natural Law," *Dine Israel*, III (1972), p. xxi, overlooks that, for Saadia, one uses moral criteria independent of revelation to evaluate the claims of prophetic authority. According to Saadia, moral norms have a rational status distinct from certain ritual norms which are only utilitarian. Saadia justifies the need for revelation regarding moral norms by arguing that without revelation, there would be disagreement concerning the details and the application of moral norms. If Fox is correct, Saadia should have claimed that without revelation there is no rational ground for moral obligation.
14. See *M.T., Hilkhot Yesodei ha-Torah*, VIII; *Iggeret Teman*, pp. 53–57; Halevi, *Kuzari*, I, 87 and IV, 11; Saadia, *The Book*

of Beliefs and Opinions, III, 6; see Halkin's fine treatment on the polemical aspect of *Iggeret Teman*, pp. xiii–xxi.

15. "We have been given adequate Divine assurance that not only did all the persons who were present at the Sinaitic Revelation believe in the prophecy of Moses and in his Law, but that their descendants likewise would do so, until the end of time, as it is written, 'I will come to you in a thick cloud, in order that the people may hear when I speak with you and so trust you ever after' (Ex. 19:9). Consequently it is manifest that he who spurns the religion that was revealed at that theophany, is not an offspring of the folk who witnessed it." *Iggeret Teman*, B. Cohen, trans. p. vi.

16. *Guide*, III, 24, p. 500; *M.T., Hilkhot Yesodei ha-Torah*, VII, 1, 2.

17. Compare *M.T., Hilkhot Yesodei ha-Torah*, VIII, with *Guide*, II, 35, and *Treatise on Resurrection*, 45–46, pp. 31–32. Compare *M.T., Hilkhot Yesodei ha-Torah*, X, with Saadia, III, 4, concerning the authentication of the prophet by miracles. See Wolfson, "The Veracity of Scripture from Philo to Spinoza," *Religious Philosophy: A Group of Essays* (New York: Atheneum, 1965), pp. 217–45.

18. *M.T., Hilkhot Yesodei ha-Torah*, VII, 2.

19. This only applies to the political function of the prophet and not to prophecy which is related to individual perfection. See *M.T., Hilkhot Yesodei ha-Torah*, VII, 7; see Soloveitchik, "The Lonely Man of Faith," p. 37.

20. Introduction to *C.M.*, p. 4.

21. See *M.T., Hilkhot Yesodei ha-Torah*, IX, 4, and comment of *Kesef Mishneh*. See *M.T., Book of Knowledge*, S. Lieberman, ed. (Jerusalem: Mossad Harav Kook, 1964), p. 134, nn. 35–36.

22. Introduction to *C.M.*, p. 14.

23. Ibid., pp. 3, 4, 19–20. See Levinger, *Maimonides' Techniques of Codification*, chap. 2.

24. See Ibn Daud, *The Book of Tradition (Sefer ha-Qabbalah)*, critical edition with notes by G. D. Cohen, trans. (Philadelphia: The Jewish Publication Society of America, 1967), pp. lvii–lxii.

25. Cf. comments of Ramban on Second Principle in *Book of Commandments*; see Urbach, "Halakhah u-Nevuah," p. 21, n. 177. On the place of human reasoning and tradition in Islamic law, see Coulson, *Conflicts and Tensions*, pp. 4–7, 19–24, and *Islamic Surveys: A History of Islamic Law* (Edin-

burgh: Edinburgh University Press, 1964), pp. 36–73; J. Schacht, *An Introduction to Islamic Law* (London: Oxford University Press, 1964), pp. 43–48 (hereafter cited as *Islamic Law*). Because talmudic law contains both law based on tradition from Sinai and law derived from human reasoning, it is understandable why Maimonides placed *pardes*-knowledge within the framework of the study of Talmud. The cognitive disciplines contained in *pardes* can have the same religious status as legal knowledge not based on revelation. See *M.T., Hilkhot Talmud Torah*, I, 11, 12. For a similar justification of philosophic knowledge in Islam, see Averroes, *Harmony of Religion*, p. 46.

26. Introduction to *C.M.*, p. 4.
27. See Perelman, *Justice*, pp. 104–10; cf. *Hinukh, Mitzvah 78*, where he suggests that majority rule is not only a legal procedure for adjudication but is also a reliable method to arrive at the truth; see Ramban to Deuteronomy 17:11 where he claims that divine grace protects the courts from error.
28. See Mishnah Eduyyot, I, 5, and comment of *Tosafot Shantz* which confirms our analysis of halakhic disagreement. For a mystic understanding of halakhic disagreement see Scholem, "Revelation and Tradition as Religious Categories," *Messianic Idea*, pp. 297–303.
29. *M.T., Hilkhot Mamrim*, III, 4, p. 144; see T.B. Sanhedrin 88b, and Bava Meẓia 59b, where the reason for not forgiving one who rebels against the decision of the majority is "so that contention may not increase in Israel."
30. *M.T., Hilkhot Mamrim*, III, 6, p. 145; T.B. Sanhedrin 96b.
31. *C.M., Sanhedrin*, XI, 2, pp. 221–22; *M.T., Hilkhot Mamrim*, III, 1, p. 143.
32. Ibn Daud, *The Book of Tradition*, p. 3. See remarks by Cohen in introduction, p. lviii and n. 71; Saadia, *Beliefs and Opinions*, p. 13.
33. Ibid., p. 107, nn. 16, 17.
34. Introduction to *C.M.*, p. 20.
35. Ibid., pp. 20–21.
36. Ibid., p. 35.
37. *Guide*, I, 31, p. 66.
38. See Perelman, "What the Philosopher May Learn from the Study of Law," *Justice*, p. 105; H. L. A. Hart, *The Concept of Law* (London: Oxford University Press, 1961), p. 200; R. A. Wasserstrom, *The Judicial Decision* (Stanford: Stanford University Press, 1969), pp. 14–38.
39. Introduction to *C.M.*, p. 14.

40. See Urbach, "Halakhah u-Nevuah," pp. 20–22, and his comments on the approach of the Rabad; *Kuzari*, III, 39–41. For an explanation of the Aggadah in T.B. Bava Meẓia 59b, see *Sefer ha-Ḥinukh* (Jerusalem: Eshkol, 1961), Mitzvah 496, pp. 299–300; Joseph Albo, *Sefer ha-Ikkarim*, Husik, trans. (Philadelphia: The Jewish Publication Society of America, 1946), III, 23. According to both *Ḥinukh* and Albo, prophecy can decide a legal argument. Both appeal, therefore, to the political need for social order to explain why the rabbis disagreed with the legal opinion of Rabbi Eliezer. Maimonides, by insisting that legal argumentation is not subject to appeals to divine authority, is not forced to appeal to social order to defend the rabbis' decision.

41. Introduction to *C.M.*, pp. 12–13. For an insight into Maimonides' keen capacity for discrimination and selectivity, see his response to Islam in *Iggeret Teman*, pp. 15–19, *M.T.*, *Hilkhot Ma'akhalot Asurot*, XI, 7 and comment of *Kesef Mishneh; R. Moses ben Maimon: Responsa*, J. Blau, ed. (Jerusalem: Mekitze Nirdamin, 1957), vol. I, res. 149, pp. 284–85. Compare Wolfson, "Maimonides on the Unity and Incorporeality of God," *JQR*, 56, (1965), p. 132, n. 76, with *M.T.*, *Hilkhot Avodah Zarah*, IX, 4.

42. See Spinoza, *Tractatus*, V; Husik, "Hellenism and Judaism," pp. 3–14. Husik does not appreciate the legal and spiritual changes which have occurred in the Jewish tradition. He is insensitive to the fact that Jewish spiritual creativity is both rooted to the past yet excitingly innovative. Critical selectivity and change in emphasis characterize much of the legal and aggadic process of historical Judaism. It is a clear mistake to attribute such creativity to the influence of Hellenism. Husik's portrayal of the Jewish tradition as a mindless process in which the only concern was action and not critical reflection ignores the variety of approaches to Torah in the tradition. Husik does not understand that novelty in the Jewish tradition was respectfully expressed in traditional forms. For a better understanding of how novelty and innovation were expressed in traditional Judaism, see Scholem, *Messianic Idea*, pp. 282–303; *On the Kabbalah and Its Symbolism*, pp. 32–86; S. Rawidowicz, "On Interpretation."

Strauss' evaluation of Spinoza is correct: "Genuine fidelity to a tradition is not the same as literalist traditionalism and is in fact incompatible with it. It consists in preserving not simply the tradition but the continuity of the tradi-

tion . . . the loveless Spinoza sees only the ashes, not the flame, only the letter, not the spirit" (Preface to *Spinoza's Critique of Religion*, p. 24).
43. *Guide*, I, 71; III, 17, 21; *Treatise on Resurrection*, 42, pp. 29–30.
44. *Guide*, I, 71; III, 28.
45. Ibid., II, 16, pp. 293–94.
46. Ibid., II, 25, p. 328; see I, 28, p. 60.
47. Ibid., II, 33, p. 364.
48. Maimonides ascribed the last eight commandments of the Decalogue to the legal authority of the prophet. This does not prove, however, that Maimonides believed that without revelation there is no rational basis for moral obligation. One should not confuse the statement "moral norms are logically subject to prophetic authority" with the statement "without prophetic authority, there is no rational basis for moral obligation." Maimonides makes the first statement; Fox attributes the second to him. For an understanding of the educative function of prophetic authority concerning demonstrative truths, see *Guide*, I, 33, 34. In Maimonidean thought, it is incorrect to restrict the concept of rationality to the logic of demonstrative arguments. Abraham rationally convinced his generation to accept belief in creation even though, according to Maimonides, there is no demonstrative argument for creation. Cf. Strauss, "Notes" p. 279. Cf. Fox, "Maimonides and Aquinas on Natural Law," pp. xxi–xxii; Strauss, *Spinoza's Critique of Religion*, preface, pp. 23–24; "How To Study *The Guide*," pp. xxii–xxvii; B. Z. Bokser, "Morality and Religion in the Theology of Maimonides," *Essays on Jewish Life in Honor of Salo W. Baron* (New York: Columbia University Press, 1959), pp. 139–57.
   If it is correct to claim that Maimonides believed that there is no ground for moral obligation without appeals to divine authority, and given Maimonides' insistence that appeals to divine authority began only with Moses, how does one explain the moral life of pre-Mosaic man? See Chapter Five, n. 38; Wolfson, *Philo*, Vol. II, pp. 165–85, 303–15.
49. *M.T.*, *Hilkhot Mamrim*, II, 2. See comment of Rabad on *Hilkhot Mamrim*, II, 2; Ha-Meiri on T.B. Beẓah 5 regarding repeal of legislation when the original reason for the legislation is no longer applicable.
50. Ibid., II, 1; cf. Mishnah Eduyyot, I, 5, comment of Maimonides and n. 31 of Kafiḥ, and the explanation of the *Kesef Mishneh* to *Hilkhot Mamrim*, II, 1.

51. It is clear from the introduction to the *M.T.*, p. 4a, that Maimonides is aware of this distinction. He therefore introduces a new legal principle, i.e., "acceptance by the total community," to explain why post-talmudic legal courts may not disagree with talmudic legislation. Maimonides states that one may disagree with gaonic legislation because such legislation lacks universal acceptance by the community. Baron is mistaken in applying the Islamic legal principle of *Ijma* to explain Maimonides' position. "Acceptance by the total community" is different from *Ijma* ("my community will never agree upon an error"). Unlike *Ijma*, "acceptance by the total community" is not used to establish the truthfulness of traditions nor to reveal the divine intention. "Acceptance by the community" provides a new legal status to legislated laws of the courts in terms of the legal conditions required for repeal. See *M.T.*, *Hilkhot Mamrim*, II, 5–7, and the suggestive comment of *Kesef Mishneh* to 7, which supports our analysis. See Baron, *A Social and Religious History of the Jews*, 2nd ed., vol. VI (New York and London: Columbia University Press; Philadelphia: The Jewish Publication Society of America, 1958), p. 100. For an understanding of *Ijma* in Islam see Schacht, *Islamic Law*, p. 30; Coulson, *Conflicts and Tensions*, pp. 23–24, *Islamic Surveys*, pp. 59–60, 76–80.
52. *Guide*, II, 8, p. 267.
53. For the difference between the authority of biblical and talmudic Aggadah, see *Guide*, introduction to first part, pp. 9–10.
54. *Guide*, II, 11, p. 276.
55. See Pines, "The Philosophic Sources," pp. lviii–lix, for Maimonides' approach to the teachings of Aristotle.
56. *The Code of Maimonides*, Book III, *Treatise 8: Sanctification of the New Moon*, S. Gandz, trans. (New Haven: Yale University Press, 1956), XVIII, 25, p. 73.
57. Hourani makes the identical point with regard to Averroes' approach to Aristotle. ". . . Although his veneration for Aristotle is very great . . . it is not a veneration for authority as such, but only a respect for the sage as a medium of truth about the world" (*Harmony of Religion*, introduction, p. 25).
58. *Guide*, I, 71, pp. 175–76; see II, 11, p. 276. Maimonides' claim that an oral tradition existed in philosophy is not, in spirit, different from the claim of talmudic rabbis that the entire Oral Law goes back to Moses or that Abraham ob-

served all the *mitzvot*. See Urbach, *The Sages*, pp. 266–78, 295.

59. Foreword to *Eight Chapters*, pp. 35–36. For a discussion of the philosopher referred to in the foreword to the *Eight Chapters*, see H. Davidson, "Maimonides' *Shemonah Peraqim* and al-Farabi's *Fusul al-Madani,*" *PAAJR*, XXXI (1963), pp. 33–50. Averroes expresses the same conviction: "But if someone other than ourselves has already examined that subject, it is clear that we ought to seek help toward our goal from what has been said by such a predecessor on the subject, regardless of whether this other one shares our religion or not" (*Harmony of Religion*, pp. 46–47). See pp. 48–49, where Averroes argues that the ill effects of philosophy upon believers is not the fault of philosophy, but of the people studying philosophy. See *Guide*, I, 32, 33.

60. The argument in the *Guide* is similar to the argument in the introduction to *Ḥelek* in which Maimonides shows his reader that a symbolic understanding of Aggadah is a traditional mode of understanding.

61. See Spinoza, *Tractatus*, VII, XV. Spinoza fails to mention that Maimonides only appeals to the authority of tradition with questions which cannot be resolved by demonstrative argument. See *Guide*, I, 71, p. 180; II, 23, p. 322; Strauss, *Spinoza's Critique of Religion*, pp. 156–65.

62. Cf. Strauss, "How To Study *The Guide,*" p. xiv, where he denies that Maimonides is a philosopher because Maimonides accepts the Jewish belief in creation.

63. Maimonides' epistemology explains the legitimate function of appeals to authority, it is not meant to provide a justification for revelation. Cf. Strauss, *Spinoza's Critique*, pp. 156–58.

64. *Guide*, I, 31, p. 67.

65. Ibid., I, 71, p. 180; II, 23, p. 322, should be read together with Maimonides' concluding remarks in II, 25.

66. "Now it is certain that if there had been cogent demonstrations with regard to this question, Aristotle would not have needed to buttress his opinion by means of the fact that the physicists who preceded him had the same belief as he." *Guide*, II, 15, p. 290.

67. *Commentary to Mishnah Avot*, V, 7, p. 105; see Aristotle, *Nicomachean Ethics*, I, 3, 1094b.

68. T.B. Hagigah, 14b.

69. *Guide*, I, 32, pp. 68–69.

70. See Guttmann, *The Guide*, abr. ed., C. Rabin, trans. (London: East and West Library, 1952), p. 217, n. 50.

71. Ibid., II, 25, p. 329.
72. Ibid., p. 330.
73. See *Treatise on Resurrection,* pp. 29–30, for a defense of the belief in resurrection on the basis of certain epistemological distinctions.
74. *Letter on Astrology*, R. Lerner, trans., in *Medieval Political Philosophy*, R. Lerner and M. Mahdi, eds. (New York: Free Press of Glencoe, 1963), p. 228.
75. Ibid., pp. 234–35.
76. Ibid., p. 234.
77. Ibid., p. 229.
78. Ibid., p. 234.
79. Ibid.
80. *Guide*, I, 71, p. 180.
81. Ibid., I, 75, p. 226.
82. Ibid., I, 71, p. 180; cf. III, 51, p. 519.
83. For example, *M.T.*, *Hilkhot Yesodei ha-Torah*, I, 1; VII, 1; *Hilkhot Teshuvah*, V, 5; *Guide*, II, 23; *Treatise on Resurrection*, 36, pp. 24–25, 44, p. 31.

FOUR
The Philosophic Religious Sensibility

1. Pines, "The Philosophic Sources," pp. cxxxiii–cxxxiv.
2. *Guide*, I, 71, pp. 180–82.
3. See *M.T.*, *Hilkhot Shemitah ve-Yovel*, XIII, 13; "Letter to Ḥasdai Ha-Levi," *Collection of Responsa of Maimonides and His Letters*, reprint ed. (Israel: Gregg International, 1969), pp. 23–24.
4. Cf. Husik, "Jewish Philosophy," *Philosophical Essays*, p. 66, where he states: "The medieval Jewish philosophy is of historical interest only." See Atlas, "The Contemporary Relevance of the Philosophy of Maimonides," *CCAR Yearbook*, LXIV (1954), pp. 186–213; Diesendruck, "The Philosophy of Maimonides," *CCAR Yearbook*, XLV (1935), pp. 355–68. What makes a philosopher perenially significant is not that he addresses a "universal" audience without roots in a specific cultural tradition, but that he attempts to clarify problems which have implications beyond the philosopher's particular culture. That Maimonides is a traditional Jew addressing Jews does not imply that the problem with which he deals is a particularly Jewish problem. Just as one cannot properly understand Maimonides' thought separated from its specific socio-cultural milieu, so, too, one cannot fully

understand Plato's and Aristotle's political and ethical thought in isolation from a particular culture. See E. Barker, *Greek Political Theory* (London: Methuen, Ltd., 1964), p. 16; A. W. H. Adkins, *Merit and Responsibility* (London: Oxford University, Press, 1960), pp. 348–51; A. MacIntyre, *A Short History of Ethics* (New York: The Macmillan Co., 1966), pp. 1–15, 84–109; E. R. Dodds, *The Greeks and the Irrational* (Berkeley: University of California Press, 1964), pp. 207–24; cf. Strauss, "How To Study *The Guide*," p. xiv.

5. See *The Passover Haggadah*, arranged by M. Kasher, ed. (New York, 1956), pp. 68–70; Urbach, *The Sages*, pp. 21–24; and *M.T., Hilkhot Teshuvah*, III, 20, p. 85a.

6. *M.T., Hilkhot Teshuvah*, II, 8, p. 83a.

7. "I beg you to send a copy of this missive to every community in the cities and hamlets, in order to strengthen the people in their faith and to put them on their feet. Read it at public gatherings and in private, and you will thus become a public benefactor. . . . When I began writing this letter I had some misgivings about it, but they were overruled by my conviction that the public welfare takes precedence over one's personal safety." *Iggeret Teman*, p. xx. See *Iggeret Hashmad*, II.

8. Cf. Wolfson, "Maimonides and Halevi," pp. 314–15.

9. Pines, "The Philosophic Sources," p. cxxi. See Plato, *Theaetetus*, 176; Aristotle, *Nicomachean Ethics* X, 8; L. V. Berman, "The Political Interpretation of the Maxim: The Purpose of Philosophy Is the Imitation of God," *Studia Islamica*, XV (1962), pp. 53–63.

10. Plato's and Aristotle's positions with regard to the relationship of individual perfection and commitment to community are subject to much controversy. F. Rahman, in *Prophecy in Islam* (London: George Allen and Unwin, 1958), contrary to A. E. Taylor, writes: "The teaching that there is an inner compulsion in philosophy and wisdom to create a state is not Platonic but Aristotelian" (p. 88, n. 89). Jaeger, in *Aristotle*, pp. 426–40, adopts the opposite position. Jaeger maintains that Aristotle's later works introduce a separation between theoretical and practical virtue not present in Plato. According to Adkins there is no difference between Plato and Aristotle on this subject: ". . . but it must be emphasized that Aristotle has succeeded no better than Plato in demonstrating why a man capable of philosophizing should at any moment choose rather to perform any individual moral or political action" (*Merit and Responsibility*, p. 347).

See Adkins, pp. 290–93, 344–48; Ross, *Aristotle* (New York: Meridian Books, 1959), pp. 225–27, 231–32; Barker, *The Politics of Aristotle* (London: Oxford University Press, 1968), pp. xlvii–lii, for a discussion of Aristotle's statement in *Politics:*" [Man is thus intended by nature to be a part of a political whole, and] there is therefore an imminent impulse in all men toward an association of this . . . order" (*Politics* 1253a). See Pines, "The Philosophic Sources,"pp. lxxxvi–xcii, which supports Jaeger's position.

11. *M.T., Hilkhot Issurei Biah*, XIV, 1–5.
12. The unity of "Egypt" and "Sinai," which embraces 1) identification and concern with the political liberation of an oppressed group, and 2) the founding of a covenant-community, presents a dilemma to one who attempts to understand contemporary Jewish history. The "unity of Egypt and Sinai" does not exist today. Auschwitz, the contemporary symbol of "Egypt," serves as the fundamental impetus for Jewish unity. Since identification with the liberation from Egypt is also a fundamental spiritual memory in Judaism, it is impossible to decide whether this is a secular, political symbol or a deeply spiritual category. For works which illuminate contemporary Jewish thought and experience see E. Fackenheim, *God's Presence in History* (New York: New York University Press, 1970); N. Rotenstreich, *Tradition and Reality* (New York: Random House, 1972); *Jewish Philosophy in Modern Times* (New York: Holt, Rinehart and Winston, 1968); Schweid, *Israel at the Crossroads* (Philadelphia: The Jewish Publication Society of America, 1973), and *Le'umiut Yehudit* [Hebrew] (Jerusalem: S. Zack and Co., 1972).
13. See Pines, "The Philosophic Sources," pp. cvi–cvii, for the difference between Ibn Bajja and al-Farabi regarding the relationship of the philosopher to political activity; E. I. J. Rosenthal, *Studia Semitica*, vol. 2, *Islamic Themes* (London: Cambridge University Press, 1971), pp. 35–60, 93–115, for the place of politics in the philosophy of Ibn Bajja and al-Farabi.
14. Scholem, *Major Trends in Jewish Mysticism*, pp. 28–29.
15. Cf. Ibn Daud, *Emunah Ramah* (Jerusalem 1967), p. 4.
16. *M.T., Hilkhot De'ot*, I, 7; *Eight Chapters*, VI; introduction to *C.M.*, p. 42; *Guide*, III, 17, p. 470.
17. *Eight Chapters*, VI, pp. 75–76.
18. See Schweid, *Iyyunim be-Shmoneh Perakim le-Rambam*, chap. 6.

19. *Eight Chapters*, pp. 76–77. See *Book of Commandments*, Negative Commandments, 365, and *M.T.*, *Hilkhot Meilah*, VIII, 8, where Maimonides suggests the approach to the commandments he took in the *Guide*. Compare *C.M.*, *Berakhot*, V, 3 and *M.T.*, *Hilkhot Tefilah*, IX, 7, with *Guide*, III, 48, p. 600. For treatments of rabbinic sources, see A. Buchler, *Studies in Sin and Atonement in the Rabbinic Literature of the First Century* (New York: Ktav, 1967), pp. 36–37, 54–63; Urbach, *The Sages*, pp. 320–41; I. Heinemann, *Taame ha-Mitzvot be-Safrut Yisrael*, 2 vols. (Jerusalem: Jewish Agency, 1959), I, pp. 22–35.

20. *Treatise on Resurrection*, 42, p. 30.

21. Chapters 6, 7, and 8 of the *Eight Chapters* reflect this spirit. Cf. Spinoza, *Tractatus*, VI, p. 89.

22. *Treatise on Resurrection*, 32, p. 22.

23. See *Guide*, II, 47.

24. *C.M.*, *Avot*, II, 6, p. 34; cf. *Guide*, III, 17, p. 470; see *C.M.*, *Peah*, I, 1, pp. 94–95.

25. *M.T.*, *Hilkhot Teshuvah*, VI, 11, pp. 88b-89a. Cf. explanation of Ramban to Genesis 15:13. See *Guide*, II, 48, for Maimonides' interpretation of biblical statements which suggest a divine scheme in history independent of human choice.

26. Ibid., VI, 8, pp. 88b. Compare the analogy Maimonides uses in *Eight Chapters*, VIII, p. 95, to explain the loss of freedom with the withholding of prophecy from one who has met the natural requirements of prophecy, *Guide*, II, 32, p. 361. One can understand the gift of prophecy in the same way as one understands the "gift" of freedom. See *Hilkhot Teshuvah*, VI, 9, p. 88b. Maimonides' belief in creation enables him to translate human and natural events into categories involving the will of God. Belief in eternal necessity does not allow for this translation. See Strauss, "How To Study *The Guide*," pp. lii–liii.

27. *Hilkhot Teshuvah* VI, 10, p. 88b. One should pay careful attention to the way Maimonides understands the statement of the sages: "Whoever comes to purify himself receives aid" (T.B. Yomah 38b, Avodah Zarah 55a, Shabbat 104a, Menahot 29b).

28. Cf. S. Rawidowicz, "Knowledge of God: A Study in Maimonides' Philosophy of Religion," *Jewish Studies Issued in Honor of the Chief Rabbi J. L. Landau* (Tel Aviv, 1936), specifically pp. 103–108, for a different understanding of grace in Maimonidean thought. For support of our position, see introduction to *C.M.*, p. 36.

29. *Guide*, III, 12, p. 448.
30. *M.T.*, *Hilkhot Teshuvah*, VII, 5, pp. 89a–89b.
31. *Guide*, III, 36, pp. 539–40. See *Treatise on Resurrection*, 48, pp. 33–34; 51, p. 36. *M.T.*, *Hilkhot Ta'anit*, I, 1–3.
32. See Urbach, "Redemption and Repentance in Talmudic Judaism," in *Types of Redemption*, R. J. Z. Werblowsky and C. J. Bleeker, eds. (Leiden: E. J. Brill, 1970), pp. 190–206, and *The Sages*, pp. 585–623; A. H. Silver, *A History of Messianic Speculation in Israel* (Boston: Beacon Press, 1959), pp. 3–30.
33. Our explanation of Maimonides' theory of messianism runs counter to certain aspects of Scholem's understanding of Maimonides. We agree completely with Scholem's claim that Maimonides rejects the approach of the apocalyptists; we disagree with him when he writes: "But Maimonides nowhere recognizes a causal relationship between the coming of the Messiah and human conduct. It is not Israel's repentance which brings about the redemption; rather, because the eruption of redemption is to occur by divine decree, at the last moment there also erupts a movement of repentance in Israel itself" (*Messianic Idea*, p. 31).
   Our difficulty with this statement is that it is contrary to Maimonides' attempt to understand divine action within natural categories. This separation of the divine and the human is not healed by claiming that suddenly—at the moment of redemption—Israel miraculously decides to repent. Our thinking unites the spiritual aspiration of messianism with Maimonides' aversion to separating divine action from the intelligible processes of nature and history. Maimonides would be guilty of a serious inconsistency if his theory of messianism were based on an understanding of the divine-human relationship that differs from his philosophic approach to Jewish spirituality. See Halkin, *Iggeret Teman*, part four of introduction, pp. 12–13.
34. *Guide*, III, pp. 440–41. See *Guide*, II, 36, p. 373, for Maimonides' explanation of the absence of prophecy in exile and its return in the messianic era. Compare this with Halevi, *Kuzari*, II, 14.
35. The description of the Messiah in *M.T.* concerning the performance of miracles is different from the description of the Messiah in *Iggeret Teman*. See Scholem, *Messianic Idea*, p. 342, n. 25, and Halkin, *Iggeret Teman*, p. xxviii and n. 278, for an explanation of this difference; Pines, "Histabrut ha-Tekumah mi-Ḥadash shel Medina Yehudit lefi Yoseph ibn Kaspi u-lefi Spinoza," *Riv'on Philosophe*, 14 (1964), pp. 301–

309, and p. 303, n. 16, for a similar understanding of the *Iggeret Teman*.

Pines rightly claims that Maimonides is silent about the transition from *galut* to messianism. However it is consistent with Maimonides' overall approach to claim that were he alive after this transition, he would attempt to understand it without appealing to miracles. Messianism, as distinct from resurrection, is organically related to Maimonides' philosophy of Judaism. Resurrection is a miracle which Maimonides accepted simply because the tradition demanded this of him. He did not attempt to explain its significance. His extended treatment of the significance of messianism in his legal writings suggests that messianism (as distinct from resurrection) indeed is essentially related to his philosophy of Judaism. See chap. 2, n. 43.

36. *M.T., Hilkhot Teshuvah*, IX, 9, p. 92a. See *Hilkhot Melakhim*, XI, 4.

37. Cf. Commentary of Ramban to Deuteronomy 30:6, for a completely different approach to grace and the messianic age. See Scholem, "Toward an Understanding of the Messianic Idea in Judaism," in *Messianic Idea*, for a careful analysis of the differences between utopian and restorative elements in Jewish conceptions of messianism. For an analysis of activist and quietist approaches to messianism see G.D. Cohen, "Messianic Postures of Ashkenazim and Sephardim," *The Leo Baeck Memorial Lecture* (New York: Leo Baeck Institute, 1967).

38. See *M.T., Hilkhot Melakhim*, XI, 3; W. D. Davies, *Torah in the Messianic Age and/or the Age to Come* (Philadelphia: Society of Biblical Literature, 1952); Scholem, "The Crises of Tradition in Jewish Mysticism," *Messianic Idea*, pp. 49–77; "The Meaning of the Torah in Jewish Mysticism," *On the Kabbalah and Its Symbolism*, pp. 32–86; Urbach, *The Sages*, pp. 261–78.

39. See non-censored version of *Hilkhot Melakhim*, XI, 4, in Mossad Harav Kook edition. Maimonides' description of Christianity and Islam as preparing the world for the messianic triumph of Judaism is in harmony with his philosophical approach to miracles. Without Christianity and Islam, the messianic hope would have to be based upon a belief in a miraculous transformation of world history. See remarks and translation of uncensored edition by A. M. Hershman in *The Code of Maimonides*, Book Fourteen, *The Book of Judges*, pp. 22–24. See Halkin, *Iggeret Teman*, p. 14.

40. See *Iggeret Teman*, and *M.T. Hilkhot Issurei Biah* XIV, 1, 4, 5; *Kuzari*, I, 4, 112–15.
41. *Guide*, II, 48, pp. 409–10. See Pines, "Spinoza, Maimonides, Kant," pp. 6–8.
42. See *Guide*, III, 25, p. 504.
43. *Guide*, II, 12, p. 280.
44. See Spinoza, *Tractatus*, VI, pp. 81–82.
45. Cf. Strauss, "Notes," p. 273.
46. *Guide*, III, 25, p. 506.
47. The *Eight Chapters*, VIII, p. 90. See *M.T., Hilkhot Teshuvah*, V, 8, for an application of this approach to human freedom.
48. *Guide*, I, 71, p. 182.
49. One notices the difference between the spiritual outlooks of the Mutakallimun and of Maimonides when one examines the different ways they both attempt to establish a conception of the universe which makes possible a personal relationship with God. See Pines, "The Philosophic Sources," pp. cxxiv–cxxxi.
50. See Wolfson, *Philo*, Vol. I, pp. 347–59, p. 51, n. 24; J. Heller, "Maimonides' Theory of Miracles," *Between East and West*, A. Altmann, ed. (London: East and West Library, 1958), pp. 112–27. What Heller fails to recognize is that Maimonides is looking to the rabbinic sources to discover a spiritual sensibility rather than an articulate theory of miracles. Placing miracles within nature at the moment of creation illustrates the spiritual orientation of one who does not require belief in ongoing miracles to prove God's providential concern. As a philosophical answer to the problem of miracles, it is weak. As a guide for the development of a religious sensibility, it is philosophically significant. See *Guide*, II, 29, p. 345.
51. See *Treatise on Resurrection*, 42, pp. 29–30, in which Maimonides appeals to belief in creation to legitimize the belief in resurrection.
52. One of the reasons for Maimonides' attempt to orient the community toward the "reward" of *olam ha-ba* was that it provided a conception of reward and punishment not based on miracles. See *Treatise on Resurrection*, 46, p. 32; see Strauss, *Spinoza's Critique*, pp. 185–91, for the distinction between the interest in miracles and the logical possibility of miracles.
53. *Guide*, II, 6, pp. 263–64.
54. *Treatise on Resurrection*, 32, p. 22; 34, pp. 23–24.
55. *Guide*, Introduction, pp. 3–17.
56. Ibid., III, 32, pp. 525–26. See Pines, "The Philosophic

Sources," pp. lxxii–iv; *Midrash Va-Yikra Rabbah*, critical
edition with notes by M. Margulies (Jerusalem: Wahrmann
Books, 1972), part three, 22:8, and n. 5, p. 517.
57. For a somewhat similar description of the development of
religious forms in Islam, see H. A. R. Gibb, *Studies on the
Civilization of Islam* (Boston: Beacon Press, 1962), pp. 166–
87.
58. *Guide*, III, 32, pp. 529–30.
59. *M.T., Hilkhot Tefilah*, I, 1–3, and comment of Ramban to
Book of Commandments, Positive Commandments 5.
60. *M.T., Hilkhot Tefilah*, I, 6, p. 98b. See T.B. Berakhot 34a,
which supports our contention that the petitional element
is the core of the *Amidah*.
61. For the relationship between knowledge and adorational
prayer *(shevaḥ)* see *Guide*, I, 59, 64. For the relationship
between *teshuvah* and petitional prayer, see *Guide*, III, 36.
The verbal expressions of adoration for God, for Maimonides, have an educative-social function and are not intrinsic
to the act of adoration.
62. The following midrash illustrates how the Talmud provided
a new understanding of God for a defeated people in exile:

> . . . R. Joshua b. Levi said: Why were they called Men of the Great
> Synod? Because they restored the Crown of the Divine Attributes
> to its ancient completeness. [For] Moses had come and said: "The
> great, the mighty, and the awesome God" (Deut. 10:17). Then Jere-
> miah came and said: Aliens are destroying His Temple. Where then,
> are, His awful deeds? Hence he omitted [the attribute] the "awe-
> some" (Jer. 32:17 ff.). Daniel came and said: Aliens are enslaving his
> sons. Where are His mighty deeds? Hence he omitted the word
> "mighty" (Dan. 9:4 ff.). But they came and said: On the contrary!
> Therein lie His mighty deeds that He suppresses His wrath, that He
> extends long-suffering to the wicked. Therein lie His awesome pow-
> ers: for but for the fear of Him, how could one [single] nation persist
> among the [many] nations? But how could [the earlier] Rabbis abol-
> ish something established by Moses? R. Eleazar said: Since they
> knew that the Holy One, blessed be He, insists on truth, they would
> not ascribe false [things] to Him. (T.B. Yoma 69b.)

See Urbach, *The Sages*, pp. 384–96, for different rabbinic
attempts at theodicy.
63. See Soloveitchik, "The Lonely Man of Faith," pp. 35–36, n.
2.
64. Cf. Pines, "The Philosophic Sources," p. cii.
65. Guttmann, *Philosophies of Judaism*, p. 206.
66. See T.B. Yoma 69b; Sanhedrin 64a; Y. Kaufmann, *The Religion of Israel*, pp. 133–47.

67. In his exoteric work, *The Treatise on Resurrection,* Maimonides applies the same method to explain why the doctrine of the resurrection of the dead was only mentioned in the book of Daniel. This shows that he believed that the masses would not be upset to know that later Jewish history represents a higher stage of spiritual development than biblical history. See *Treatise on Resurrection,* 44–47, pp. 31–33; Strauss, "How To Study *The Guide,*" pp. xxxiii, xxxix–xliv; cf. *Eight Chapters,* IV, p. 68, for a different evaluation of the community at the time of Moses. Cf. T.B. Shabbat 112b, and comment of Rashi to Kohelet VII, 10.

68. *Guide,* III, 26, pp. 506–507.

69. Ibid., p. 507. See Wolfson, *Philo,* vol. II, p. 311.

70. *Guide,* III, 27, p. 510.

71. Ibid., p. 511.

72. Ibid., III, 28, pp. 513–14. We accept Hyman's understanding of this chapter. See "Spinoza's Dogmas of Universal Faith," pp. 188–90. See Dodds, *The Greeks and the Irrational,* p. 234, n. 85, for a similar approach to levels of religious insight in Plato.

73. *Guide,* III, 29, p. 515.

74. Ibid., p. 518.

75. Ibid., p. 521.

76. Ibid., pp. 521–22.

77. Ibid., III, 31, pp. 523–24. See Wolfson, *The Philosophy of the Church Fathers,* Vol. I, chapter 5, pp. 102–105, and "The Double-Faith Theory in Clement, Saadia, Averroes, and St. Thomas, and its Origin in Aristotle and the Stoics," *JQR,* XXXIII, 2 and 3 (October 1942-January 1943), p. 243.

78. Cf. Commentary of Shem Tov to *Guide,* III, 31.

79. Ibid., p. 524.

80. Ibid., III, 32, pp. 527–28.

81. Ibid., p. 529.

82. The following words of the daily evening service show how both the giving and the study of the Torah lend expression to the love-relationship between God and Israel:

Thou hast loved the house of Israel Thy people with everlasting love; Thou hast taught us Torah and precepts, laws and judgments. Therefore, Lord our God, when we lie down and when we rise up we will speak of Thy laws, and rejoice in the words of Thy Torah and in Thy precepts forevermore. Indeed, they are our life and the length of our days; we will meditate on them day and night. Mayest Thou never take away Thy love from us. Blessed art Thou, O Lord, who lovest Thy people Israel. (*Ma'ariv* service, *The Daily Prayer*

Book, P. Birnbaum, trans. [New York: Hebrew Publishing Co., 1949], p. 192.)

Although from a broader political and historical perspective one can justifiably claim that the faith of the halakhic Jew helped develop a passive orientation to his political destiny, one must also appreciate the mature and responsible activism that characterized his daily religious life. The model of God as a teacher of Torah sets into motion a religious life in which man feels adequate to unfolding his spiritual capacities through his own efforts.

83. See Maimonides' distinction between eternity *a parte post* and eternity *a parte ante, Guide*, II, 26–28; and comment of Hourani to Averroes, *Harmony of Religion*, p. 115, n. 192. Maimonides' belief in eternity *a parte post* has important implications for his theory of messianism. See his explanation of the duration of the messianic period in introduction to *Ḥelek*, p. 44.

84. Ibid., III, 34, p. 534.

85. Ibid., II, 39, p. 380; III, 32; 34; 49, pp. 605–606.

86. Cf. J. B. Agus, *The Evolution of Jewish Thought* (London and New York: Abelard-Schuman, 1959), p. 202.

87. *M.T., Hilkhot Melakhim*, XI, 1, p. 238.

88. *Guide*, III, 34, pp. 534–35. See E. S. Rosenthal, "For the Most Part," *P'raqim*, Vol. I, E.S., Rosenthal, ed. (Jerusalem: 1967–68), pp. 183–224.

89. See Pines, "The Philosophic Sources," pp. cxii–cxiii.

90. *Guide*, III, 41, pp. 562–63. See Levinger, "The Oral Law in Maimonides' Thought," *Tarbiẓ*, XXXVII, 3 (March 1968), pp. 282–93, for an explanation of this chapter in the light of *Guide*, II, 39; see commentary of Narboni to *Guide*, III, 34.

91. *M.T., Hilkhot Mamrim*, II, 2.

92. *Guide*, III, 29, p. 519.

93. *M.T., Hilkhot Melakhim*, XI, 1, 3.

94. See *Commentary to Avot*, II, 5.

95. *M.T., Hilkhot Teshuvah*, I, 1, p. 81b.

96. Ibid., II, 10, p. 83a.

97. *M.T., Hilkhot Teshuvah*, II, 5 (which suggests the emergence of a new human being) should be interpreted by that which Maimonides writes in *Hilkhot Teshuvah*, VII, 10. The new identity that is brought about by the act of *teshuvah* does not entail the loss of memory of previous sins. See VII, 6–9, for an understanding of what constitutes the new identity of the *ba'al teshuvah*.

98. T.B. Pesaḥim 116b. See *M.T., Hilkhot Ḥametz u-Matzah,* VII, 6.
99. *Guide,* III, 46, p. 589.
100. T.B. Pesaḥim 116a; *M.T., Hilkhot Ḥametz u-Matzah,* VII, 4.
101. This rationale for maintaining sacrifices should be understood within the genre of midrashic explanations which offer new interpretations for commandments which are accepted as unalterable divine imperatives. Other midrashic interpretations are possible. For example, one may suggest that sacrifices reenact the first stages of Israel's spiritual journey; that concomitant with the individual's heightened capacity for worship, the collective halakhic memory of sacrifices still finds expression. Such explanations, however, do not claim to reflect the original reasons for the commandments.
102. For an excellent study of Maimonides' *ta'amei ha-mitzvot,* see I. Heineman, *Ta'amei ha-Mitzvot be-Safrut Yisrael,* pp. 69–97.
103. *Guide,* III, 48, pp. 572–74. The rich symbolism which midrashic writers gave to the four species should be contrasted with the simple explanations in the *Guide.* See *Yalkut Shimoni* or *Va-Yikrah Rabbah* on Leviticus 23.
104. Ibid., III, 45, p. 578. See *Guide,* III, 47, pp. 596–97.
105. *Sifre on Deuteronomy,* L. Finkelstein, ed. (New York: The Jewish Theological Seminary of America, 1969), 33, 6, p. 59. See *M.T., Hilkhot Ḥagigah,* III, 6.
106. *Guide,* III, 41, p. 558. See Levinger, "The Oral Law in Maimonides' Thought."

FIVE
Morality and the Passionate Love for God

1. Strauss, "The Literary Character of the *Guide of the Perplexed,*" p. 92. For Strauss' understanding of the ascent-descent model in the *Guide,* see pp. 90–92.
2. See Guttman, *Philosophies of Judaism,* pp. 176, 199; Rawidowicz, "Knowledge of God," pp. 78–121 and "Philosophy as a Duty," *Moses Maimonides' VIII Centenary Volume,* Epstein, ed. (London, Soncino Press, 1935), p. 187. For the significance of knowledge in Islamic culture see F. Rosenthal, *Knowledge Triumphant* (Leiden: E. J. Brill, 1970).
3. *Guide,* III, 51, p. 619.
4. Ibid., p. 618.

5. See Rawidowicz, "Knowledge of God," p. 105. The mediated spirituality of Halakhah is balanced in Maimonidean thought by the immediacy of demonstrative knowledge. Demonstrative knowledge, as opposed to knowledge based upon authority, is the ground for immediacy with God. See *Guide*, I, 50; III, 51, p. 619. According to Maimonides, the leap of faith is not the ground for immediacy. Buber does not appreciate the lived moment of immediacy in Maimonidean thought which presupposes knowledge of God. See Buber, "The Faith of Judaism," *Israel and the World*, pp. 14, 22–23; Strauss, "How To Study *The Guide*," p. xxvii; Soloveitchik, "The Lonely Man of Faith," p. 32, n. 1, for an existentialist reading of Maimonides' conception of knowledge.

6. *Guide*, III, 51, p. 620.

7. Ibid., pp. 620–21.

8. *Guide*, III, 51, pp. 623, 628; III, 54, p. 636; *M.T.*, *Hilkhot Teshuvah*, X, 5.

9. *Guide*, III, 51, p. 620.

10. Ibid., p. 625.

11. It is interesting to observe that after the individual has acquired demonstrative knowledge of God's existence, he returns to nature with the intention of showing that the interconnections of phenomena point ultimately to God:

> There are those who set their thought to work after having attained perfection in the Divine science, turn wholly toward God, may He be cherished and held sublime, renounce what is other than He, and direct all the acts of their intellect toward an examination of the beings with a view to drawing from them proof with regard to Him, so as to know His governance of them in whatever way it is possible. These people are those who are present in the ruler's council. This is the rank of the Prophets. (*Guide*, III, 51, p. 620.)

This passage suggests that in the descent, the theoretical quest is not replaced by practical wisdom. Cf. Strauss, "Der Ort der Vorsehungslehre nach der Ansicht Maimunis," *Monatsschrift für Geschichte und Wissenschaft des Judentums*, LXXXI (1937), pp. 93–105; "The Literary Character of the *Guide*," pp. 89–94; and *Guide*, I, 10, 15. The religious philosopher's study of nature is unlike that of a pure research scientist in that the primary goal of this study is to understand how phenomena confirm God's existence and reveal His governance. Maimonides writes in the *Mishneh Torah*:

> All beings, except the Creator, from the highest angelic form to the tiniest insect that is in the interior of the earth, exist by the power

of God's essential existence. And as He has self-knowledge, and realizes His greatness, glory and truth, He knows all, and nought is hidden from Him. (*M.T., Hilkhot Yesodei ha-Torah*, II, 9, p. 36a.)

The religious philosopher imitates, as it were, divine knowledge when he perceives the world solely in relationship to God. For a discussion of the contradictory statements regarding divine knowledge in the *Guide*, see Pines, "The Philosophic Sources," pp. xcv–xcviii.

12. Guide III, 51, p. 627. For a discussion of the need for divine grace as a condition for man's ultimate perfection in Maimonides' thoughts, see S. Rawidowicz, "Knowledge of God," pp. 103–108. For an analysis of the notion of grace in Ibn Bajja see Altmann, "Ibn Bajja on Man's Ultimate Felicity," *Studies in Religious Philosophy and Mysticism* (Ithaca, N.Y.: Cornell University Press, 1969), pp. 88–93. See above, Chapter Four and nn. 26, 28 for the reasons we disagree with Rawidowicz. One can distinguish between the subjective *appropriation* of the constant, natural, divine overflow that one experiences at rare moments, and a conception of grace which implies a miraculous and unpredictable act of divine will. See Dodds, *Pagan and Christian in an Age of Anxiety* (New York: W.W. Norton, 1970), pp. 86–90, and *Guide*, II, 12, pp. 279–80.

It may be fruitful to explore the difference between apostolic prophecy and prophecy as a personal religious perfection through the necessity to appeal to the notion of divine will to explain prophecy. The prophet as messenger of God speaks on the basis of divine authority (divine will). In the prophet's quest for intellectual love of God, this appeal is unnecessary. Maimonides' distinction between Abraham and Moses may suggest such an approach. See *Guide*, I, 63; II, 39; *M.T., Hilkhot Yesodei ha-Torah*, VII, 1, 7; *Guide*, II, 37; Strauss, "Notes," p. 275; Pines, "The Philosophic Sources," pp. cv–vi, cxvi; Soloveitchik, "The Lonely Man of Faith," p. 37, n. 1.

13. Maimonides' description of the passionate love for God, at the end of the *Guide*, is similar to his description of this love at the end of the *Book of Knowledge:*

What is the love of God that is befitting? It is to love the Eternal with a great and exceeding love, so strong that one's soul shall be knit up with the love of God, and one should be continually enraptured by it, like a love-sick individual, whose mind is at no time free from his passion for a particular woman, the thought of her filling his heart at all times, when sitting down or rising up, when he is eating or drinking. Even more intense should be the love of God in the heart of those who love Him. And this love should continually possess them, even as He commanded us in the phrase, "with all your heart and with all your soul" (Deut. 6:5). This, Solomon expressed allegorically in the sentence, "for I am love-sick" (Song of Songs 2:5). The entire Song of Songs is indeed an allegory descriptive of this love. (*M.T., Hilkhot Teshuvah*, X, 5, p. 92b.)

14. *Guide*, III, 51, p. 621.
15. Ibid., p. 623. Night, here representing the time when one can legitimately devote oneself to contemplative love of God, was considered the most valuable time for the study of Torah. See *M.T., Hilkhot Talmud Torah*, III, 13. The study of Torah at night is recommended for those unique individuals who strive to acquire the crown of Torah. There is a striking similarity between the spiritual way Maimonides suggests in the *Guide*, III, 51, and the spiritual way he outlines for these individuals in chapter three of *Hilkhot Talmud Torah*.
16. See *Guide*, II, 36, p. 371; III, 12, p. 446; III, 27, p. 511; *M.T., Hilkhot De'ot*, III, 2; *Eight Chapters*, 5.
17. Ibid., III, 51, pp. 621–22.
18. Ibid., III, 27, 28.
19. Ibid., III, 51, pp. 622–23.
20. *M.T., Hilkhot Keriat Shema*, II, 1; *Hilkhot Tefillah*, X, 1. See *Hilkhot Tefillah* IV, 15, 16, and Soloveitchik, "The Lonely Man of Faith," p. 35, n. 2.
21. *Guide*, III, 44, p. 574.
22. See the beautiful discussion between Moses and the ministering angels in T.B. Shabbat 88b. Compare Aristotle, *Nicomachean Ethics*, X, 8, 1178b, which should be related both to this midrash and to Maimonides' discussion, in *Helek*, of the contemplative joy of the angels.
23. T.B. Sanhedrin 21b; see *Book of Commandments*, Negative Commandment 365, where Maimonides shows, from the example of Solomon, the danger of revealing the purposes of the commandments. A prerequisite for exposure to the deeper meanings of Torah is full respect for the perennial vulnerability of man. A person prone to self-deception would misunderstand the significance of theoretical knowledge.
24. See *Guide*, II, 36, p. 371; II, 23, p. 321.
25. Ibid., pp. 629–30.
26. Ibid., III, 51, pp. 623–24. See Scholem, "Devekut, or Communion with God," *Messianic Idea* p. 205, where he points to a strong similarity between Maimonides and Nahmanides

regarding the relationship of the contemplation of God and social action. See Heschel, "The Last Days of Maimonides," *The Insecurity of Freedom* (New York: Farrar, Straus and Giroux, 1966), pp. 285–98.

27. See *M.T., Hilkhot Yesodei ha-Torah*, VII, 6, for the difference between the sporadic prophetic moments of most prophets and Mosaic prophecy. Considering the natural explanation, in this chapter of the *Guide*, of the difference between most men and Moses, one can understand the differences between the other prophets and Moses, discussed in *Hilkhot Yesodei ha-Torah*, in terms of the capacity to sustain intellectual love amid political and human concerns. See Soloveitchik, "The Lonely Man of Faith," p. 52, n. 1. For a radically different approach to Maimonides' naturalism, see A. J. Reines, *Maimonides and Abrabanel on Prophecy* (Cincinnati: Hebrew Union College 1970) and "Maimonides' Concept of Mosaic Prophecy," *HUCA*, XL–XLI (1970), pp. 325–62. Reines' claim that Maimonides believed Moses had a demonstrative proof for creation is unconvincing. Reines does not appreciate the force of religious convictions which are not derived from demonstrative knowledge. See *Maimonides and Abrabanel on Prophecy*, pp. xix, n. 12, xxxv, n. 82.

28. *Guide*, III, 51, p. 624. Heschel claims that Maimonides yearned for prophetic illumination and that, in the end of the *Guide*, Maimonides attempted to lead his student to prophetic inspiration. Heschel's position is based on the assumption that Maimonides believed that the prophet has access to knowledge unavailable to discussive reasoning. We believe that the end of the *Guide* is not an attempt to lead the reader to new cognitive discoveries but, rather, to a higher form of worship. See Heschel's article, "Ha-he'emin ha-Rambam she-zekhah la-Nevuah?," *Louis Ginzberg Jubilee Volume* (New York: 1945), pp. 159–88. See Pines, "The Philosophic Sources," p. cxvi, for an understanding of the nature of prophetic knowledge and the meaning of Maimonides' parable of the Palace of the King which accords with our approach.

29. See *Guide*, III, 51, pp. 622–23.

30. See *Guide*, I, 1, and *M.T., Hilkhot Yesodei ha-Torah*, IV, 8, for Maimonides' understanding of "the image of God."

31. It is interesting that those mitzvot which train one in contemplative love of God, discussed at the end of the *Guide*, are precisely those commandments discussed in the *Book of Love* of the *Mishneh Torah*. The one exception is the inclu-

sion of the commandment of circumcision in the *Book of Love.* See introduction to *M.T.*, p. 18a, for Maimonides' explanation of this inclusion.
32. *Guide*, II, 36, p. 372. See comment of Shem Tov which supports our approach.
33. See Pines, "The Philosophic Sources" p. cvii, for the possible similarity between Maimonides and Ibn Bajja; L.V. Berman, *Ibn Bajja and Maimonides: A Chapter in the History of Political Philosophy*, Unpublished thesis (Jerusalem: The Hebrew University 1959).
34. *Guide*, II, 36, pp. 371–72.
35. See Plato, *Republic*, VII, 520e–521a, for an identical approach to the fitness of the philosopher for political leadership. For contrasting evaluations of Plato's approach to the philosopher's disdain for political power see K. R. Popper, *The Open Society and Its Enemies* (London: Routledge and Kegan Paul, 1966), vol. I, p. 155, and A. E. Taylor, *Plato: The Man and His Work* (New York: Meridian Books, 1956), pp. 282–85.
36. *Guide*, II, 36, pp. 372–73. See comments of Efodi and Abravanel on the effect of suffering on Moses' prophecy.
37. Ibid., II, 37. See the concluding comments of Shem Tov and Efodi.
38. Ibid., II, 40, pp. 383–84. Maimonides, counter to what Fox ascribes to him, does not claim that *nomos* (as distinct from Torah) lacks a legitimate ground for moral obligation. Maimonides only distinguishes between a law that aims solely at political well-being, and a law that leads man to spiritual perfection. If Fox is correct that Maimonides believed a moral system lacking the sanction of divine authority does not bind a rational man, it is difficult to understand how "a *nomos* society" could realize its own goal. Maimonides only claims that law exclusively concerned with social and political well-being is limited; he does not say it fails as a moral system. See Fox, "Maimonides and Aquinas on Natural Law," pp. xxii–vi. For an understanding of morality similar to that of Fox, see Strauss, "The Law of Reason in the *Kuzari,*" *Persecution*, especially pp. 134, 140. See Rosenthal, "Torah and 'Nomos' in Medieval Jewish Philosophy," *Studies in Rationalism, Judaism, and Universalism*, R. Loewe, ed. (London: Routledge and Kegan Paul, 1966), pp. 215–30, and "Maimonides' Conception of State and Society," *Moses Maimonides*, I. Epstein, ed., pp. 191–206; Wolfson, *Philo*, vol. II, pp. 374–95. For an understanding of prophecy in

Islam, which bears directly upon Maimonides' understanding of the ideal law, see F. Rahman, *Prophecy in Islam*, pp. 52–64. See Lerner and Mahdi *Medieval Political Philosophy*, introduction, pp. 1–20; M. Mahdi, *Ibn Khaldun's Philosophy of History* (Chicago: University of Chicago Press, 1964), pp. 63–132.

39. *Guide*, II, 37, p. 375. See al-Farabi, *Philosophy of Plato and Aristotle*, Mahdi, trans. (New York: The Free Press of Glencoe, 1962), pp. 43–50. It is not accidental that Maimonides describes the prophetic response to failure in order to illustrate the meaning of prophetic overflow. It is in the response to failure that one may grasp the difference between the Platonic and the prophetic commitment to community. The movement of detachment from community, which Jaeger and Strauss describe in their discussions of Socrates, Plato, and Aristotle, is different from a religious commitment to the biblical god of history. In the former, withdrawal may be a legitimate response to failure; in the latter, steadfast hope despite repeated failure and prolonged exile is the response.

Withdrawal into the private city of God can never be the option for one who organizes his individual spiritual life on the basis of the prophetic demand "And I will be sanctified in the midst of the children of Israel." The prophets' messianic vision sustained Maimonides' yearning for messianism in a way which would be difficult to understand if his prophetology is explained solely within the categories of Platonic political philosophy. Cf. Strauss, "Quelques Remarques," pp. 28–29. Maimonides' commitment to the Torah which relates God essentially to history enabled him to understand prophetic political leadership as the imitation of the God of nature. See Plato's seventh letter; W. Jaeger, "Plato and Dionysius: The Tragedy of Paideia," *Paideia: The Ideals of Greek Culture*, vol. III, trans. G. Highet (New York: Oxford University Press, 1969), pp. 197–212; Karl Lowith, *Meaning in History* (Chicago: University of Chicago Press, 1949), pp. 6, 204–17; Strauss, "Jerusalem and Athens," pp. 23–28. For a profound observation on messianism in the context of modern Jewish history, see Scholem, *Messianic Idea*, pp. 35–36.

40. *Guide*, III, 54, p. 635.
41. Ibid.
42. Ibid., p. 636.
43. Ibid., p. 637.

44. Rahman, in summarizing his discussion of prophecy in Islam, writes:

> The fundamental gap, as we pointed out while discussing Al-Ghazali and Ibn Taymiya, between the orthodox and the philosophical *Weltanschauung*, concerns the nature of man and therefore the nature of the divine message to the prophet. According to the philosophers the goal of man in which his ultimate bliss consists is the contemplation of reality; in their thoroughly intellectualistic-mystical attitude to life, life of religio-moral action is at best a ladder which is to be transcended. The orthodox impulse is activist; it does not reject intellectualism but subordinates it to the end of moral dynamism. (*Prophecy in Islam*, pp. 109–10.)

See *Prophecy in Islam*, p. 64, and Scholem, *Major Trends*, pp. 30, 35, for an explanation of why the community responded differently to the intellectual elitism of the philosophers than to that of the mystics. Scholem's analysis has important implications for the way personal spiritual aspirations develop within the context of community. See his discussion, pp. 25–28, on the differences between an allegorical and a symbolic explanation of Scripture. The risks that are involved in both philosophic and mystic approaches are clearly recognized by Scholem:

> I have said before that Jewish philosophy had to pay a high price for its escape from the pressing questions of real life. But Kabbalism, too, had to pay for its success. Philosophy came dangerously near to losing the living God; Kabbalism, which set out to preserve Him, to blaze a new and glorious trail to Him, encountered mythology on its way and was tempted to lose itself in its labyrinth. (*Major Trends*, pp. 36–37.)

One wonders whether the mystic understanding of mitzvot as cosmic symbols can find its place in the modern Jew's struggle to find his way back to his tradition. Perhaps Maimonides' sober understanding of Judaism is more in harmony with modern man's spiritual sensibilities than is the mystic's approach to Judaism. See E. Simon, "Law and Observance in Jewish Experience," *Tradition and Contemporary Experience*, A. Jospe, ed. (New York: Schocken Books, 1970), pp. 221–38.

45. Guttmann, *Philosophies of Judaism*, p. 200; see Guttman's introduction to *The Guide of the Perplexed*, pp. 34–35.
46. Guttmann, *Philosophies of Judaism*, p. 200.
47. See comment of Rabad to *M.T., Hilkhot Teshuvah*, VIII, 2. Rabad correctly perceived that Maimonides' analysis of *olam ha-ba* makes the doctrine of resurrection insignificant.

Why would one who longs for *olam ha-ba* (freedom from the limitations of the body) desire to return to corporeal existence? Compare *Kesef Mishnah*.

48. Compare H. Cohen, "Charakteristik der Ethik Maimunis," *Moses Ben Maimon*, W. Bacher, M. Brann, and D. Simonsen, eds. (Leipzig: G. Fock, 1908, 1914), pp. 63–134, for an analysis of the nature of knowledge of God in Maimonidean thought. See Pines, "The Philosophic Sources," pp. xcvi, cxv, for a different approach to *Guide*, I, 54. Pines' understanding of Maimonides appears to border on a fact-value distinction of moral descriptions of God's actions in nature. One may legitimately wonder whether this is an accurate description of how a religious man, like Maimonides, perceives nature. In *Guide*, I, 54, Maimonides corrects the false inference that moral descriptions of God entail ascribing change to God. He does not claim that moral descriptions are human projections which, in fact, are incorrect descriptions of reality.

49. Pines, "The Philosophic Sources," pp. cxxi–cxxii and "Spinoza, Maimonides, Kant," pp. 27–28. Maimonides' statements in *Guide*, I, 54, "Scripture has restricted itself to mentioning only those 'thirteen characteristics' although [Moses] apprehended 'all His goodness'—I mean to say all His actions . . ." and in *Guide*, III, 54, "But he says that one should glory in the apprehension of Myself *and* in the knowledge of My attributes," support Pines' understanding of Maimonides.

50. *Guide*, III, 54, pp. 635–36. Maimonides' statement in *Guide*, III, 27, "It is clear that to this ultimate perfection there do not belong either actions or moral qualities and it consists only of opinions toward which speculation has led and that investigation has rendered compulsory," should be understood in the same way we have analyzed his evaluation of morality in III, 54.

51. Ibid., p. 636.

52. Ibid., p. 638.

53. The end of the *Guide* is similar to I, 54. However, in the latter, Maimonides emphasizes the significance of imitation of God for the ruling prophet. In the end of the *Guide* the significance of imitation of God is related to the individual practice of the *ḥasid* who is not necessarily a political leader. Compare Pines, "The Philosophic Sources," pp. cxxi–cxxii.

54. See *Guide*, I, 54, 72; III, 12, 53.

55. See *Guide*, I, 2, for a description of how different states of cognition affect practical judgments. *Guide*, III, 8–14, shows how human choices are influenced by an understanding of the whole of being and of man's place within it. See Efodi

on *Guide*, I, 2. Efodi rightly recognized the connection between I, 2, and III, 12. The liberating influence of knowledge on Job (*Guide*, III, 23) was not due to his acquiring a philosophical answer to the problem of suffering. Job's new knowledge of being gave him a new perspective which enabled him to bear his suffering. Compare L. S. Kravitz, "Maimonides and Job: An Inquiry as to the Method of the Moreh," *HUCA*, XXXVIII (1967), pp. 149–58 and Husik, "The Philosophy of Maimonides," pp. 22–23.

There are numerous statements in the Talmud which indicate that moral conflicts are often resolved by insights whose content is not exhausted by moral rules. For example, see T.B. Berakhot 5a, regarding how one struggles with the evil impulse within oneself; Sotah 36b, regarding how Joseph overcame his desire to commit adultery; Avoth III, 1, and comment of Maimonides.

For a contemporary discussion of an ancient insight as to how man constructs a moral life, see R. W. Hepburn and I. Murdoch, "Symposium: Vision and Choice in Morality," *Aristotelian Society* sup. vol., XXX (1956), pp. 14–58, and I. Murdoch, *The Sovereignty of Good* (London: Routledge and Kegan Paul, 1970).

56. *Guide*, III, 52, p. 629.
57. Teachers in the Midrash tried to explain why the Torah does not begin with the normative revelation. See Yalkut Exodus 12 and Rashi on Genesis I, 1. For Philo's understanding of the relationship of creation to revelation, see Wolfson, *Philo*, II, pp. 209–10. See Abraham Maimonides, *Milḥamot Ha-Shem*, R. Margaliyot, ed. (Jerusalem: Mossad Harav Kook, 1953), pp. 57–58, for an interesting interpretation of why the Bible does not begin with the revelation of the law.

One of the essential differences between the approaches of Halevi and Maimonides to Jewish particularity is the way they each understand the relationship of creation to Sinai. To Maimonides, creation places Jewish particularity within the context of the universal spiritual way of reason; to Halevi, creation is totally absorbed within Jewish particularity. Halevi uses creation to explain the ontological basis of the election of Israel, see *Kuzari*, I, 95. For an understanding of the meaning of the term "Torah," see Urbach, *The Sages*, pp. 254–58, 280, and C. H. Dodd, *The Bible and the Greeks* (London: Hodder and Stoughton, 1964), pp. 25–41.

58. *Guide*, introduction to the first part, pp. 8–9.
59. *M.T.*, *Hilkhot Yesodei ha-Torah*, II, 2, p. 35b.

60. Ibid., IV, 12, p. 39b.
61. Throughout most of Maimonides' writings *yirah* (fear) is presented as a preliminary stage eventually transcended as one approaches the level of love of God. This was explained in the discussion of *yirah* and *ahavah* in chapter two. The same approach is repeated in the closing chapter of *Hilkhot Teshuvah:*

> Let not a man say, "I will observe the precepts of the Torah and occupy myself with its wisdom, in order that I may obtain all the blessings written in the Torah, or to attain life in the world to come; I will abstain from transgressions against which the Torah warns, so that I may be saved from the curses written in the Torah, or that I may not be cut off from life in the world to come." It is not right to serve God after this fashion for whoever does so, serves Him out of fear. This is not the standard set by the Prophets and Sages. Only those serve God in this way, who are illiterate, women, or children whom one trains to serve out of fear, till their knowledge shall have increased when they will serve out of love (X, 1, 2, pp. 92a-b).

However in chapters two and four in *Hilkhot Yesodei ha-Torah, yirah* is not presented as a preliminary stage leading to *ahavah* but as a condition which results from and accompanies love of God. Yet, there is no contradiction between these different descriptions of *yirah.* In the last chapter of *Hilkhot Teshuvah,* and in *Helek,* Maimonides is addressing individuals who have not yet reached the level of love of God. At this level, the first stage of religious worship, *yirah,* refers to a relationship to God based on reciprocity. When one has transcended reciprocity and loves God for His own sake, he then discovers how *yirah* accompanies love of God. See Rawidowicz, *Iyyunim,* pp. 358–59.

The categories which guide one's religious development prior to the acquisition of philosophic knowledge are also operative after this knowledge has been achieved. The categories of single-mindedness and Halakhah, discussed in chapters four and five of the *Eight Chapters,* can be used to describe the difference between Moses and the patriarchs, and those individuals whose intellectual love is limited to the disciplined framework of Halakhah. Similarly, the categories of *ahavah* and *yirah* describe the quality of the relationship with God prior to and subsequent to philosophic knowledge of God. Although the structures and categories remain the same, their meanings alter according to the spiritual level of the individual. Since the forms are identified with more than one meaning, they are capable of being appropriated by different individuals with different spiritual capacities and orientations.

62. See Guttmann, *Philosophies of Judaism*, p. 199, and "Hamotivim ha-Dati'im be-filosophia shel ha-Ramban," translated into Hebrew from the German by S. Esh, *Dat u-Mada* (Religion and Knowledge), S. H. Bergman, and N. Rotenstreich eds. (Jerusalem: The Magnes Press, 1955), p. 96; S. Rawidowicz, "Knowledge of God," p. 106; Cohen, "The Song of Songs and the Jewish Religious Mentality," *The Samuel Friedland Lectures* (New York: The Jewish Theological Seminary of America, 1966), pp. 1–21; Scholem, *Messianic Idea*, pp. 203–27.

63. The performance of *mitzvot* engenders awe and humility insofar as the *mitzvot* provide a continuous structure for living in the presence of God. Compare Guttmann, *The Guide of the Perplexed*, p. 224, n. 87.

64. *Guide*, III, 53, pp. 629–30.

65. This method of relating particularity to universality is implicit in Maimonides' *Eight Chapters*. He begins the *Eight Chapters* with a discussion of reason's understanding of the psyche. After showing that the health of the psyche is achieved through balance and moderation of the different psychic forces in man, he explains in chapter four how Halakhah provides a life-system which reflects reason's understanding of the psyche. What the psyche requires is known by reason; the value of moderation is not known exclusively from the Talmud. Maimonides understands Halakhah as a way of life which actualizes that which philosophic reason understands to be essential for man.

66. *M.T., Hilkhot Ta'anit,* I, 1–3; Twersky, *A Maimonides Reader,* pp. 113–14. See *M.T., Hilkhot Teshuvah,* III, 17, 36; *Iggeret Teman,* p. xiv; *Letter on Astrology,* pp. 232–34.

67. See *Treatise on Resurrection,* 48, p. 34; 50, pp. 35–36.

68. *Guide*, III, 51, pp. 625–26.

69. Ibid., pp. 627–28.

70. Ibid., p. 619.

71. See commentary of Shem Tov to *Guide,* III, 51; Friedlander, in his translation of the *Guide,* III, n. 2, p. 281; A. Ginzberg (Aḥad Ha-am), "The Supremacy of Reason," *Maimonides Octocentennial Series,* cipher one (New York: Maimonides Octocentennial Committee, 1935), p. 29.

72. The non-halakhic life of pre-Mosaic man in the Torah is used by Maimonides for two purposes: 1) to convince the halakhic Jew of the primacy of Aggadah (philosophy), and 2) to explain the spiritual integrity of the non-Jew who devotes his

life to the knowledge of God. Once one appreciates the spiritual value of philosophy, one's commitment to Halakhah will not blind one to the spiritual life of non-Jews. See "Letter to Ḥasdai ha-Levi, *Collection of Responsa;* introduction to *C.M.,* p. 39.

73. See Abraham Maimonides, *Milḥamot ha-Shem,* p. 59, for an interesting parallel between acquiring legal knowledge and acquiring philosophical knowledge from individuals with whom one is not in total agreement. Maimonides' son was influenced by his father's method, but he also distinguished between what he believed was the truth of a statement and its author. For an analysis of Maimonides' philosophical influence on his son, see Cohen, "The Soteriology of R. Abraham Maimuni," *PAAJR,* XXXV–XXXVI, pp. 75–98, 33–56 (1968). Maimonides' approach to Jewish particularity should be contrasted with the approaches of Judah Halevi and Spinoza. Maimonides does not support Jewish particularity, as Halevi does, by appealing to an ontological difference between the Jew and the rest of mankind. Maimonides, in contrast to Spinoza, believed that Jewish particularity is compatible with an openness to the spiritual integrity of the non-Jew. See *Responsa,* vol. II, 293, pp. 548–50; *Kuzari,* I, 27, 95, 103, 115; Spinoza, *Tractatus,* III; V, p. 72; VI, p. 89; XII, p. 170; Pines, "Spinoza, Maimonides, Kant," pp. 37–38. In "The Philosophic Sources," p. cxvi, n. 96, Pines notes that Maimonides' disciples and commentators did not achieve the same integration of philosophy and commitment to the law as did their teacher. Wolfson, in his article, "Halevi and Maimonides on Prophecy," *JQR,* XXXIII, I (July 1942), pp. 58–75, is unconvincing in his attempt to harmonize the views of Halevi and Maimonides through the position of the non-Jew in prophecy. One cannot ignore, when considering this question, the vast differences between Halevi's and Maimonides' appreciation of the function of reason in man's spiritual life and their approaches to the chosenness of Israel and to the purpose of Torah. For a clarification of the status of the non-Jew in biblical thought, see M. Greenberg, "The Biblical Grounding of Human Value," *The Samuel Friedland Lectures* (New York: The Jewish Theological Seminary of America, 1966), pp. 39–52, and "Mankind, Israel, and the Nations in the Hebraic Heritage," *No Man Is Alien: Essays on the Unity of Mankind,* J. R. Nelson, ed. (Leiden: E. J. Brill, 1971), pp. 15–40.

SELECTED BIBLIOGRAPHY

This bibliography does not purport to be exhaustive. It lists the titles of those books and articles which were consulted while preparing this book. For list of abbreviations see p. 215.

Works of Maimonides

Maimonides, Moses. *The Guide of the Perplexed.* Translated from the Arabic, introduction and notes by Shlomo Pines. Chicago and London: Chicago University Press, 1963.

———. *Moreh ha-Nevukhim.* 3 volumes. Original Arabic and Hebrew translation by Joseph Kafiḥ. Jerusalem: Mossad Harav Kook, 1972.

———. *Le guide des égarés.* Translated from the Arabic into French with notes and commentary by Solomon Münk. Paris: A. Franck, 1856–66.

———. *Moreh Nevukhim.* Translated into Hebrew by Samuel ibn Tibbon, with five commentaries: Efodi, Shem Tov, Crescas, Abravanel, and Hanarboni. New York: Om Publishing Co., 1946.

———. *Moreh Nevukhim.* 3 volumes. Translated by Samuel ibn Tibbon, edited and commentary by Yehuda Evenshamuel (Kaufman). Jerusalem: Mossad Harav Kook, 1958.

———. *The Guide of the Perplexed.* Translated from the original, annotated by Michael Friedländer. London: 1881, 1885.

———. *The Guide of the Perplexed.* Edited by Hugo Bergman, abridged edition with introduction and commentary by Julius Guttmann, translated from the Arabic by Chaim Rabin. London: East and West Library, 1952.

———. *Mishneh Torah.* Jerusalem: El Hamekorot, 1954.

———. *Mishneh Torah: The Book of Knowledge.* Edited by Saul Lieberman, annotation of sources, notes, and elucidations by Jacob Cohen, Variae lectiones, Moshe Hayim Katzenelenbogen. Jerusalem: Mossad Harav Kook, 1964.

———. *Sefer ha-Madah.* Edited by Mordecai D. Rabinowitz, commentary Samuel T. Rubinstein. Jerusalem: Mossad Harav Kook, 1958.

———. *Sefer Shoftim.* Commentary by Samuel T. Rubinstein. Jerusalem: Mossad Harav Kook, 1966.

———. *The Book of Knowledge: Mishneh Torah.* Edited according to the Bodleian (Oxford) Codex with introduction, biblical, and talmudical references, notes and English translation by Moses Hyamson. Jerusalem: Boys' Town Publishers, 1965.

———. *The Book of Adoration: Mishneh Torah.* Edited according to the Bodleian (Oxford) Codex with English translation by Moses Hyamson, talmudical references of Hebrew footnotes by Chaim M. Brecher. Jerusalem: Boys' Town Publishers, 1965.

———. *The Code of Maimonides: Book III, Treatise 8, Sanctification of the New Moon.* Translated from the Hebrew by Solomon Gandz. New Haven: Yale University Press, 1956.

———. *The Code of Maimonides: Book XI, The Book of Torts.* Translated by Hyman Klein. New Haven: Yale University Press, 1954.

———. *The Code of Maimonides: Book XIV, The Book of Judges.* Translated by Abraham M. Hershman. New Haven: Yale University Press, 1949.

———. *Sefer Hamitzvot.* Arabic original with Hebrew translation and commentary by Joseph Kafih. Jerusalem: Mossad Harav Kook, 1971.

———. *Sefer Hamitzvot.* Translated into Hebrew by Moses ibn Tibbon, critical text, notes, and introduction by Chaim Heller. Jerusalem-New York: Mossad Harav Kook, 1946.

———. *Sefer Hamitzvot.* Translated into Hebrew by Moses ibn Tibbon. Jerusalem: Lewin-Epstein, 1959.

———. *Sefer Hamitzvot: The Book of Commandments.* Translated into English, notes, glossary, appendices, and indices by Charles B. Chavel. London-New York: Soncino Press, 1967.

———. *Commentary to the Mishnah.* 7 volumes. Arabic original with Hebrew translation by Joseph Kafih. Jerusalem: Mossad Harav Kook, 1963-1968.

———. *Hakdamot le-Perush ha-Mishnah.* Notes and translation

into Hebrew by Mordecai D. Rabinowitz. Jerusalem: Mossad Harav Kook, 1960.

———. *Commentary to Mishnah Avot.* Commentary by Mordecai D. Rabinowitz. Jerusalem: Mossad Harav Kook, 1969.

———. *The Eight Chapters of Maimonides on Ethics.* Edited, annotated and translated by Joseph I. Gorfinkle. New York: AMS Press, 1966.

———. "Maimonides on the Jewish Creed": Introduction to *Ḥ elek.* Translated into English by Joshua Abelson. *JQR*, October, 1906; pp. 24–58.

———. *The Commentary to Mishnah Avot.* Translated and notes by Arthur David. New York: Bloch Publishing, 1968.

———. *Hilkhot ha-Yerushalmi (The Laws of the Palestinian Talmud of Rabbi Moses Ben Maimon).* Edited by Saul Lieberman. New York: The Jewish Theological Seminary of America, 1947.

———. *Iggerot.* Arabic original with translation and commentary by Joseph Kafiḥ. Jerusalem: Mossad Harav Kook, 1972.

———. *Teshuvot ha-Rambam (Responsa).* Translated into Hebrew by Joshua Blau. 3 volumes. Jerusalem: Mekitze Nirdamim, 1957, 1960, 1961.

———. *Kobez Teshuvot ha-Rambam ve-Iggerotav.* Leipzig: A. Lichtenberg, 1859.

———. *Iggerot ha-Rambam (Epistulae).* Edited by David H. Baneth. Jerusalem: Mekitze Nirdamim, 1946.

———. *Iggerot.* Edited by Mordecai Ravidowitz. Jerusalem: Mossad Harav Kook, 1944.

———. *Iggeret Teman (Epistle to Yemen).* Edited, with introduction and notes by Abraham S. Halkin, English translation by Boaz Cohen. *PAAJR*, 1952.

———. *Ma'amar Teḥiyyat ha-Metim (Treatise on Resurrection).* Edited by Joshua Finkel, translated into Hebrew by Samuel ibn Tibbon. *PAAJR*, 1939.

———. *Letter on Astrology (Letter to Rabbis of Marseilles).* Translated from Hebrew by Ralph Lerner in *Medieval Political Philosophy*, edited by Ralph Lerner and Muhsin Mahdi. New York: Free Press of Glencoe, 1963.

———. "The Correspondence Between the Rabbis of Southern France and Maimonides about Astrology." Edited by Alexander Marx, *HUCA*, III (1926), pp. 311–58.

———. *Milot ha-Higayon (Treatise on Logic).* Arabic original and three Hebrew translations. Edited and translated into English by Israel Efros. *PAAJR*, 1938.

272 | Selected Bibliography

———. *A Maimonides Reader*. Edited by Isadore Twersky. New York: Behrman House, 1972.

Background Literature and General Philosophy

Adkins, Arthur W. H. *Merit and Responsibility: A Study in Greek Values*. London: Oxford University Press, 1960.

Afnan, Soheil M. *Avicenna: His Life and Works*. London: G. Allen and Unwin, 1958.

Al-Farabi. *Philosophy of Plato and Aristotle*. Translated with introduction by Muhsin Mahdi. New York: Free Press of Glencoe, 1962.

———. *Aphorisms of the Statesman (Fusul al-Madani)*. Edited and English translation by Douglas M. Dunlop. Cambridge: Cambridge University Press, 1961.

———. *The Political Regime (Al-Siyasa Al-Madaniyyah)*. Arabic text, edited with introduction and notes by Fauzi M. Najjar. Beyrouth: Imprimerie Catholique, 1964. Partly translated into English by Fauzi M. Najjar in *Medieval Political Philosophy: A Sourcebook*. Edited by Ralph Lerner and Muhsin Mahdi. New York: Free Press of Glencoe, 1963.

Al-Ghazali. *Incoherence of the Philosophers (Tahafut Al-Falasifah)*. Translated into English by Sabih Ahmad Kamali. Lahore: The Pakistan Philosophical Congress, 1958.

Allan, Donald J. *The Philosophy of Aristotle*. London: Oxford University Press, 1970.

Arberry, Arthur J. *Avicenna on Theology*. London: J. Murray, 1951.

———. *Revelation and Reason in Islam*. London: G. Allen and Unwin, 1957.

———. *Sufism: An Account of the Mystics of Islam*. London: G. Allen and Unwin, 1950.

Aristotle. *The Basic Works of Aristotle*. Edited with introduction by Richard McKeon. New York: Random House, 1941.

———. *The Politics of Aristotle*. Edited and translated by Ernest Barker. New York and London: Oxford University Press, 1968.

———. *Nicomachean Ethics*. Translated by Harris Rackham. Cambridge, Mass.: Harvard University Press, 1934.

Averroes. *The Incoherence of the Incoherence*. 2 volumes. English translation with introduction and notes by Simon van den Bergh. London: Luzac, 1954.

———. *On the Harmony of Religion and Philosophy*. English translation with introduction and notes by George F. Hourani. London: Luzac, 1967.

Baḥya ibn Pakuda. *Duties of the Heart.* Translated by Moses Hyamson. Jerusalem: Boys' Town Publishers, 1962.

Barker, Ernst. *Greek Political Theory.* London: Methuen, Ltd., 1964.

Collingwood, Robin G. *The Idea of Nature.* New York: Oxford University Press, 1960.

Coulson, Noel J. *A History of Islamic Law.* Edinburgh: Edinburgh University Press, 1964.

——. *Conflicts and Tensions in Islamic Jurisprudence.* Chicago and London: University of Chicago Press, 1969.

De Boer, Tjitze J. *The History of Philosophy in Islam.* Translated by Edward R. Jones. New York: Dover Publications, 1967.

Dodds, Eric R. *The Greeks and the Irrational.* Berkeley and Los Angeles: University of California Press, 1964.

——. *Pagan and Christian in an Age of Anxiety.* New York: W. W. Norton, 1970.

Fakhry, Majid. *A History of Islamic Philosophy.* New York: Columbia University Press, 1970.

Frankfort, Henri, et al. *Before Philosophy: The Intellectual Adventure of Ancient Man.* Baltimore: Penguin Books, 1967.

Friedrich, Carl J. *The Philosophy of Law in Historical Perspective.* Second edition. Chicago and London: University of Chicago Press, 1963.

Fuller, Lon L. *The Morality of Law.* New Haven and London: Yale University Press, 1964.

Gibb, Hamilton A.R. *Studies on the Civilization of Islam.* Boston: Beacon Press, 1962.

——. "Law and Religion in Islam," *Judaism and Christianity.* Volume 3. Edited by Erwin I. J. Rosenthal. New York: Ktav, 1969.

Gilson, Étienne H. *Reason and Revelation in the Middle Ages.* New York: Charles Scribner's Sons, 1938.

Goldziher, Ignác. *Muslim Studies.* 2 volumes. Translated from the German by C. R. Barber and Samuel M. Stern. London: G. Allen and Unwin, 1967, 1971.

——. *The Zahiris: Their Doctrine and Their History.* Translated and edited by Wolfgang Behr. Leiden: E. J. Brill, 1971.

——. *Vorlesungen uber den Islam.* Translated into Hebrew by Yoseph Rivlin. Jerusalem: Bialik Institute, 1951.

Grunebaum, Gustave E. von. *Medieval Islam: A Study in Cultural Orientation.* Second edition. Chicago and London: University of Chicago Press, 1953.

Guthrie, William K.C. *The Greeks and Their Gods.* London: Methuen, 1968.

Hardie, William F.R. *Aristotle's Ethical Theory.* London: Oxford University Press, 1968.

Hart, Herbert L.A. *The Concept of Law.* London: Oxford University Press, 1961.

Hepburn, Ronald W. and Iris Murdoch. "Symposium: Vision and Choice in Morality," *Proceedings of the Aristotelian Society,* sup. vol. XXX (1956), pp. 14–53.

Hyman, Arthur and James J. Walsh (editors). *Philosophy in the Middle Ages: The Christian, Islamic, and Jewish Traditions.* New York: Evanston and London: Harper and Row, 1967.

Jaeger, Werner. *Aristotle: Fundamentals of the History of His Development.* Translated by Richard Robinson. London: Oxford University Press, 1948.

———. *The Theology of the Early Greek Philosophers.* London: Oxford University Press, 1967.

———. *Early Christianity and Greek Paideia.* London: Oxford University Press, 1969.

———. *Paideia: The Ideals of Greek Culture.* 3 volumes. Translated by Gilbert Highet. New York: Oxford University Press, 1969.

Kaufmann, Walter. *Critique of Religion and Philosophy.* New York: Anchor Books, 1961.

Kierkegaard, Sorën. *Concluding Unscientific Postscript.* Translated by David F. Swenson. Princeton: Princeton University Press, 1941.

———. *Fear and Trembling and the Sickness unto Death.* Translated by Walter Lowrie. New York: Doubleday-Anchor, 1954.

Klibansky, Raymond. *The Continuity of the Platonic Tradition During the Middle Ages.* London: Warburg Institute, 1939.

Lerner, Ralph and Mushin Mahdi (editors). *Medieval Political Philosophy: A Sourcebook.* New York: Free Press of Glencoe, 1963.

Levy, Raphael. *The Social Structure of Islam.* Cambridge: Cambridge University Press, 1969.

Lloyd, Geoffrey E.R. *Aristotle: The Growth and Structure of His Thought.* Cambridge: Cambridge University Press, 1968.

Lovejoy, Arthur O. *The Great Chain of Being.* New York: Harper & Row, 1960.

Löwith, Karl. *Meaning in History.* Chicago: University of Chicago Press, 1949.

MacIntyre, Alasdair C. *A Short History of Ethics.* New York: The Macmillan Co., 1966.

———. "The Nature and Destiny of Man: On Getting the Question Clear," *The Modern Churchman,* 45, Number 3 (September 1955), pp. 171–76.

Mahdi, Muhsin. *Ibn Khaldun's Philosophy of History.* Chicago: University of Chicago Press, 1964.

Murdoch, Iris. *The Sovereignty of Good.* London: Routledge and Kegan Paul, 1970.

Nygren, Anders. *Agape and Eros.* Translated by Philip S. Watson. New York and Evanston: Harper & Row, 1969.

Perelman, Chaim. *The Idea of Justice and the Problem of Argument.* New York: Humanities Press, 1963.

———. *Justice.* New York: Random House, 1967.

Pines, Shlomo. "Philosophy," *Cambridge History of Islam.* Volume 2. Edited by Peter M. Holt, Ann K. S. Lambton, Bernard Lewis. Cambridge: Cambridge University Press, 1970, pp. 780–823.

———. "Some Problems of Islamic Philosophy," *Islamic Culture,* 11 (1938), pp. 66–80.

Plato. *The Collected Dialogues of Plato.* Edited by Edith Hamilton and Huntington Cairns. New York: Bollingen Foundation, 1961.

Popper, Karl R. *The Open Society and Its Enemies.* London: Routledge and Kegan Paul, 1966.

Rahman, Fazlur. *Prophecy in Islam.* London: G. Allen and Unwin, 1958.

———. *Avicenna's Psychology.* An English translation of Kitab Al-Najat, book II, chapter 6, with historico-philosophical notes and textual improvements. London: Oxford University Press, 1952.

Rosenthal, Erwin I.J. *Studia Semitica.* Volume 2. *Islamic Themes.* London: Cambridge University Press, 1971.

Rosenthal, Franz. *Knowledge Triumphant: The Concept of Knowledge in Medieval Islam.* Leiden: E. J. Brill, 1970.

Ross, William D. *Aristotle.* New York: Meridian Books, 1959.

Schacht, Joseph. *An Introduction to Islamic Law.* London: Oxford University Press, 1964.

Spinoza, Baruch. *A Theological-Political Treatise.* Translated by Robert H.M. Elwes. New York: Dover Publications, 1951.

Stone, Julius. *Legal System and Lawyers' Reasonings.* London: Stevens and Sons, 1964.

Strauss, Leo. *What Is Political Philosophy and Other Studies.* New York: The Free Press of Glencoe, 1959.

———. "Farabi's *Plato,*" *Louis Ginzberg Jubilee Volume.* PAAJR, 1945.

———. *Liberalism: Ancient and Modern*. New York-London: Basic Books, 1968.

———. *Spinoza's Critique of Religion*. Translated by Elsa M. Sinclair. New York: Schocken Books, 1965.

———. *Natural Right and History*. Chicago and London: University of Chicago Press, 1965.

Taylor, Alfred E. *Plato: The Man and His Work*. New York: Meridian Books, 1956.

Walzer, Richard. *Greek into Arabic: Essays on Islamic Philosophy*. Oxford: Bruno Cassirer, 1962.

———. "Early Islamic Philosophy." *The Cambridge History of Later Greek and Early Medieval Philosophy*. Edited by Arthur H. Armstrong. Cambridge: Cambridge University Press, 1967.

Wasserstrom, Richard A. *The Judicial Decision: Toward a Theory of Legal Justification*. Stanford: Stanford University Press, 1969.

Watt, William M. *The Faith and Practice of Al-Ghazali*. London: G. Allen and Unwin, 1953.

———. *Islamic Political Thought: The Basic Concepts*. Edinburgh: Edinburgh University Press, 1968.

———. *A History of Islamic Spain*. Edinburgh: Edinburgh University Press, 1965.

———. *Islamic Philosophy and Theology*. Edinburgh: Edinburgh University Press, 1962.

Winch, Peter. "Authority," *Proceedings of the Aristotelian Society* (1958), pp. 225–40.

Wolfson, Harry A. *The Philosophy of the Church Fathers*. Volume I. *Faith, Trinity, Incarnation*. Second edition. Cambridge, Mass.: Harvard University Press, 1964.

———. *The Philosophy of Spinoza*. 2 volumes. New York: Meridian Books, 1958.

———. *Religious Philosophy: A Group of Essays*. New York: Atheneum, 1965.

Literature on Maimonides and Jewish Thought

Abravanel. *Rosh Amana*. Tel Aviv: Sifreati, 1958.

Agus, Jacob B. *The Evolution of Jewish Thought from Biblical Times to the Opening of the Modern Era*. London and New York: Abelard-Schuman, 1959.

Albo, Joseph. *Sefer ha-Ikkarim*. Edited with translation and notes by Isaac Husik. Philadelphia: The Jewish Publication Society of America, 1946.

Altmann, Alexander. *Studies in Religious Philosophy and Mysticism.* Ithaca, New York: Cornell University Press, 1969.
———. "Judaism and World Philosophy from Philo to Spinoza," *The Jews: Their Role in Civilization.* Edited by Louis Finkelstein. New York: Schocken Books, 1971.
Atlas, Samuel. "The Contemporary Relevance of the Philosophy of Maimonides," *CCAR Yearbook*, LXIV (1954), pp. 186–213.
———. "Solomon Maimon and Spinoza," *HUCA*, XXX (1959), pp. 233–85.
———. "Moses in the Philosophy of Maimonides, Spinoza, and Solomon Maimon," *HUCA*, XXV (1954), pp. 369–400.
———. "Maimon and Maimonides," *HUCA*, XXIII (1950–51), pp. 517–48.
Bacher, Wilhelm, Marcus Brann, et al. *Moses ben Maimon: Sein Leben, seine Werke und sein Einfluss.* Leipzig: G. Fock, 1908, 1914.
———. "*Ha-Rambam Parshan ha-Mikra.* Translated from German into Hebrew by A. Z. Rabinowitz. Tel Aviv: Achdut, 1932.
Bamberger, Benjamin J. "Fear and Love of God in the Old Testament" *HUCA*, VI (1929), pp. 39–53.
Baron, Salo W. "The Historical Outlook of Maimonides," *PAAJR*, VI (1934–35), pp. 5–113.
———. editor. *Essays on Maimonides.* New York: Columbia University Press, 1941.
———. *A Social and Religious History of the Jews.* 14 volumes. Philadelphia: The Jewish Publication Society of America, 1952–69.
Beker, Jacob. *Mishnato hafilosofi shel Rabbenu Moshe ben Maimon.* Tel Aviv: Simoni Publishing House, 1955.
Berman, Lawrence V. "The Political Interpretation of the Maxim: The Purpose of Philosophy Is the Imitation of God," *Studia Islamica*, XV (1962), pp. 53–63.
———. "A Reexamination of Maimonides' 'Statement on Political Science,'" *Journal of the American Oriental Society*, LXXXIX (1969), pp. 106–12.
———. *Ibn Bajja and Maimonides: A Chapter in the History of Political Philosophy.* Unpublished thesis. Jerusalem: The Hebrew University, 1959.
Blumenfeld, Samuel M. "Toward a Study of Maimonides the Educator," *HUCA*, XXIII (1950–51), pp. 555–91.
Bokser, Ben Zion. "Morality and Religion in the Theology of Maimonides," *Essays on Jewish Life in Honor of Salo W.*

Baron. New York: Columbia University Press, 1959.
————. *The Legacy of Maimonides*. New York: Hebrew Publishing Co., 1962.
Buber, Martin. *Israel and the World: Essays in a Time of Crises*. New York: Schocken Books, 1948.
————. *Moses: The Revelation and the Covenant*. New York: Harper & Brothers, 1958.
Buchler, Adolf. *Studies in Sin and Atonement in the Rabbinic Literature of the First Century*. New York: Ktav, 1967.
————. *Types of Jewish-Palestinian Piety from 70 B.C.E. to 70 C.E.—The Ancient Pious Men*. New York: Ktav, 1968.
Chajes, Zevi H. *Torat Nevi'im*. Jerusalem: Divre Hakhamim, 1958.
Cohen, Arthur. *The Teachings of Maimonides*. Prolegomenon by Marvin Fox. New York: Ktav, 1968.
Cohen, Boaz. "The Classification of the Law in the Mishneh Torah," *JQR*, XXV, number 4 (1935), pp. 519–40.
————. *Law and Tradition in Judaism*. New York: Ktav, 1969.
Cohen, Gerson D. "The Song of Songs and the Jewish Religious Mentality," *The Samuel Friedland Lectures*. New York: The Jewish Theological Seminary of America, 1966.
————. "Messianic Postures of Ashkenazim and Sephardim," *The Leo Baeck Memorial Lecture*. New York: Leo Baeck Institute, 1967.
————. "The Soteriology of R. Abraham Maimuni," *PAAJR*, XXXV, pp. 75–98, XXXVI, pp. 33–56 (1968).
————. "The Talmudic Age." *Great Ages and Ideas of the Jewish People*. Edited by Leo W. Schwarz. New York: Random House, 1956.
Cohen, Hermann. "Charakteristik der Ethik Maimunis," *Moses Ben Maimon*. Edited by Wilhelm Bacher, Marcus Brann, and David Simonsen. Leipzig: G. Fock, 1908, 1914.
Daube, David. "Rabbinic Methods of Interpretation and Hellenistic Rhetoric," *HUCA*, XXII (1949), pp. 239–64.
Davidson, Herbert "Maimonides' *Shemonah Peraqim* and al-Farabi's *Fusul al-Madani*," *PAAJR*, XXXI (1963), pp. 33–50.
Davies, William D. *Torah in the Messianic Age and/or the Age to Come*. Philadelphia: Society of Biblical Literature, 1952.
Dienstag, Jacob I. "The Prayer Book of Maimonides," *The Leo Jung Jubilee Volume*. Edited by Menahem M. Kasher, Norman Lamm, Leonard Rosenfeld. New York: The Jewish Center, 1962.
————. "Biblical Exegesis of Maimonides in Jewish Scholarship," *Samuel K. Mirsky Memorial Volume*. Edited by Gersion

Appel. New York: Sura Institute for Research, 1970.
Diesendruck, Zevi. "Maimonides' Lehre von der Prophetie," *Jewish Studies in Memory of Israel Abrahams.* New York: Jewish Institute of Religion, 1927.
———. "The Philosophy of Maimonides." *CCAR Yearbook,* XLV (1935), pp. 355–68.
———. "Maimonides' Theory of the Negation of Privation," *PAAJR,* VI (1934–1935), pp. 139–52.
Dodd, Charles H. *The Bible and the Greeks.* London: Hodder and Stoughton, 1964.
Efros, Israel. *Philosophical Terms in the Moreh Nebukim.* New York: AMS Press, 1966.
Eichrodt, Walther. *Theology of the Old Testament.* 2 volumes. Translated by J. A. Baker. Philadelphia: Westminster Press, 1961, 1967.
Epstein, Isidore. "Maimonides' Conception of the Law and the Ethical Trend of His Halacha," *Moses Maimonides' VIII Centenary Volume.* Edited by Isadore Epstein. London: Soncino Press, 1935.
Fackenheim, Emil L. "The Possibility of the Universe in al-Farabi, Ibn Sina, and Maimonides," *PAAJR,* XVI (1947), pp. 39–70.
———. *God's Presence in History.* New York: New York University Press, 1970.
———. *Quest for Past and Future: Essays in Jewish Theology.* Boston: Beacon Press, 1970.
Feldman, R.V. "The Union of Prophetism and Philosophism in the Thought of Maimonides," *Moses Maimonides.* Edited by Isadore Epstein. London: Soncino Press, 1935.
Feldman, William M. "Maimonides as Physician and Scientist," *Moses Maimonides.* Edited by Isadore Epstein. London: Soncino Press, 1935.
Finkelstein, Louis. "Maimonides and the Tannaitic Midrashim," *JQR,* XXV, 4 (April 1935), pp. 469–99.
Flusser, David. "A New Sensitivity in Judaism and the Christian Message." *HTR,* 61 (1968), pp. 107–27.
Fox, Marvin. "Maimonides and Aquinas on Natural Law," *Dine Israel,* III (1972), v–xxxvi.
Fromm, Erich. *You Shall Be as Gods.* New York: Holt, Rinehart and Winston, 1966.
Ginzberg, Asher (Aḥad Ha-am). "The Supremacy of Reason," *Maimonides Octocentennial Series,* 1. New York: Maimonides Octocentennial Committee, 1935.
Ginzberg, Louis. *On Jewish Law and Lore.* New York: Meridian

Books and Philadelphia: The Jewish Publication Society of America, 1962.

———. *The Legends of the Jews.* 7 volumes. Philadelphia: The Jewish Publication Society of America, 1968.

Goitein, Shlomo D. "The Title and Office of the Nagid: A Reexamination," *JQR*, LIII, 2 (October 1962), pp. 93–119.

———. "Maimonides as Chief Justice," *JQR*, XLIX, 3 (January 1959), pp. 191–204.

———. *Jews and Arabs: Their Contacts through the Ages.* New York: Schocken Books, 1964.

———. "Abraham Maimonides and His Pietist Circle," *Jewish Medieval and Renaissance Studies.* Edited by Alexander Altmann. Cambridge, Mass.: Harvard University Press, 1967.

Goldman, Eliezer. "The Worship Peculiar to Those Who Have Apprehended True Reality," Hebrew. *Annual of Bar-Ilan Studies in Judaica and the Humanities*, VI. Ramat Gan: Bar Ilan University, 1968.

Greenberg, Moshe. "The Biblical Grounding of Human Value," *The Samuel Friedland Lectures.* New York: The Jewish Theological Seminary of America, 1966.

———. "Mankind, Israel, and the Nations in the Hebraic Heritage," *No Man Is Alien: Essays on the Unity of Mankind.* Edited by J. R. Nelson. Leiden: E. J. Brill, 1971, pp. 15–40.

Guttman, Michel. "Maimonide sur l'universalité de la morale religieuse," *REJ*, V, 89 (1935), pp. 34–45.

Guttmann, Julius. *Dat u-Mada.* Translated by Saul Esh. Edited by Shmuel H. Bergman and Nathan Rotenstreich. Jerusalem: The Magnes Press, 1955.

———. *Philosophies of Judaism.* Translated by David W. Silverman. New York: Anchor Books, 1966.

Halevi, Judah. *Book of Kuzari.* Translated from the Arabic by Hartwig Hirschfeld. New York: Pardes Publishing House, 1946.

Halkin, Abraham S. "Classical and Arabi c Material in Ibn 'Aknin's *Hygiene of the Soul,*" *PAAJR*, XIV (1944), pp. 25–148.

———. "Ibn 'Aknin's Commentary on the Song of Songs," *Alexander Marx Jubilee Volume.* New York: The Jewish Theological Seminary of America, 1950.

———. "The Judeo-Islamic Age," *Great Ages and Ideas of the Jewish People.* Edited by Leo W. Schwarz. New York: Random House, 1956.

———. "Judeo-Arabic Literature." *The Jews: Their Religion and Culture.* Edited by Louis Finkelstein. New York: Schocken Books, 1971.

———. "The Ban on the Study of Philosophy." Hebrew. *P'raqim,* Volume I. Edited by Eliezer S. Rosenthal. Jerusalem: 1967–68.

Ha-Meiri, Menaḥem. *Bet ha-Beḥirah on Avot.* Edited by Samuel Waxman. New York, 1944.

Heinemann, I. "Maimuni und die arabischen Einheitslehrer." *Monatsschrift für Geschichte und Wissenschaft des Judentums.* LXXIX. (1935), pp. 102–48.

———. *Ta'amei ha-Mitzvot be-Safrut Yisrael.* 2 volumes. Jerusalem: Jewish Agency, 1959.

Heller, Joseph. "Maimonides' Theory of Miracles." *Between East and West.* Edited by Alexander Altmann. London: East and West Library, 1959.

Herzog, Isaac. "Maimonides as Halachist." *Moses Maimonides.* Edited by Isadore Epstein. London: Soncino Press, 1935.

Heschel, Abraham J. "Ha-He'emin ha-Rambam She-zakhah la-Nevuah?" *Louis Ginzberg Jubilee Volume. PAAJR,* 1945 (Hebrew section, pp. 159–88).

———. "The Quest for Certainty in Saadia's Philosophy," *JQR,* XXXIII (1942–43), pp. 213–64.

———. "The Last Days of Maimonides." *The Insecurity of Freedom.* New York: Farrar, Straus and Giroux, 1966.

———. *Maimonides Eine Biographie.* Berlin: Erich Reiss, 1935.

———. *God in Search of Man.* New York: Farrar, Straus and Cudahy, 1955.

Hoffmann, Ernst. *Die Liebe zu Gott bei Mose ben Maimon.* Breslau: M. and H. Marcus, 1937.

Husik, Isaac. "An Anonymous Medieval Christian Critic of Maimonides," *JQR,* II, 2 (October 1911), pp. 159–90.

———. "The Law of Nature, Hugo Grotius, and the Bible," *HUCA,* II (1925), pp. 381–417.

———. "The Philosophy of Maimonides," *Maimonides Octocentennial Series,* 4. New York: Maimonides Octocentennial Committee, 1935.

———. *A History of Medieval Jewish Philosophy.* New York: Meridian Books and Philadelphia: The Jewish Publication Society of America, 1958.

———. *Philosophical Essays.* Edited by Milton C. Nahm, Leo Strauss. Oxford: Blackwell, 1952.

Hyman, Arthur. "Spinoza's Dogmas of Universal Faith in Light of Their Medieval Jewish Background." *Biblical and Other Studies.* Edited by Alexander Altmann. Cambridge, Mass.: Harvard University Press, 1963, pp. 183–95.

———. "Some Aspects of Maimonides' Philosophy of Nature,"

La Filosofia della natura nel Medioevo. Milan: Societa Editrice Vita e Pensiero.

———. "Maimonides' 'Thirteen Principles.'" *Jewish Medieval and Renaissance Studies.* Edited by Alexander Altmann. Cambridge, Mass.: Harvard University Press, 1967.

Ibn Daud, Abraham. *The Book of Tradition (Sefer ha-Qabbalah).* Critical edition, with a translation and notes by Gerson D. Cohen. Philadelphia: The Jewish Publication Society of America, 1967.

———. *Emunah Ramah.* Jerusalem: 1967.

Kaufmann, Yehezkel. *The Religion of Israel.* Translated and abridged by Moshe Greenberg. Chicago: University of Chicago Press, 1960.

Krakovski, Menahem. *Avodat ha-Melekh.* Jerusalem: Mossad Harav Kook, 1971.

Kravitz, Leonard S. "Maimonides and Job: An Inquiry as to the Method of the Moreh," *HUCA,* XXXVIII (1967), pp. 149–58.

Levinger, Jacob. *Maimonides' Techniques of Codification.* Hebrew. Jerusalem: The Magnes Press, 1965.

———. "The Oral Law in Maimonides' Thought." Hebrew. *Tarbiz,* XXXVII, (March 1968), pp. 282–93.

Lieberman, Saul. *Greek in Jewish Palestine.* New York: Philipp Feldheim, 1965.

———. *Hellenism in Jewish Palestine.* New York: Jewish Theological Seminary of America, 1950.

Loewe, Herbert (editor). *The Contact of Pharisaism and Other Cultures.* Library of Biblical Studies, Volume 2. New York: Ktav, 1969.

Loewe, Raphael. (editor). *Studies in Rationalism, Judaism, and Universalism.* London: Routledge and Kegan Paul, 1966.

Maimonides, Abraham. *Milḥamot ha-Shem.* Edited by R. Margaliyot. Jerusalem: Mossad Harav Kook, 1953.

Marmorstein, Arthur. *The Doctrine of Merits in Old Rabbinical Literature and the Old Rabbinic Doctrine of God.* New York: Ktav, 1968.

———. "The Place of Maimonides' *Mishneh Torah* in the History and Development of the Halacha," *Moses Maimonides.* Edited by Isadore Epstein. London: Soncino Press, 1935.

———. *Studies in Jewish Theology.* Edited by Joseph Rabinowitz, Myer S. Low. London: Oxford University Press, 1950.

Marx, Alexander. "Moses Maimonides," *Maimonides Octocentennial Series,* 2. New York: Maimonides Octocentennial Committee, 1935.

———. (editor). "Texts By and About Maimonides," *JQR,* XXV (April 1935).

Moore, George Foot. *Judaism in the First Centuries of the Christian Era: The Age of the Tannaim.* 3 volumes. Cambridge, Mass.: Harvard University Press, 1954.

Neumark, David. *Toledot ha-Ikkarim be-Yisrael.* Odessa: 1919.

———. *Essays in Jewish Philosophy.* Edited by Samuel S. Cohon. Amsterdam: *CCAR,* 1971.

Osterley, William O.E. (editor). *Judaism and Christianity: The Age of Transition.* Library of Biblical Studies, Volume 1. New York: Ktav, 1969.

Pines, Shlomo. "The Philosophic Sources of *The Guide of the Perplexed,*" *The Guide of the Perplexed.* Chicago and London: University of Chicago Press, 1963.

———. "Spinoza's Tractatus Theologico-Politicus, Maimonides, and Kant," *Scripta Hierosolymitana,* XX (1968), pp. 3–54.

———. "Histabrut ha-Tekumah mi-Hadash shel Medinah Yehudit Lefi Yoseph ibn Kaspi ue-lefi Spinoza." *Riv'on Philosophe,* 14 (1964), pp. 289–317.

———. "A Tenth-Century Philosophical Correspondence." *PAAJR,* XXIV (1955), pp. 103–36.

———. *History of Jewish Philosophy from Philo to Maimonides.* Hebrew. Edited from lecture notes by Yisroel Igra. Jerusalem: Akademon, 1966.

———. "Ibn Khaldun and Maimonides: A Comparison Between Two Texts." *Studia Islamica,* 32 (1970), pp. 265–74.

Rawidowicz, Simon. "Philosophy as a Duty." *Moses Maimonides' VIII Centenary Volume.* Edited by Isadore Epstein. London: Soncino Press, 1935.

———. "Perek be-Torat ha-Musar le-ha-Rambam." *Sefer Yovel for Mordecai M. Kaplan.* New York: The Jewish Theological Seminary of America, 1953.

———. "On Maimonides' Sefer ha-Madda." *Essays in Honour of Joseph H. Hertz.* London: St. Ann's Press, 1942.

———. "Knowledge of God: A Study in Maimonides' Philosophy of Religion." *Jewish Studies Issued in Honor of the Chief Rabbi Joshua L. Landau.* Tel Aviv: 1936.

———. *Iyyunim be-Mahashevet Yisrael (Hebrew Studies in Jewish Thought),* Volume I. Edited with introduction by Benjamin C. I. Ravid. Jerusalem: Rubin Mass, 1969.

———. "On Interpretation," *PAAJR,* XXVI (1957), pp. 83–126.

Reines, Alvin J. *Maimonides and Abrabanel on Prophecy.* Cincinnati: Hebrew Union College Press, 1970.

———. "Maimonides' Concept of Mosaic Prophecy," *HUCA,* XL–XLI (1970), pp. 325–62.

Rosenthal, Erwin I.J. "Maimonides' Conception of State and Society," *Moses Maimonides.* Edited by Isadore Epstein. London: Soncino Press, 1935, pp. 191–206.

——. *Judaism and Islam.* London: Thomas Yoseloff, 1961.

——. "Avicenna's Influence on Jewish Thought," *Avicenna: Scientist and Philosopher.* Edited by George M. Wickens. London: Luzac, 1952.

——. "Torah and 'Nomos' in Medieval Jewish Philosophy." *Studies in Rationalism, Judaism, and Universalism.* Edited by Raphael Loewe. London: Routledge and Kegan Paul, 1966.

——. (editor). *Law and Religion.* Library of Biblical Studies, Volume 3. New York: Ktav, 1969.

Rosenthal, Eliezer S. "For the Most Part." *P'raqim*, Volume I, pp. 183–224. Edited by Eliezer S. Rosenthal. Jerusalem: 1967–68.

Rosin, D. *Die Ethik des Maimonides.* Breslau: F.W. Jungfer 1876.

Rotenstreich, Nathan. *Tradition and Reality: The Impact of History on Modern Jewish Thought.* New York: Random House, 1972.

——. *Jewish Philosophy in Modern Times: From Mendelssohn to Rosenzweig.* New York: Holt, Rinehart and Winston, 1968.

Roth, Leon. *Spinoza, Descartes, and Maimonides.* London: Oxford University Press, 1924.

——. *The Guide of the Perplexed: Moses Maimonides.* London: Hutchinson's Universal Library, 1948.

Saadia Gaon. *The Book of Beliefs and Opinions.* Translated from the Arabic and the Hebrew by Samuel Rosenblatt. New Haven: Yale University Press, 1948.

Saadya Studies. Edited by Erwin I.J. Rosenthal. Aberdeen: Manchester University Press, 1943.

Sarachek, Joseph. *The Doctrine of the Messiah in Medieval Jewish Literature.* New York: Hermon Press, 1968.

——. *Faith and Reason: The Conflict over the Rationalism of Maimonides.* New York: Hermon Press, 1970.

Schecter, Solomon. *Aspects of Rabbinic Theology.* New York: Schocken Books, 1961.

——. "The Dogmas of Judaism," *Studies in Judaism.* First series. Philadelphia: The Jewish Publication Society of America, 1958, pp. 73–104.

Scholem, Gershom G. *Major Trends in Jewish Mysticism.* New York: Schocken Books, 1941.

——. *On The Kabbalah and Its Symbolism.* New York: Schocken Books, 1965.

——. *Jewish Gnosticism, Merkavah Mysticism, and Talmudic Tradition.* New York: The Jewish Theological Seminary of America, 1960.

——. *The Messianic Idea in Judaism and Other Essays on Jewish Spirituality.* New York: Schocken Books, 1971.

Schwarzschild, Steven S. "On Maimonides' Philosophy of Halacha." Unpublished, 1948.

——. "Aristotelianism and Neo-Platonism in Maimonides' Concept of God." Hebrew Union College. Unpublished, 1946.

——. "Do Noachites Have to Believe in Revelation?" *JQR*, LII, 4 (April 1962), pp. 297–365.

Schweid, Eliezer. *Iyyunim be-Shmoneh Perakim le-Rambam.* Jerusalem: Offset Ha'amanim, 1969.

——. *Feeling and Speculation.* Hebrew. Ramat Gan: Massada, 1970.

——. *Israel at the Crossroads.* Philadelphia: The Jewish Publication Society of America, 1973.

——. *Le'umiut Yehudit.* Jerusalem: S. Zack and Co., 1972.

Sefer ha-Rambam shel ha-Tarbiz (The Maimonides Book of Tarbiz). Jerusalem: Hebrew University Press, 1935.

Silberg, Moshe. *Principia Talmudica.* Hebrew. Jerusalem: Mif'al ha-Shikhpul, 1964.

Silver, Abba H. *A History of Messianic Speculation in Israel.* Boston: Beacon Press, 1959.

Silver, Daniel J. *Maimonidean Criticism and the Maimonidean Controversy: 1180–1240.* Leiden: E. J. Brill, 1965.

Simon, Ernst. "Law and Observance in Jewish Experience," *Tradition and Contemporary Experience.* Edited by Alfred Jospe. New York: Schocken Books, 1970.

Snaith, Norman H. *The Distinctive Ideas of the Old Testament.* New York: Schocken Books, 1964.

Soloveitchik, Joseph B. "Ish ha-Halakhah," *Talpioth,* 1944, pp. 651–735.

——. "The Lonely Man of Faith," *Tradition,* VII, 2 (Summer 1965), pp. 5–67.

Sonne, Isaiah. "A Scrutiny of the Charges of Forgery Against Maimonides' 'Letter on Resurrection,' " *PAAJR*, XXI (1952), pp. 101–18.

Strauss, Leo. "Notes on Maimonides' Book of Knowledge," *Studies in Mysticism and Religion Presented to Gershom G. Scholem.* Jerusalem: The Magnes Press, 1967.

——. "Jerusalem and Athens," *The City College Papers,* Number 6. pp. 3–28. New York: 1967.

————. "Quelques remarques sur la Science Politique de Maimonides et de Farabi," *REJ,* 100 (January-June 1936), pp. 1–37.

————. *Philosophie und Gesetz.* Berlin: Schocken Verlag, 1935.

————. "Der Ort der Vorsehungslehre nach der Ansicht Maimunis," *Monatsschrift für Geschichte und Wissenschaft des Judentums,* LXXXI (1937), pp. 93–105.

————. "How To Begin To Study the Guide of the Perplexed," *The Guide of the Perplexed.* Translated by Shlomo Pines. Chicago: University of Chicago Press, 1963, pp. xi–lvi.

————. *Persecution and the Art of Writing.* Glencoe, Illinois: The Free Press, 1952.

Tchernowitz, Chaim. "Maimonides as Codifier," *Maimonides Octocentennial Series,* 3. New York: Maimonides Octocentennial Committee, 1935.

————. *Toledot ha-Halakhah: History of Hebrew Law.* 2 Volumes. New York: Jubilee Committee, 1945.

Teicher, Jacob. "Observations critiques sur l'intérpretation traditionelle de la doctrine des attributes négatifs chez Maimonides," *REJ,* 99 (1935), pp. 56–67.

Twersky, Isadore. *Rabad of Posquières.* Cambridge: Harvard University Press, 1962.

————. "Some Non-Halakhik Aspects of the *Mishneh Torah,*" *Jewish Medieval and Renaissance Studies.* Edited by Alexander Altmann. Cambridge, Mass.: Harvard University Press, 1967.

————. "The Beginnings of *Mishneh Torah* Criticism," *Biblical and Other Studies.* Edited by Alexander Altmann. Cambridge, Mass.: Harvard University Press, 1963.

Urbach, Efraim E. "Studies in Rabbinic Views Concerning Divine Providence." *Yehezkel Kaufmann Jubilee Volume.* Edited by Menahem Haran (Hebrew section, pp. 122–48). Jerusalem: The Magnes Press, 1960.

————. "Derashot Hazal al Neviei Umot ha-Olam v-al Parshat Bil'am le-Or ha-Vikuah ha-Yehudi-Notzri." *Tarbiz,* 25 (1956), pp. 272–89.

————. "Halakhah u-Nevuah." *Tarbiz,* 18 (1946), pp. 1–27.

————. "The Traditions about Merkavah Mysticism in the Tannaitic Period," Hebrew. *Studies in Mysticism and Religion Presented to Gershom G. Scholem.* Jerusalem: The Magnes Press, 1967.

————. *Hazal: Pirkei Emunot ve-De'ot (The Sages: Their Concepts and Beliefs).* Jerusalem: The Magnes Press, 1969.

————. "Redemption and Repentance in Talmudic Judaism,"

Types of Redemption. Edited by R. J. Zwi Werblowsky and C. Jouco Bleecker. Leiden: E. J. Brill, 1970.

———. "Ascesis and Suffering in Talmudic and Midrashic Sources," Hebrew. *Yitzhak F. Baer Jubilee Volume.* Jerusalem: Historical Society of Israel, 1960.

———. "The Homiletical Interpretations of the Sages and the Expositions of Origin on Canticles, and the Jewish-Christian Disputation," *Studies in Aggadah and Folk Literature.* Edited by Joseph Heinemann and Dov Noy. Jerusalem: The Magnes Press, 1971, pp. 247–75.

Vajda, Georges. *Introduction à La Pensée Juive du Moyen Age.* Paris: Librairie Philosophique J. Vrin, 1947.

———. *L'amour de Dieu dans la théologie Juive du Moyen Age.* Paris: Librairie Philosophique J. Vrin, 1957.

Wolfson, Harry A. *Crescas' Critique of Aristotle.* Cambridge, Mass.: Harvard University Press, 1929.

———. *Philo: Foundations of Religious Philosophy in Judaism, Christianity, and Islam.* 2 volumes. Cambridge, Mass.: Harvard University Press, 1968.

———. "Notes on Proofs on the Existence of God in Jewish Philosophy," *HUCA,* I (1924), pp. 575–96.

———. "Maimonides and Halevi," *JQR,* II, 3 (January 1912), pp. 279–337.

———. "Maimonides on the Internal Senses," *JQR,* XXV, 4 (April 1935), pp. 441–67.

———. "Note on Maimonides' Classification of the Sciences," *JQR,* XXVI, 4 (April 1936), pp. 369–77.

———. "Halevi and Maimonides on Prophecy," *JQR,* XXXII, 4 (April 1942), pp. 345–70; XXXIII, I (July 1942), pp. 49–82.

———. "Halevi and Maimonides on Design, Chance, and Necessity," *PAAJR,* XI (1941), pp. 105–63.

———. "Maimonides on Negative Attributes," *Louis Ginzberg Jubilee Volume. PAAJR,* 1945.

———. "The Double-Faith Theory in Clement, Saadia, Averroes, and St. Thomas and Its Origin in Aristotle and the Stoics," *JQR,* XXXIII, 2 and 3 (October 1942–January 1943), pp. 213–64.

———. "Maimonides and Gersonides on Divine Attributes as Ambiguous Terms," *Mordecai M. Kaplan Jubilee Volume.* New York: The Jewish Theological Seminary of America, 1953.

———. "The Aristotelian Predictables and Maimonides' Division of Attributes," *Essays and Studies in Memory of Linda R.*

Miller. New York: The Jewish Theological Seminary of America, 1938.

———. "Maimonides on the Unity and Incorporeality of God," *JQR,* 56 (1965), pp. 112–36.

———. "The Jewish Kalam," *The Seventy-fifth Anniversary Volume of the JQR.* Edited by Abraham Neuman and Solomon Zeitlin. Philadelphia: *JQR,* 1967.

Yellin, David and Israel Abrahams. *Maimonides.* Philadelphia: The Jewish Publication Society of America, 1903.

Zeitlin, Solomon. *Maimonides.* New York: Bloch Publishing Co., 1955.

INDEX

Abraham
  archetype of universal way to
    God, 57–62, 73, 83–84,
    224n75, 236n2, 238n12,
    242n48
  community of, 58–60, 238n12
  his influence on history,
    170–171, 238n12
  his worship from love, 228n16
  in relationship to Moses, 61–62,
    170, 225n86
  in revolt against idolatry, 54,
    57–59, 170
  midrashic treatment of, 57–58,
    67
Account of the Chariot (Maaseh
  Merkavah). See Metaphysics
Account of Creation (Maaseh
  Bereshit). See Physics
Adkins, Arthur W.H.,
  246–247n10
Aggadah
  as spiritual way of singular
    individuals, 37–39, 42, 60, 86
  importance of, 29–30, 42, 44,
    46, 48, 54, 86, 218n8,
    266n72
  in relationship to Halakhah,
    30–33, 36, 126, 218n8
  in relationship to philosophy,
    30–31, 35, 47, 122

interpretation of, 31–34, 39,
  41, 70, 77, 159, 244n60; in
  Bible, 126; in Talmud, 29,
  57, 98, 134
Akiva, 51, 131–133, 228n15
Albo, Joseph, 226n92, 241n40
Al-Farabi, 23–24, 76, 128
Al-Ghazali, 229n30, 262n44
Allegory. See Aggadah,
  interpretation of; Language,
  religious and symbolic
Am ha-arez
  communal role of, 220n43
  definition of, 45
  in contrast to hasid, 45, 48, 86
  observance of, 86, 91–92, 94
  self-understanding of, 98
Anthropomorphism, 230n33,
  235n69
  See also God, unity and
  incorporeality of
Aristotle, 20, 22, 24–26, 53,
  126–128, 130, 133, 141, 157,
  and Averroes, 243n57
  and creation of the world, 133,
    157, 244n66
  and Torah, 53
  concept of nature, 6, 158
  spiritual ideal of, 6,
    246–247n10
  theory of virtues, 21

Creation of the world
Abraham's belief in, 242n48
and belief in Torah, 132–133
and philosophic understanding
of God, 49, 136–137, 157
epistemological basis for,
122–123, 130, 132–133, 136,
156, 242n48
in relationship to Sinai, 264n57

David, 190
Day of Atonement, 140, 151
Decalogue
and demonstrative reason, 124,
242n48
spiritual significance of the first
commandment, 49, 221n51
See also Commandments
Derashot, definition of, 29
See also Aggadah
Din (strict requirement of law),
90–91, 93–94, 96, 98–99,
143, 188.
See also Halakhah, as
communal discipline;
Morality, of legal duty;
Worship, levels of
Divine providence, 135–136,
152, 210–211, 248n25
views of the rabbis on, 228n15
Divine revelation, 3, 9, 104, 108,
144, 148, 176, 186, 188
and human reason, 9, 14–16,
117, 122–124, 144–145, 151,
160, 183, 223n62
and talmudic tradition, 29,
106, 117
See also Sinai
Divination. See Idolatry

Egypt, exodus from,
as archetype of political
struggle and communal
identification, 60, 84, 141,
181–182, 247n12
as symbol of God's action in
history, 5, 69–70
Eight Chapters (Shemoneh
Perakim), 88, 147, 159, 167,
171, 266n65

Eliezer, Rabbi, 73, 241n40
Eliezer ben Yaacov, 181
Elisha ben Abuya, 131–133
Epistemology
and concept of God, 16, 77
and conception of man, 47
and language usage, 17
and law, 30, 39, 105, 109–110,
112–116, 221n51, 224n74,
243n51, 244n63
and morality, 10–12, 238n13,
242n48
religious importance of, 7–9,
129–133, 134–138, 159, 173
See also Creation of the world,
epistemological basis for;
Knowledge
Eschatology, 68, 79, 82–83, 85
See also Messianism;
Repentance; Resurrection;
World to come
Esoteric teachings of Judaism, 4,
23–24, 30–31, 36–37, 42, 76
See also Community of Israel,
education of
Ever, 40, 219n29
Exile. See Community of Israel,
exile of
Evil, problem of, 209–211,
263–264n55
See also Divine providence;
Job, interpretation of

Fox, Marvin, 238n13, 260n38
Free will, 149–150, 248n25–26
Fromm, Erich, 237n4
Fuller, Lon L., 231n47

Garden of Eden, 68
Gentiles, 50, 52–53, 92, 226n92,
266–267n72, 267n73
God
as educator, 174, 175,
253–254n82
as legislator, 86, 93, 119,
177–179, 219n25, 221n51
fear of, 44, 50, 76, 94, 207–208,
221–222n56, 230n33, 265n61
imitation of, 6, 93, 96, 141,
202, 204, 263n53

POSTSCRIPT

POSTSCRIPT

A central theme of this book was my disagreement with the dualistic approach to Maimonides by scholars such as Isaac Husik and Leo Strauss (see Introduction). Their working hypothesis was that there were two Maimonides: Maimonides the halakhist, the responsible judge who served his community in terms of its temporal and spiritual needs, and Maimonides the philosopher, who served God through knowledge of the structure of nature within the privacy of his esoteric Aristotelian universe. This dichotomy is reflected in Maimonides' two major works: *The Guide of the Perplexed*, which was addressed to the singular individual capable of emulating Maimonides' philosophic quest, and the *Mishneh Torah*, which was addressed to the general public—those who required a clear and comprehensive normative framework by which to live.

In *Torah and Philosophic Quest*, I argued that this binary understanding of Maimonides and of his works, the *Guide* and the *Mishneh Torah*, was fundamentally mistaken. I proposed "the way of integration" as my interpretive model and tried to show that Maimonides the philosopher and Maimonides the halakhist were one and the same person. I argued that the author of the *Guide* and of the *Mishneh Torah* held a unified worldview in which the God of Abraham, Isaac, and Jacob and the God of the Philosophers were integrated harmoniously into a full and rich religious life.

A key text that I used to corroborate this thesis was the following section at the end of the Guide:

From here on I will begin to give you guidance with regard to the form of this training so that you should achieve this great end. The first thing that you should cause your soul to hold fast onto is that, while reciting the *Shema*, you should empty your mind of everything and pray thus. You should not content yourself with "being intent" while "reciting the first verse of *Shema*" and saying "the first benediction" [of the *Amidah*]. When this has been carried out correctly and has been practiced consistently for years, cause your soul, whenever you read or listen to the Torah, to be constantly directed—the whole of you and your thought—toward reflection on what you are listening to or reading. When this too has been practiced consistently for a certain time, cause your soul to be in such a way that your thought is always quite free of distraction and gives heed to all that you are reading of the other discourses of the Prophets and even when you read all the benedictions, so that you aim at meditating on what you are uttering and at considering its meaning. If, however, while performing these acts of worship you are free from distraction and not engaged in thinking upon any of the things pertaining to this world, cause your soul—after this has been achieved—to occupy your thought with things necessary for you or superfluous in your life, and in general with "worldly things," while you eat or drink or bathe or talk with your wife and your small children or while you talk with the common run of people.[1]

I interpreted this description of the philosophic Jew's new appreciation of Halakhah as follows:

Although the Halakhah, as stated in the *Mishneh Torah*, only requires that one have *kavvanah* [intent] during the first verse of the *Shema* and the first benediction of the *Amidah*, the philosophic Jew of the *Guide* is not satisfied with this minimal standard. (*Torah and Philosophic Quest*, p. 194)

I understood Maimonides' recommendation about extending *kavvanah* beyond the minimal halakhic requirement to mean that after achieving knowledge and love of God the philosophic Jew would adopt a more stringent and demanding attitude toward Halakhah.

My original contention was that Maimonides proposed that the student of the *Guide* approach Halakhah by practicing more rigorous observance with more conscientious *kavvanah* (intention), thus adopting a stricter, more demanding standard of legal obligation. My claim that the philosophic Jew's religious state of mind (*kavvanah*) was essentially halakhic supported my rejection of a dichotomous view of Maimonides in favor of an integrative one. In contrast to this interpretation, I now contend that the object of the *kavvanah* Maimonides described was not legal authority and obligation but rather the ritual acts of worship themselves and/or God, the ultimate object of religious worship. In this context, kavvanah is less a legal, halakhic category—like *kavvanah la'tseit*, the intention to fulfill one's legal obligation—than a cognitive state of reflection on the content of one's action. Although the philosophic Jew continues to practice Halakhah, the practice of Halakhah before and after exposure to the philosophic quest is significantly, if not radically, changed.

The disciplined practice of Halakhah Maimonides recommends to the student of the *Guide* provides times for attending to "worldly things" ("Thus I have provided you with many and long stretches of time, in which you can think all that needs thinking regarding property, the governance of the household, and the welfare of the body"[2]) and for private moments of religious meditation in keeping with the student's new spiritual aspirations. Although the student also continues to perform the rituals prescribed by Halakhah, in doing these actions he consciously trains himself to concentrate fully on what he is doing and to exclude all distractions.

"While performing the actions imposed by the Law," writes Maimonides, "you should occupy your thought only with what you are doing, just as we have explained."[3] By doing so, the student begins to appreciate the meaning of meditative worship.

In reciting the *Shema* ("Hear, Oh Israel"), says Maimonides, you should focus fully on the recitation to the exclusion of all else. In addition to the significance of the *Shema* itself (traditionally, the acceptance of the kingdom of heaven), Maimonides introduces the value of total and undivided concentration on all three chapters of the *Shema*. This perspective is applied to other halakhic performances as well, such as listening to the Torah reading or reciting blessings. Any religious act not related to practical human needs (i.e., any purely expressive, symbolic act) becomes an occasion for training the philosophic individual in meditative worship. The student's attitude toward halakhic ritual emphasizes and cultivates single-mindedness rather than submissive obedience to the authority of Halakhah. Thus the student of the *Guide* no longer views Halakhah the same way as he did before he embarked on the philosophic path.

In this book I stated that "[b]y emphasizing that the observance of and perspective on Halakhah changes for the philosophic Jew, Maimonides clearly indicates that he does not adopt the way of dualism regarding tradition" (p. 195). This conclusion as it was formulated was misleading because it minimized the essential differences between the philosophic and halakhic spiritual paths. Halakhah and philosophy are distinct, albeit significant, parts of Maimonides' religious philosophy.

* * *

Although Maimonides advises his readers to view halakhic practice as an opportunity to train the individual to engage in concentrated moments of worship, this approach does not fully capture Maimonides' understanding of the relationship of philosophy to the normative practice of Judaism. The key text describing this relationship is in the *Mishneh Torah*:

1. Let not a man say, "I will observe the precepts of the Torah and occupy myself with its wisdom in order that I may obtain all the blessings written in the Torah, or to attain life in the world to come; I will abstain from transgressions against which the Torah warns, so that I may be saved from the curses written in the Torah, or that I may not be cut off from life in the world to come." It is not right to serve God after this fashion for whoever does so, serves Him out of fear. This is not the standard set by the prophets and sages. Those who may serve God in this way are illiterate, women, or children whom one trains to serve out of fear, till their knowledge shall have increased when they will serve out of love.

2. Whoever serves God out of love, occupies himself with the study of the Law and the fulfillment of commandments and walks in the paths of wisdom, impelled by no external motive whatsoever, moved neither by fear of calamity nor by the desire to obtain material benefits—such a man does what is truly right because it is truly right, and ultimately, happiness comes to him as a result of his conduct. This standard is indeed a very high one; not every sage attained it. It was the standard of the patriarch Abraham whom God called His lover, because he served only out of love. It is the standard which God, through Moses, bids us achieve, as it is said, "And you shall love the Lord your God" (Deut. 6:5). When one loves God with the right love, he will straightway observe all the commandments out of love.

3. What is the love of God that is befitting? It is to love the Eternal with a great and exceeding love, so strong that one's soul shall be knit up with the love of God, and one should be continually enraptured by it, like a love-sick individual, whose mind is at no time free from his passion for a particular woman, the thought of her filling his heart at all times, when sitting down or rising up, when he is eating or drinking. Even intenser should be the love of God in the hearts of those who love Him. And this love should continually possess them, even as He commanded us in the phrase, "with all your heart and with all your soul" (Deut. 6:5). This, Solomon expressed allegorically in the sentence, "for I am sick with love" (Song 2:5). The entire Song of Songs is indeed an allegory descriptive of this love.

6. ... One only loves God with the knowledge with which one knows Him. According to the knowledge will be the love. If the former be little or much, so will the latter be little or much. A person ought therefore to devote himself to the understanding and comprehension of those sciences and studies which will inform him concerning his Master, as far as it lies in human faculties to understand and comprehend—as indeed we have explained in the "Laws of the Basic Principles of the Torah."[4]

The relationship of philosophy to mitzvot described here differs from the functional description in the *Guide*. "When one loves God with the right love," writes Maimonides, "he will straightway observe all the commandments out of love."[5] The term Maimonides uses is *miyyad*, which means immediately, translated here as straightway. When a person becomes a philosophical lover of God, he immediately begins to perform the commandments out of love.

I understand this to mean that the relationship to God that grows out of philosophic knowledge is essentially a yearning to be in the presence of God. The human effect of this type of love is total and all-consuming. Individual self-interest, symbolized by the biblical concern with reward and punishment, is replaced by an overwhelming longing for the beloved. Philosophic knowledge of God engenders a kind of infatuation, a love-sickness, to be in God's presence.

The study of philosophy is not only an intellectual pursuit but also a process that shapes human character. Philosophy involves the transformation of a person's character as well as the acquisition of knowledge. The relationship to God that results from philosophic knowledge is not grounded in self-interest but in the joy of discerning the presence of God in nature. This change in one's basic character also affects one's relationship to Halakhah. This is the meaning of *miyyad*, immediately.

Advocating passionate love of God without allowing for

the slow but necessary change in one's character is dangerous and irresponsible. Presenting the idea of disinterested
worship to people in need of the reassurance and motivational incentives of the providential biblical framework of
reward and punishment can be disastrous. For this reason,
Maimonides describes the method of nurturing service of
God out of love as a gradual process beginning with serving
God "out of fear" (for the sake of reward) and proceeding
incrementally to service out of love ("we reveal to them this
secret truth little by little, and train them by easy stages till
they have grasped and comprehended it, and serve God out
of love"⁶).

It is noteworthy that one of the paradigms of love of
God Maimonides cites is Abraham ("It was the standard of
the patriarch Abraham whom God called His lover, because
he served only out of love"⁷). As I explained in this book, for
Maimonides, Abraham is the archetypal lover of God independent of Halakhah, who established a religious community
based on knowledge of God. Moses is the figure who established Halakhah and legal authority as a result of the historical realization that Abraham's community of knowledge
was insufficiently strong to withstand the pagan influences of
Egyptian culture. It was this contingent fact of history that
made it necessary to transform the Abrahamic community
into a legal community.

The relationship between Abraham and Moses as archetypal figures mirrors the relationship between the God of
nature and the God of revelation. Moses is the source of legal authority; he was the prophet of the revelatory God who
legislated and demanded compliance with Torah as a way of
life. Yet the models of Abraham and of the God of nature
continue to serve as ideals and to exert corrective influences
on the possible distortions of the halakhic framework, specifically the belief in its self-sufficiency. The Abraham-Creator

God motif acts as a corrective to the use of the Sinai-revelation motif to exclude spiritual and moral influences outside of Halakhah and mitzvah. Sinai, on the other hand, acts as a corrective to the belief that human beings can establish a community solely on the basis of disinterested contemplative love. Legal authority, discipline, and structure are necessary for maintaining a communal framework in which the human potential to transcend self-interest can be nurtured.

Two biblical figures, two images of God: the God of Abraham and the God of Moses, the God of nature and the God of revelation. The Abrahamic God of nature inspires the yearning to understand and be passionately related to the source of existence. Passionate love of God, however, is not the only ideal of Judaism. The other ideal is to establish a covenantal community that can survive in history. Halakhah and its theological counterpart, the God of history, are necessary to create a community that can persist in an unredeemed world replete with pagan allurements.

* * *

The spiritual life of Maimonides' philosophic Jew involves meditative worship of God both within and outside the framework of Halakhah. Maimonides believed that Halakhah served an indispensable role in the development of human beings and in the establishment of an ordered society. Nonetheless, the purpose and ultimate goal of this framework was the knowledge and love of God as described at the end of the *Guide*. This religious ideal cannot be realized in a relationship to God based on the paradigm of petitional prayer, where a person turns to God for help in coping with his human condition. In contrast to this paradigm, the philosophic individual turns to God because of his attraction to the ultimate reality whose perfection is revealed in the existence and structure of the world. The self, with its particular needs and concerns, recedes from the worshiper's consciousness when entering into the theocentric context of philosophic love of God.

The ideal of knowledge, which leads to love of God, appears not only in the *Guide* but also in the *Mishneh Torah*, the code of Jewish law. Therein, Maimonides openly acknowledges and discusses a hierarchy of forms of worship. I shall now analyze three texts from the *Mishneh Torah* in which Maimonides discusses the relationship between halakhic and philosophic religious sensibilities. I shall also show how his commentary offers an alternative to the traditional belief in halakhic exclusivity, which denies the legitimacy of spiritual commitments outside of Halakhah.

In the *Mishneh Torah*, Maimonides publicly states that the philosophical quest for God through the study of physics and metaphysics is superior to the legal discussions of halakhic jurisprudence:

13. The topics connected with these five precepts, treated in the above four chapters, are what our wise men called *pardes*, [Paradise], as in the passage "Four went into *pardes*" (Hagigah 14). And although those four were great men of Israel and great Sages, they did not all possess the capacity to know and grasp these subjects clearly. Therefore, I say that it is not proper to dally in *pardes* till one has first filled oneself with bread and meat; by which I mean knowledge of what is permitted and what forbidden, and similar distinctions in other classes of precepts. Although these last subjects were called by the Sages "a small thing"—when they say, "A great thing, *Ma'aseh Merkavah* [the story of the chariot: see Ezekiel 10, Isaiah 6]; a small thing, the discussions of Abaye and Rava"—still they should have the precedence. For the knowledge of these things gives primarily composure to the mind. They are the precious boon bestowed by God, to promote social well-being on earth, and enable men to obtain bliss in the life hereafter. Moreover, the knowledge of them is within the reach of all, young and old, men and women; those gifted with great intellectual capacity as well as those whose intelligence is limited.[8]

The distinction and relationship between these two frameworks, Halakhah and philosophic love of God, is best explained in Maimonides' treatment of messianism. The messianic idea refers to a historical period when the majority of human beings will be sufficiently free of economic, social, and political concerns to be able to devote themselves to reflection and to the acquisition of knowledge. Under such historical conditions, the majority of people will have the opportunity to develop morally and intellectually to the level of love of God. Pure love of God—the goal and fulfillment of human nature—is ultimately an individual achievement, which Maimonides identifies with *olam ha-ba*, the world to come. *Olam ha-ba*, the ahistorical, immaterial world of pure intellects, represents human fulfillment in its most perfect form.

According to Maimonides, the rationale behind messianic hope is that favorable social and political conditions are necessary for the majority of individuals to be engaged in the kinds of activities that lead to the knowledge and love of God. In the absence of such conditions (i.e., in a pre-messianic world), only a few exceptional individuals can acquire the practical and intellectual virtues that lead to love of God. Given this conception of messianism, we can say that the *Guide* was written for those singular individuals capable of achieving the goal of *olam ha-ba*, intellectual love of God, in a pre-messianic society. For the vast majority of people, however, messianism expresses the hope that historical conditions will change so that they too will be able to pursue and possibly realize the goal of love of God.

Hence, all Israelites, their prophets and sages, longed for the advent of Messianic times, that they might have relief from the wicked tyranny that does not permit them properly to occupy themselves with the study of the Torah and the observance of the commandments; that they might have ease, devote themselves to getting wisdom, and thus attain to life in the world to come [*olam haba*)][9]

The functional relationship between *olam ha-ba* and messianism is analogous to the distinction between the "great thing," philosophic knowledge that leads to love of God, and the "small thing," knowledge of what is permitted and forbidden.

The second text in the *Mishneh Torah* that I have chosen is Maimonides' description of how a Jew ideally should organize his day:

> For example, if one is an artisan who works at his trade three hours daily and devotes nine hours to the study of the Torah, he should spend three of these nine hours in the study of the Written Law, three in the study of the Oral Law, and the remaining three in reflecting on how to deduce one rule from another ... This plan applies to the period when one begins learning. But after one has become proficient and no longer needs to learn the Written Law, or continually be occupied with the Oral Law, he should, at fixed times, read the Written Law and the traditional dicta, so as not to forget any of the rules of the Torah, and should devote all his days exclusively to the study of Talmud, according to his breadth of mind and maturity of intellect.[10]

It is important to notice that Maimonides places the study of philosophy under the rubric of Talmud. The significance of this becomes apparent when considering the subsequent statement, "... after one has become proficient and no longer needs to learn the Written Law, or continually be occupied with the Oral Law... [one] should devote all his days exclusively to the study of Talmud..."[11] In other words, after a person is confident in his knowledge of Halakhah, he should devote the majority of his time to the study of philosophy. Again we see the hierarchical, functional relationship between Halakhah—the normative rules of conduct and social organization—and Talmud—the study of nature, and of God as manifest in nature, which leads to love of God.

It is interesting that Maimonides uses the expression "according to his breadth of mind and maturity of intellect" with respect to the study of Talmud, but not with respect to the study of Halakhah. Halakhah is a legal system and therefore must be comprehensible to and achievable by the vast majority of the public. By contrast, philosophic love of God is conditional on the study and mastery of philosophy. Its realization is dependent not only on will and determination but also on a person's intellectual capacities and powers of concentration.

The third text that demonstrates the religious significance of philosophic spirituality is Maimonides' dramatic demystification of divine worship in the cultic practices of the Temple:

12. Why did the tribe of Levi not acquire a share in the Land of Israel and in its spoils together with their brothers? Because this tribe was set apart to serve God and to minister to Him, to teach His straight ways and righteous ordinances to the multitudes, as is written: "They shall teach Jacob Your ordinances and Israel Your law" (Deut. 33:10). Therefore, they were set apart from the ways of the world; they do not wage war like the rest of Israel, nor do they inherit land or acquire anything for themselves by their physical prowess. They are rather the army of God, as is written: "Bless, Lord, his substance" (Deut. 33:11). He, blessed be He, acquires [goods] for them, as is written: "I am your portion and your inheritance" (Num. 18:20).

13. Not only the tribe of Levi but every single individual from among the world's inhabitants whose spirit moved him and whose intelligence gave him the understanding to withdraw from the world in order to stand before God to serve and minister to Him, to know God, and he walked upright in the manner in which God made him, shaking off from his neck the yoke of the manifold contrivances which men seek—behold, this person has been totally consecrated and God will be his portion and inheritance forever and ever. God will acquire for him sufficient goods in this world just as he did for the priests and Levites. Behold, David, may he rest in peace, says: "Lord, the portion of my inheritance and of my cup, You maintain my lot" (Ps. 16:5).[12]

The tribe of Levi is freed from ordinary worldly activities in order to be engaged fully in the worship of God. The cultic role assigned to them by Jewish law is not based on individual merit or achievement (e.g., the "breadth of mind and maturity of intellect," noted above with regard to the mastery of Talmud). The qualifications of the priests and Levites derive from their birth. The child of a priest is a priest. The child of a Levite is a Levite. Their special status and prerogatives are defined by halakhic norms. Thus, the service of God in the Temple cult has nothing in common with the knowledge and love of God that Maimonides describes in the *Guide* and the *Mishneh Torah.*

Nevertheless, after describing the unique role of the Levites, who are "set apart from the ways of the world" to serve God and to teach Torah, Maimonides states: "Not only the tribe of Levi but every single individual from among the world's inhabitants ..."[13] can also become God's portion and inheritance. The spiritual vocation of the tribe of Levi is not the exclusive prerogative of that tribe alone. Any individual who is sufficiently motivated and capable of devoting his life to God can reach the spiritual level represented by the tribe of Levi, regardless of lineage, of social class, or even of membership in the Jewish people.

It is as if Maimonides were telling the reader not to be misled by the particular symbolic categories by which Halakhah organizes communal life, such as the tribe of Levi. In the end, Levites and *Kohanim* (Priests) represent the ideal of consecrating one's life to God. This ideal is independent of the particular ritualistic or structural forms of Jewish Halakhah or any other tradition. Any individual, Jew or non-Jew, anywhere in the world can achieve what the Priests and Levites represent.

Maimonides counters a possible exclusivist interpretation of halakhic worship by declaring that the ideal of passionate love of God which he described in the *Guide* (III: 51) and in the *Mishneh Torah's* "The Laws Concerning the Study of the

Torah" (1:12) has significance independent of any particular tradition or revelatory system. This kind of internal commentary on the law is not uncommon in the *Mishneh Torah*. In these descriptive digressions from the otherwise prescriptive content of his code of Jewish law, Maimonides provides what he believes is the proper context in which to understand the law or laws in question. Though these comments are non-binding in the strict legal sense, they reveal the dialectical relationship between Maimonides the philosopher and Maimonides the judge.

* * *

The conclusion I draw from the above three texts is that while he believed in the value and importance of both Halakhah and philosophic love of God, Maimonides placed the latter above the former in the hierarchy of human activities. As mentioned previously, Maimonides' conceptions of messianism and *olam ha-ba* expressed his multidimensional world view. By freeing people from the debilitating demands of physical and social survival, messianism makes contemplation of God in nature into a realistic goal for the community at large.

This functional relationship between Halakhah and philosophy may not be adequately described by the "the way of integration," which I argued for in this book. I feel uncomfortable with this formulation now because I believe that "integration" is not the only way of appreciating and embracing two different traditions. While the term "integration" is preferable to "synthesis" because it does not connote the transformation and loss of original identities, nevertheless, it does not adequately express the difficulty of combining these two traditions. What is needed is a concept that would capture the human struggle of living with two world views, two loyalties, two traditions that are desirable, meaningful but at times irreconcilable. Maimonides was a complex religious personality who felt the claims of these two passions: his passion for the

We hope that you enjoy your JPS book and use it to enrich your life.

Title of your JPS book

Did you ☐ Purchase it? ☐ Receive it as a gift? Occasion
Store name / website   Comments

We invite you to learn more about JPS by visiting www.jewishpub.org, where you will find a listing of all our books, a complete online ordering center for books and gift certificates, and information about the benefits of becoming a member of the Society.

Please send me:
☐ Membership benefits information   ☐ Email about new books and special offers
☐ Gift certificate options   ☐ Book catalog

Name

Address

City   State   Zip Code   Email

☐ Please send a JPS book catalog to my friend:

Name

Address

City   State   Zip Code

The Jewish Publication Society ◆ 2100 Arch Street, 2nd Floor ◆ Philadelphia, PA 19103
(800) 234-3151 ◆ www.jewishpub.org

halakhic tradition and his passion for philosophical spirituality. Both lived side by side within him. Both influenced his
creativity and activities as an individual and as a leader.

The individual infused by the theocentric passion described at the end of the *Guide* is not necessarily a person who
is interested in the synthesis of philosophic contemplation
and halakhic jurisprudence. Such a person is primarily interested in enabling the two frameworks to live together without
excluding one another. Consequently, one of Maimonides'
tasks in the *Mishneh Torah* was to circumscribe the traditionalists' belief in the complete all-inclusive nature of Halakhah.
According to this not uncommon approach, Halakhah claims
the totality of one's life while proscribing allegiance to any
other spiritual framework.

As if to counteract this insular conception of Judaism,
the very first rabbinic text Maimonides deals with in the introduction to his *Commentary on the Mishnah* is "From the day
that the Temple was destroyed, the Holy One, blessed is He,
dwells only in [has nothing in His world except for] the four
cubits of halakhah" (T.B., Berakhot 8a). Maimonides couldn't
accept this statement at face value because, as he argued, this
would exclude our acknowledgment that the generations of
Noah and of Abraham *who lived before Sinai* served God. Maimonides therefore felt compelled to interpret this statement
so as to neutralize its implications regarding the exclusivity of
Halakhah in defining what constitutes authentic Judaism.

Maimonides' efforts at countering halakhic exclusivity took two basic forms. First, he repeatedly informed his
readers about the ideal of love of God mediated by philosophic knowledge. As shown above, there are several places
in the *Mishneh Torah* where Maimonides openly declares the
supremacy of the philosophic spiritual ideal.

Second, as a halakhic commentator and codifier, Maimonides shunned strict formalism when dealing with morally

problematic rulings, choosing instead to acknowledge the legitimacy of "extra-legal" moral arguments. By allowing what I call "self-corrective mechanisms" into halakhic discussions in the *Mishneh Torah* he challenged the doctrine of Halakhah's completeness and self-sufficiency. Maimonides' comments on halakhic legislation in the *Mishneh Torah* include moral and theological arguments that, from a purely formal legal point of view, have no relevance. Although these "extra-legal" considerations have no immediate impact on halakhic legislation, the very fact that they were included shows that Maimonides wanted them to be part of the broader context in which the Jew viewed Halakhah. The acknowledgment of "self-corrective mechanisms" in Halakhah weakens the claim to exclusivity by empowering Jews to critically evaluate halakhic legislation on the basis of values and ideals not derived exclusively from formal halakhic hermeneutics.

For example, Halakhah makes a distinction between Jewish and non-Jewish slaves with respect to the prohibition of working a slave with rigor (*befarech*) (Lev 25:43):

It is permitted to work a heathen slave with rigor. Though such is the rule, it is the quality of piety and the way of wisdom that a man be merciful and pursue justice and not make his yoke heavy upon the slave or distress him, but give him to eat and to drink of all foods and drinks.

The sages of old were wont to let the slave partake of every dish that they themselves ate of and to give the meal of the cattle and of the slaves precedence over their own. Is it not said: "As the eyes of slaves to the hand of their master, as the eyes of a female servant to the hand of her mistress" (Ps. 123:2)?

Thus also the master should not disgrace them by hand or by word, because Scriptural law has delivered them only to slavery and not to disgrace. Nor should he heap upon the slave oral abuse and anger, but should rather speak to him softly and listen to his claims. So it is also explained in the good paths of Job, in which he prided himself:

"If I did despise the cause of my manservant,
Or of my maidservant, when they contended with me ...

Did not He that made me in the womb make him?
And did not One fashion us in the womb?" (Job 31:13,15)[14]

Biblical legislation against treating a slave with rigor (*be-farech*), which was interpreted in the tradition to refer to de-humanizing work (tasks with no useful purpose or end: "do this until I return"), was limited to the Hebrew slave. From a strict halakhic point of view, a Jew may treat a non-Jew-ish slave harshly. Nonetheless, writes Maimonides, there are compelling reasons to ignore this distinction and to adopt a higher standard of behavior. First, the "quality of piety and the way of wisdom" preclude treating any slave, Jew or heathen, harshly. The Jewish tradition commends the "sag-es of old" for their merciful treatment of heathen slaves.

Maimonides also offers a legalistic halakhic argument to the effect that the power given to the master over the slave does not override the latter's right to human dignity. Enslave-ment does not entail degradation. Furthermore, the teleology of this system develops compassion towards others and, as a consequence, cruelty is infrequent among Jews who "are merciful people who have mercy upon all" (Ps. 145:9).

Another argument invokes theological motifs by setting the Divine Legislator against His alter ego, the Divine Cre-ator. Drawing on a midrashic source, Maimonides quoted Job's use of the egalitarian implications of creation ("Did not He that made me in the womb make him?") to argue against the discriminatory treatment of non-Jewish slaves, which the Halakhah based on revelation permits.

Apart from biblical images and narratives, knowledge of God in nature awakens and instills in us a love for and desire to imitate the source of existence whose perfection (good-ness) overflows to all beings. The yearning for and knowledge of God in nature provides a person with a theological *and moral* outlook independent of revelation.

On the basis of the multiple arguments Maimonides presents, one can conclude that the two main ideas his religious universe is organized around can be represented by two theological models: 1. the God of revelation, the source of law and legal authority; and 2. God as He is unto Himself, the ultimate source of all contingent existence. Torah and Halakhah mediate the will and authority of the personal God of history; nature mediates the divine presence by enabling us to discover and imitate the "moral" qualities of the Creator manifest in the world. [15]

This two-fold theological perspective of creation and revelation has implications for the way in which the philosophic Jew relates to the tradition. In terms of Halakhah, this means that the revelatory framework does not exhaust the sources of spiritual meaning and moral inspiration in Jewish life. The currently codified law may permit treating pagan slaves in ways that conflict with the goodness we associate with the God of creation. The divine actions we strive to imitate may not coincide with the principles embodied in current halakhic practice. This is the meaning of living with two frameworks and accepting their differences. The "way of integration" oversimplifies the complexity of living in multiple religious frameworks.

The presentation of forceful moral arguments against legislation by the codifier of that legislation is, in Maimonides' case, an indication of his rejection of halakhic exclusivity. The halakhic system does not exhaust the divine word. While the word of God is expressed in mitzvot, it is not expressed only in mitzvot. Love of God and imitation of God are not dependent on revelation; they can be achieved by any human being. This awareness, this knowledge that "His mercies are over all His works," (Ps. 145:9) can act as a corrective to an overly obedient and submissive attitude toward halakhic legislation.

* * *

As I explained at the beginning of this postscript, in *Torah and Philosophic Quest*, I argued extensively against the polarized view of Maimonides that both Isaac Husik and Leo Strauss advocated. Although I am now more sympathetic to the dualistic approach, I still disagree strongly with Leo Strauss's dismissal of the central role Halakhah plays in Maimonides' philosophic world view. However, my main disagreement is with scholars who depreciate the spiritual role philosophy plays for Maimonides, specifically Yeshayahu Leibowitz. Leibowitz rejects both the ways of dualism and integration because of his firm belief that Maimonides confined the worship of God exclusively to the halakhic framework of rabbinic Judaism. Leibowitz can be classified as advocating "the way of insulation" insofar as he rejects the vital role of the philosophic quest for God in Maimonides' conception of religious life.

The key to Leibowitz's understanding of Maimonides is his interpretation of the following passage in the *Guide*:

Know that all the practices of the worship, such as reading the Torah, prayer and the performance of the other commandments, have only the end of training you to occupy yourself with His commandments, may He be exalted, rather than with matters pertaining to this world; You should act as if you were occupied with Him, may He be exalted, and not with that which is other than He.[16]

The crucial sentence for Leibowitz is: "You should act as if you were occupied with Him ... and not with that which is other than He," which he interprets to mean that worship of God can only be realized through the observance of Halakhah. According to Leibowitz, Maimonides believed that there could be no genuine worship outside of the normative tradition of Judaism. Furthermore, he defines worship of God in terms of the duty to perform mitzvot, commandments. Love of God is equated with a person's unconditional acceptance and disinterested observance of Halakhah. You love God by observing Halakhah because you are obligated to do so. Love of God and worship of God are fully exhausted by halakhic observance. Outside of this framework, they have no meaning.

This approach to Halakhah and to Maimonides is diametrically opposed to my own. As I argued previously, Maimonides countered the claim of halakhic exclusivity in two ways. First, he challenged the spiritual hegemony of halakhic legislation by emphasizing the value of philosophy and contemplative love of God grounded in philosophic knowledge. Second, he challenged the claim of normative completeness and self-sufficiency by allowing for the presence of self-corrective mechanisms within the tradition.

While I agree with Leibowitz's approach to Maimonides in terms of his appreciation of the importance of Halakhah and his analysis of disinterested love independent of metaphysical knowledge of God's essence, in contrast to Leibowitz, I ascribe great importance to the non-halakhic, cosmic motif in Maimonides' religious worldview.

The passionate yearning for God and love-sickness experienced by the lover of God when meditating on nature are integral parts of Maimonides' religious worldview. Although Maimonides developed his "negative theology" because he believed that knowledge of God in terms of essential attributes was impossible, he nonetheless maintained in the *Mishneh Torah* and throughout all his works that love of God is proportionate to knowledge. While both Leibowitz and I accept Maimonides' avowed skepticism with regard to knowledge of God's essence, I maintain that for Maimonides the knowledge of and interest in nature—the philosophic quest—nurtures a religious personality grounded in passionate love of God.

I accept Maimonides' emphasis on the centrality of philosophy and nature in terms of the existential goal of love of God. Leibowitz, however, rejects the religious significance of the philosophical quest altogether. For him, the one and only framework for worship of God is the practice of Halakhah. He, therefore, places Maimonides' concept of love of God exclusively within Halakhah. Disinterested love of God means doing mitzvot because one is commanded to and not for any self-serving reason. It is with Leibowitz's pan-Halakhism—confining a Jew's religious life to the "four cubits of Halakhah"—that I strongly disagree.

1. This God, honored and revered, it is our duty to love and fear; as it is said "You shall love the Lord your God" (Deut. 6:5), and it is further said "You shall fear the Lord your God" (Deut. 6:15).

2. And what is the way that will lead to the love of Him and the fear of Him? When a person contemplates His great and wondrous works and creatures and from them obtains a glimpse of His wisdom which is incomparable and infinite, he will straightway love Him, praise Him, glorify Him, and long with an exceeding longing to know His great Name; even as David said, "My soul thirsts for God, for the living God" (Ps. 42:3). And when he ponders these matters, he will recoil frightened, and realize that he is a small creature, lowly and obscure, endowed with slight and slender intelligence, standing in the presence of Him who is perfect in knowledge. And so David said, "When I consider Your heavens, the work of Your fingers—what is man that You are mindful of him?" (Ps. 8:4–5). In harmony with these sentiments, I shall explain some large, general aspects of the works of the Sovereign of the Universe, that they may serve the intelligent individual as a door to the love of God, even as our sages have remarked in connection with the theme of the love of God, "Observe the Universe and hence, you will realize Him who spoke and the world was."[17]

In this description of the meaning of love and fear of God at the beginning of the *Mishneh Torah*, Maimonides clearly describes the connection between these religious attitudes and philosophic knowledge. "When a person contemplates His great and wondrous works and creatures ... he will straightway love Him." For Leibowitz, the philosophic quest is bereft of spiritual meaning. Love of God is related exclusively to the individual's decision to submit to the authority of the Halakhah and the commandments. I, however, maintain that Maimonides wanted to check the exclusivity of Halakhah by making philosophy and the study of nature constitutive elements of his philosophy of Judaism.

* * *

I would summarize my position in terms of Maimonides' parable of the palace of the King,[18] which he uses to describe the proximity of human beings to God. Those Jews who believe that God can only be served from within the confines of traditional halakhic authority and legislative practice "have come up to the [King's] habitation and walk around it." They do not enter the antechambers, which are accessible only to those who "have plunged into speculation concerning the fundamental principles of religion."[19] Among the latter, differences in philosophic knowledge and love of God make for differences in closeness to the ruler. Unlike the "jurists," the halakhists who reject the legitimacy of religious worship not grounded exclusively in Halakhah, these philosophic individuals study "the natural things" and gain understanding in "divine science" and thus "come to be with the ruler in the inner part of the habitation." Given their knowledge of God as revealed in nature, they then "set their thought to work on God alone."[20]

As I have suggested in my analysis of the religious significance of philosophy for Maimonides, knowledge of God in nature engenders a distinct religious passion: "This is the worship peculiar to those who have apprehended the true realities; the more they think of Him and of being with Him, the more their worship increases."[21] Knowledge of God in nature gives the individual a perspective on God independent of tradition and revelation. The goal of his religious practice (as indicated in our earlier analysis of Maimonides' instruction to the student of the *Guide* regarding halakhic ritual) is to "engage in totally devoting yourself to Him." Unlike religious practice based on submission to legal authority, the goal of this kind of worship is to "endeavor to come closer to Him, and strengthen the bond between you and Him—that is, the intellect."[22]

For Maimonides, Halakhah and philosophy constitute two valid and vital religious perspectives. This duality is reflective of the complex world of a medieval Jew committed to Jewish history and Halakhah, as well as to the reigning science of his day, the Aristotelian conception of the "natural" and "divine sciences." This is Maimonides' legacy to Jews in any age seeking a way—or ways—to express their commitment to and love for Jewish history and its tradition, as well as their yearning for God who "is good to all; and his tender mercies are over all His works" (Ps. 145:9).

* * *

I asked Warren Harvey to respond to this revised last chapter of my book *Torah and Philosophic Quest* and, as usual, the questions he posed were very helpful in rewriting my rewriting. Warren has always been a dear friend and a brilliant scholar of medieval Jewish philosophy—especially of Maimonides and Crescas. Over the years, he has been one of the singular figures who sympathetically and critically responded to the approach I took to Maimonides. Although I engaged Maimonides as if he were a contemporary philosopher offering Jews a different and compelling way of understanding

Judaism, this was not the way people were accustomed to treating Maimonides and therefore their responses were often dismissive. Warren was a humble, quiet, and brilliant student who was not afraid to meet Maimonides as a contemporary voice in modern Judaism. I am deeply grateful to him for his encouragement over the years and for his contribution to this postscript. He helped me make certain that my thinking did not lose contact with the text of Maimonides.

Postscript Notes

1. *Guide*, III, 51, pp. 622–23.
2. Ibid.
3. Ibid.
4. *M.T.*, *Hilkhot Teshuvah*, X.
5. *M.T.*, *Hilkhot Teshuvah*, X, 2.
6. *M.T.*, *Hilkhot Teshuvah*, X, 5.
7. *M.T.*, *Hilkhot Teshuvah*, X, 2.
8. *M.T.*, *Yesodei ha-Torah*, IV, 13.
9. *M.T.*, *Hilkhot Teshuvah*, IX, 2.
10. *M.T.*, *Hilkhot Talmud Torah*, I, 12.
11. Ibid.
12. *M.T.*, *Hilkhot Shemitah ve-Yovel*, XIII, 12–13.
13. Ibid.
14. *M.T.*, *Hilkhot Avadim*, IX, 8.
15. *Guide* I, 36.
16. *Guide*, III, 51.
17. *M.T.*, *Yesodei ha-Torah*, II, 1–2.
18. *Guide*, III.
19. *Guide*, III, 51.
20. Ibid.
21. Ibid., p. 620.
22. Ibid.

Breinigsville, PA USA
01 October 2009
225123BV00001B/2/P